THE ORIGINS OF THE ARAB–ISRAELI WARS

ORIGINS OF MODERN WARS
General editor: *Harry Hearder*

Titles already published:

THE ORIGINS OF THE FIRST WORLD WAR
  James Joll
THE ORIGINS OF THE ARAB-ISRAELI WARS
  Ritchie Ovendale
THE ORIGINS OF THE RUSSO-JAPANESE WAR
  Ian Nish

THE ORIGINS OF THE ARAB–ISRAELI WARS

Ritchie Ovendale

LONGMAN
London and New York

LONGMAN GROUP LIMITED
Longman House, Burnt Mill, Harlow
Essex CM20 2JE, England
Associated companies throughout the world

*Published in the United States of America
by Longman Inc., New York*

© Longman Group Limited 1984

First published 1984
Second impression 1985
Third impression 1985

BRITISH LIBRARY CATALOGUING IN PUBLICATION DATA

Ovendale, Ritchie
  The origins of the Arab-Israeli wars.—(Origins of modern wars)
  1. Israel.—Arab Border Conflicts, 1949-
  I. Title   II. Series
  956'.04   DS126.5

  ISBN 0–582–49257–2

LIBRARY OF CONGRESS CATALOGING IN PUBLICATION DATA

Ovendale, Ritchie.
  The Arab–Israeli wars.

  (Origins of modern wars)
  Bibliography: p.
  Includes index.
  1. Jewish-Arab relations—1917– .2. Israel—History, Military.   3. Arab
countries—History, Military.   I. Title.   II. Series.
DS119.7.093   1984   956'.04   83–17605
ISBN 0–582–49257–2

Set in 10/11pt Linoterm Times
Produced by Longman Group (FE) Ltd
Printed in Hong Kong

CONTENTS

EDITOR'S FOREWORD

Thomas Hobbes wrote in 1651:

> Warre consisteth not in Battell only, or the act of fighting; but in a tract of
> time, wherein the Will to contend by Battell is sufficiently known: and
> therefore the notion of *Time*, is to be considered in the nature of Warre
> . . . So the nature of Warre, consisteth not in actuall fighting; but in the
> known disposition thereto, during all the time there is no assurance to the
> contrary.

Hobbes's argument would seem to justify the policies of the more
hawkish Israeli ministers, and the more aggressive members of the
PLO, in recent times. In strict terms of international law, however, the
failure to extend diplomatic relations is not a declaration of war, and
political leaders in the Middle East – for their own sakes – would surely
be well advised not to consider themselves as being in a state of
permanent warfare. But for the historian, looking back over the
history of the past thirty-five years, it would be difficult to pretend that
the wars between Israel and the Arab states were unrelated to each
other.

Dr Ovendale's scholarly and dispassionate account traces the changing tides of relationships in the Middle East, but, above all, shows how
they were controlled by the Great Powers until the Six-Day War,
when, as Dr Ovendale says (p. 184): 'The Six Day War was fought by
the countries in the Middle East for the possession of land. It was a
Middle Eastern war and the Great Powers stood aside.'

Perhaps some comfort can be gleaned from the fact that the superpowers have been reluctant to turn the Arab-Israeli confrontation into
a clear-cut Russo-American confrontation. There have always been
cross-currents which have obfuscated the picture. And perhaps from
this, one general conclusion can be drawn: the very complexity of a
situation may give room for negotiation and compromise. The danger
points in the history of humanity have usually been when a single issue
brings a direct confrontation between Great Powers or superpowers,
and there appears to be no room for manœuvre. The Cuban crisis of

1962 is perhaps the most obvious example in recent times of such a direct confrontation. If in that crisis Kennedy or Khrushchev had made one false move it is extremely unlikely that the editor of this series would be sitting quietly at his desk writing his foreword at this moment.

The first two volumes to be published in this series deal with the origins of wars which are clearly very different in their nature. The First World War started as a comparatively local Balkan affair, but developed into a war in which every Great Power was engaged, partly because – as Professor Joll has so vividly shown – developments got beyond the control of the limited imaginations of the men in power. The Arab–Israeli Wars, on the other hand, although a constant pre-occupation of the superpowers, have not led to war between them. Yet Dr Ovendale shows in his first chapters that developments in the Middle East depended upon relationships between the Great Powers, and especially between Britain and the USA. In Ovendale's words (p. 106):

> In the years immediately following the conclusion of the Second World War the politics of the powers with their concern for prestige, oil, strategic interests and communications to a large extent controlled developments in the area. But, in the end, the crucial factor was the United States, and its domestic politics determined the fate of the Middle East.

It seems tragic that the electoral preoccupations of an American president could decide the future of hundreds of thousands of people in the Middle East – people who had no idea where Washington was, or who Harry Truman was. The fact remains that the Great Powers have not intervened in a military sense in the Middle East, apart from the single, brief aberration of the 1956 War. After the Second World War the British had soon been eager to withdraw their troops from Palestine, and the Americans were dismayed at the thought that it might become necessary for them to send troops. Both the British and the Americans over-estimated the eagerness of the Russians to be involved actively. On the whole the fears of the Great Powers have proved to be exaggerated ones. Since the Six Day War Israel and the Arab states have resisted any tendency to become satellites of the Great Powers. As Dr Ovendale says (p. 198): 'In the end the Arab states retained a surprising degree of independence, resisting both American and Russian dominance.'

Unfortunately, in Hobbes's words, 'the Will to contend by Battell' is still alive in the Middle East. To complete Dr Ovendale's story we would need a futurologist, rather than a historian. And futurology is not yet a recognized academic discipline.

ACKNOWLEDGEMENTS

Some of the research for this book was made possible by grants from the British Academy and its Small Grants Fund in the Humanities, and a visiting research fellowship from the American Council of Learned Societies tenable at the University of Virginia, Charlottesville.

I should like to thank the following for assistance: Professor Inis Claude, Professor John Garnett, Dr Keith Hamilton, Professor Agnes Headlam-Morley, Professor Ieuan John, Professor James Joll, Professor Maldwyn Mills, Dr Brian Porter, Miss Pamela Porter, Miss Eilenud Rees, and Ms Jacqueline Williams. Throughout Professor Harry Hearder was a constant source of encouragement.

I am grateful to the library staffs of many institutions and archives for their expertise. In particular I should like to thank the following and, where appropriate, acknowledge permission to quote from collections in their custody: Churchill College, Cambridge, for the *Attlee Papers*; the British Library for the *Oliver Harvey Diaries*; the British Library of Political and Economic Science for the *Dalton Papers*; the Western Manuscripts Department of the Bodleian Library, and the Master and Fellows of University College, Oxford, for the *Attlee Papers*; the Guy W. Bailey Library, the University of Vermont, for Warren R. Austin and Ernest Gibson Jr's papers; the Aldeman Library, University of Virginia, for Edward R. Stettinius Jr and J. Rives Childes's collections; the Robert Muldrow Cooper Library, Clemson University, for the *James F. Byrnes Papers*; the George C. Marshall Library, Virginia Military Institute, for George C. Marshall's papers and other collections housed there; Princeton University Libraries; the Harry S. Truman Library, Independence, Missouri; the Franklin D. Roosevelt Library; Georgetown University Library for the *Robert F. Wagner Papers*; the Library of Congress Manuscript Division; and the National Archives in Washington together with the National Records Centre at Suitland, Maryland. The staff of the Public Record Office, London, was always obliging and courteous; copyright material housed there appears by permission of Her Majesty's Stationery Office. Mrs Chris. Chadwick, Mrs Kathy Hamilton and the staff of the Hugh Owen Library, University College of Wales, Aberystwyth were willing and cheerful.

The manuscript was typed by Mrs Gloria Davies, Mrs Doreen Hamer, and Mrs Marian Weston.

Chapter 1

'THE JEWISH STATE' VERSUS 'THE ARAB AWAKENING'

At the end of 1894 a Jewish officer of the French general staff, Alfred Dreyfus, was convicted behind closed doors of espionage for Germany, and sentenced to deportation for life to Devil's Island. The officer was publicly degraded at the École Militaire: his sword was broken; he was stripped of his uniform; and taken away in chains. The mob present shouted, 'Death. Death to the Jews.' Dreyfus was a parvenu, an example of social climbing by a Jewish family seeking assimilation and acceptance by high society through launching their sons on military careers. Known for boasting about his family fortune – which he spent on women – Dreyfus was not even liked by the young Austro-Hungarian journalist, Theodor Herzl, who reported the trial. But Herzl became convinced that Dreyfus was innocent, and was shaken by the apparent hostility to the Jews that the case unleashed in France. Six months later Herzl suggested to Barons Maurice de Hirsch and Albert Rothschild 'a Jewish exodus': for nearly 2,000 years Jews had been dispersed all over the world without a state of their own; if only the Jews had a political centre they could begin to solve the problem of anti-Semitism.

The Dreyfus affair became the symbol of Jewish inequality in European society. The confession of one officer, and the suicide of another, led to Dreyfus's being pardoned in 1899, but he was never acquitted. The discovery of Dreyfus's innocence did not lead to social acceptance of the Jews. Marcel Proust, the French novelist who found similarities between the exclusion forced by his Jewishness and his homosexuality, when recalling things past observed: 'The politicians had not been wrong in thinking that the discovery of the judicial error would deal a fatal blow to anti-semitism. But provisionally, at least, a social anti-semitism was on the contrary enhanced and exacerbated by it.'[1] From Emile Zola's famous defence of Dreyfus, *J'Accuse*, to the 1931 play in Paris which had to be suspended because the government could not maintain order during the performances, to the 1950s Hollywood film starring José Ferrer, the affair has been kept before public consciousness. It focused attention on anti-Semitism, and

1

helped to give birth to the Zionist movement.[2]

The ideas of liberty, equality and fraternity embodied in the French Revolution, as well as those outlined by the American Declaration of Independence, led to a certain emancipation of the Jews: in the United States in 1781, and in France in 1790, they were freed from special restrictions. The Napoleonic armies liberated Jews in many European countries. After Napoleon's defeat there was some reaction: the 1819 'Hep! Hep!' riots, starting in Würzburg and spreading throughout the German states and into Austria, Hungary, Poland and Denmark, reflected a suspicion of Jewish financiers and bankers, and suggested that the Jews were responsible for economic difficulties. These were repeated in 1830, and some central European Jews emigrated to the United States. But many Jews were assimilated into European society during the middle decades of the nineteenth century. In Britain a baptized Jew, Benjamin Disraeli, became Prime Minister in 1868, and a professing Jew, Baron Lionel de Rothschild, was elected to the House of Commons in 1858. Around 1860, however, a new word appeared, 'anti-Semitism', and with it a new challenge to the position of the Jews. The attack was now based not on grounds of creed, but of race. Assimilation was no longer possible: according to the new doctrine racial characteristics were unchangeable and a Jew could not, for instance, become a German through baptism and a rejection of his heritage. These ideas were popularized in the 1880s through a work by Eugen Dühring entitled *The Jewish Question as a Question of Race, Morals and Civilisation*. From 1815 in Russia Jews suffered increasing restrictions. Then, following the assassination of the Tsar, Alexander II, in March 1881, Russia's difficulties were attributed to Jewish corruption, and Jews were massacred in a series of attacks in which the government either acquiesced or connived. These became known as pogroms. By 1914 it is estimated that over 2 million Jews had fled from Russia, and most had settled in the United States. But in 1882 Leon Pinsker, a Jewish doctor from Odessa, argued in his book *Auto-Emancipation* that anti-Semitism would persist where the Jews were a minority; they needed a homeland of their own. This suggestion, however, offered no immediate solution, and the waves of anti-Semitism in Europe from 1880, symbolized by the Dreyfus affair, meant that over 3 million Jews fled over three decades, settling in Britain, Canada, Australia and South Africa, but the vast majority found a new home in the United States. A few went to that area of the Ottoman Empire that was loosely known as Palestine. Palestine was, in the late nineteenth century, a geographic concept. Administratively, the south of Palestine was governed from Jerusalem, and the north from Beirut. The Ottoman government used the term for an area that became known as Palestine under the British mandate in 1922; the Arab and Jewish usage was imprecise as it depended on various historical interpretations.[3] In 1856 a British Jew, Sir Moses Montefiore, was allowed by the Ottoman Sultan to buy land for Jewish settlement in the area. This work was later supported by the Rothschild family. With the racial anti-Semitism in Europe, symbolized by the Dreyfus affair, Palestine assumed a particular importance with some of the Jewish élite. The period saw the origins of Zionism.[4]

The word 'Zionism' was probably first used by Nathan Birnbaum in an article published in 1886. It has come to be understood as meaning a movement for the re-establishment of a Jewish nation in Palestine, or as one writer insists, 'Erez-Israel'.[5] Followers of Zionism emphasize the historic links between the Jews and Palestine. In the second millenium BC immigrant Semitic tribesmen moved towards the sea across the Arabian Desert, and became known as Hebrews. One tribe, or group of tribes, claiming descent from Abraham of Ur, acquired the name of Israelites.

Migration to Egypt followed, but with the return under Moses to Palestine, it appears that by about 1100 BC the Israelites occupied most of the hill country in Palestine and were distinguished from the neighbouring tribesmen by their belief in only one god. The Israelites were occupied by the Assyrians, moved to Babylon, and for about four centuries administered as part of the Persian Empire. With the ascendence of Hellenism, however, the Jews successfully revolted against foreign domination, and from around 150 to 63 BC, when Palestine was subjected to the overlordship of Rome, the Jews maintained their independence. There were unsuccessful revolts against Roman rule, and in AD 135 Jerusalem was destroyed. The Diaspora, or dispersion of the Jews around the world, had started even before 135, and in Iraq there had been a separate community of Jews for over 600 years. Six centuries after the sack of Jerusalem the Jews even followed the Arabs into North Africa and Spain where they spoke Arabic and were distinguished only by their religion. But it was in the Christian world that the Jews began to be disliked and suffered persecution, particularly at the time of the Crusades and during the medieval Inquisition. In the middle of the seventeenth century an effort was made to stop the Jews from permeating Russia, and by then Jews were often restricted to special areas of towns which became known as ghettos, and forced to wear a distinguishing yellow badge.[6]

With the assimilation evidenced during the nineteenth century the promise of the Jewish god that the race would eventually return to Palestine assumed a largely symbolic meaning. But the rise of anti-Semitism changed that, and Zionism played on what could be considered as the old faith.

Herzl is commonly regarded as the father of political Zionism. But several writers before him had argued in terms of a separate Jewish state. In 1833, Disraeli, in his first novel, *Alroy*, outlined his scheme for a Jewish empire with the Jews ruling as a separated class. This scheme was moderated to the domination of empires and diplomacy by

Jewish money in *Coningsby*, published in 1844. In *Tancred*, Disraeli explained history in terms of race, and saw the Jews as being a superior race. But in George Eliot's novel, *Daniel Deronda* (1876), one of the characters is there to show that the Jews still have a mission to fulfil: the repossession of Palestine. Political writers like Moses Hess with *Rome and Jerusalem* (1862) and Pinsker expressed similar ideas.[7]

When writing *Der Judenstaat*, most accurately translated as *The State of the Jews*, Herzl was seemingly unaware of these earlier writings. Recent biographies reveal Herzl to have been an isolated man who probably contracted gonorrhoea as a student, and hence did not marry till fairly late for fear of passing on the infection. But this liaison was desperately unhappy, and he was only able to think creatively when separated from his family, as happened during the composition of *Der Judenstaat*. Witnessing the Dreyfus affair was probably only one of several factors that led to Herzl's conversion to Zionism. Herzl's diaries show that in formulating his ideas he was influenced by the activities of Cecil John Rhodes, the great imperialist who bestowed his name on a country: in May 1895 Mashonaland and Matabeleland became Rhodesia which was administered by a chartered company, the British South Africa Company. Herzl studied carefully how Rhodes had managed to wrest control of the land from the Matabele and Mashona. The diaries reveal the assumption that the land to form the Jewish state would already be populated by a few landowners and many poor peasants. The poor were to be removed by being denied work in the new Jewish country while being offered employment in 'transit countries'. The landowners were to be dealt with by secret agents making purchases simultaneously, and giving the impression that they were paying more than the land was worth. Rhodes, once he had obtained the concession from a Black chief, used his influence to obtain a legal charter from a 'sponsor', Britain, and then opened Rhodesia to White settlement by defeating the Matabele with guns. Herzl was aware that Rhodes had the necessary financial backing and a sponsor who saw its interests being promoted.[8]

Der Judenstaat appeared in Vienna in February 1896. In the preface Herzl stated that his idea was an old one: the establishment of a state for the Jews. Anti-Semitic fervour made this an urgent necessity: that force had shown that the Jews could not assimilate and had made them into one people. The Jews' position deteriorated whenever they lived together in any great numbers. The recent liberal laws had only encouraged anti-Semitism by enabling the Jews to become a bourgeois people, and to compete with the native middle classes. Herzl asked that the Jews be granted sovereignty over territory adequate for their national requirements. They would see to the rest. Here the influence of the Rhodesian experience is evident: a Society of Jews would establish political policies and a scientific plan; they would be executed by a 'Jewish Company' which would dispose of Jewish fortunes and organize commerce in the new land. Herzl had two possible regions in mind: Palestine or Argentina. Argentina was one of the most fertile countries, temperate, vast and sparsely populated. Palestine was the unforgettable historic homeland, and the very name would be a good rallying point. If the Sultan gave the Jews Palestine, Herzl said that they would, in return, manage Turkey's finances. The state of the Jews would be part of a wall of defence for Europe in Asia, an outpost of civilization against barbarism. The Christian places could be controlled by some international arrangement. In 1895 Argentina's population was almost 4 million, that of Palestine around 500,000. In *Der Judenstaat* Herzl did not mention how the local population was to be disposed of; those thoughts were reserved for his diary, at that time not intended for publication.[9]

With the publication of *Der Judenstaat* Herzl became the ambassador of the emerging Zionist movement. In June 1896 he travelled to Constantinople to see the Sultan, but was warned through an intermediary that the Sultan regarded Palestine as a cradle of other religions besides Judaism. Then, having failed to win the sympathy of Baron Edmond de Rothschild, he turned to organizing the Jewish masses behind his ideas, and arranged the first Zionist Congress which met in Basel in August 1897. There, following a tactical manœuvre by Max Nordau, *Heimstätte* was adopted as a synonym for state. The idea of a Jewish 'home' was thought to be less provocative than that of a state. Out of the Basel programme emerged the World Zionist Organization, a national flag, a national anthem, 'Hatıqva', and the Jewish National Fund. Herzl had further unsuccessful negotiations with the Sultan, and was photographed with the German Kaiser, but by July 1902 it was evident that he was unlikely to secure the necessary charter from the Ottoman Empire or Germany. Herzl had hopes of buying the Sultan with South African money, and wanted advice from Rhodes, but the imperial statesman died before he could meet him. There was some foundation for Herzl's hopes in that Zionism grew rapidly in South Africa, and gained the sympathies of both the High Commissioner, Sir Alfred Milner, and the Boer leader, General Jan C. Smuts.[10]

Frustrated, Herzl turned to the country most likely to benefit from the crumbling of the Ottoman Empire, Britain. It appears that he hoped that if Britain granted a Jewish land company a charter with sovereign rights, that, in time, following the Rhodesian example, would lead to a sovereign Jewish state. Herzl tried to link Zionism to British imperial interests, and to play on the anti-Semitism of British statesmen who were so concerned about the flood of Jewish refugees into England following pogroms in Russia that a royal commission had been appointed to examine the question of alien immigration. Herzl gave evidence to the commission, and also met Lord Rothschild to whom he suggested the foundation of a Jewish colony in a British possession, either in the 'Sinai Peninsula, Egyptian Palestine, Cyprus'. The diaries reveal that Herzl felt that even if he secured only Cyprus and El Arish in Sinai, they could, through their pincer position, enable the seizure of Palestine by force when the Ottoman Empire crumbled. Through the offices of Leopold Jacob Greenberg, Herzl, on 20 October 1902, had an interview with the Secretary of State for the Colonies: Joseph Chamberlain. Chamberlain, personally anti-Semitic, was worried about the number of Jews settling in Britain, and impressed with the idea that a Jewish settlement and money could further British imperial interests.[11] Herzl played on these prejudices: a British conscience, disturbed by the thought of legally restricting the immigration of Russian Jews which was causing particular problems in the East End of London, could be solved if these refugees were diverted to the Middle East. Indeed, immigration could solve the Jewish problem, and Jewish capital and labour could make the British colonies prosperous. Herzl said that he wanted Cyprus, El Arish and the Sinai Peninsula. Chamberlain explained that he could not crowd out Greek Christians and Turkish Muslims for the benefit of Jewish immigrants. But Herzl envisaged a 'golden rain' encouraging the Muslims to move away, and the Greeks to sell their lands and move to Athens or Crete. El Arish, however, lay astride the communication links between Britain and India: strategically it could be of great significance. After discovering its position on a map Chamberlain explained that as it was part of Egypt the area was the responsibility of the Foreign Secretary, Lord Lansdowne. Lansdowne insisted on consulting the British agent and consul-general in Egypt, Lord Cromer. Cromer warned that the Egyptian authorities would insist on the Jewish colonists being subject to Egyptian law and that the Zionists would not accept that. A commission went to the area, but Egypt rejected the Zionist proposals.[12]

In November 1902 Chamberlain sailed for South Africa. He stopped off in Mombasa and travelled for 500 miles (800 km) up the Uganda Railway. The land along sections of the railway line, particularly the Kikuyu and Mau escarpments, looked fertile and devoid of inhabitants. It could be suitable for Jewish settlers, and such a move could help to keep East Africa British, and out of the hands of the Germans. On 24 April 1903 Chamberlain suggested to Herzl 'Uganda' – meaning in effect the Kenya highlands – as an area for Jewish colonization. Initially Herzl rejected the proposal: the starting-point had to be in or near Palestine. But he later warmed to the idea: it could be a beginning, and in July the Zionists sent a draft 'charter' to the British government. This was rejected by the assistant legal officer, Cecil Hurst, on the grounds that the Zionists wanted 'the semblance of sovereignty'. Lansdowne feared the possibility of a state within a state: 'it is throughout an *imperium in imperio*'. A letter from the Foreign Office was read to the Zionist Congress outlining a British offer of land

and local autonomy conditional on British overall control. To some it appeared that the Zionists had a sponsor, even international recognition. But it was not Palestine, and the movement split. The Russian Zionists opposed the East Africa scheme, as did leading British Jews. At the next Zionist congress in July 1905 it was rejected, and those favouring the scheme under Israel Zangwill broke away. The White settlers in East Africa, under Sir Charles Eliot, also protested at the preferential terms being offered the Jews. British sympathy cooled, and in any case the seventh Zionist congress ruled that colonization should be confined to Palestine or its immediate environs. Herzl died in 1904. He moved into myth and became considered as the prophet of Zionism: at the end of the first Zionist congress he noted in his diary that at Basel he had founded the Jewish state; at that time such an idea would be regarded with universal laughter, but in fifty years everyone would know it. [13]

The year Herzl died his successor settled in Manchester. Chaim Weizmann, a Jew born in Russia in 1874 who attended university in Berlin, was a practical man rather than a theorizer. He was influenced by the attitude of his friend, Asher Ginsberg who wrote under the pen name of Ahad ha-am. Ha-am saw Palestine as being the focus for the renaissance of Judaism based on the positive love of Zion. [14]

Weizmann consciously chose Britain to settle in: it was the one country likely to sympathize with the Zionist movement. While researching in chemistry at Manchester University Weizmann founded what became known as the Manchester School of Zionism. Its followers included Simon Marks, Harry Sacher and Israel Sieff, all bound together by ties of marriage and by being the sons of Jewish immigrants. [15]

It was during the general election campaign of 1906 that Weizmann first met Arthur James Balfour. At one time, as Prime Minister, Balfour had shown an interest in the Jewish problem since the 1890s when he had publicly deplored anti-Semitism on the Continent. But in 1905 he supported the Aliens Act which restricted the immigration of Russian Jews on allegedly economic grounds. Balfour told the House of Commons on 10 July 1905 that it possibly would not be an advantage to Britain to admit a large number of people who would remain apart. He also supported Chamberlain's schemes for Jewish settlement in either Sinai or East Africa. Some have seen in this a latent anti-Semitism, and a desire to settle Jews somewhere other than Britain. Indeed it was Balfour's curiosity as to why the Jews had rejected the East African offer that led to his meeting with Weizmann. Balfour learnt that any deflection from Palestine was a form of idolatry. He was apparently convinced. [16]

Weizmann did visit Palestine in 1907. He agreed on the need for political activity, but argued that diplomatic pressure alone was not going to convince the governments of Europe; what was necessary was practical work, particularly in the field of colonization in Palestine. Jewish immigration into the area had started in significant numbers in 1882, following the Russian pogroms. The Turks tried to restrict this settlement, but many Jews managed to circumvent the regulations. Reliable statistics are unobtainable, but it is reasonably estimated that of the 100,000 Jews who immigrated to Palestine between 1882 and 1914 at least half left after a short time. In 1882 there were around 24,000 Jews in Palestine. By 1897 the number had probably reached around 50,000 with the creation of 18 settlements or 'agricultural colonies'. The colonization was organized partly by Baron Edmond de Rothschild, partly by the 'Lovers of Zion' societies founded mainly in Russia, later by the Jewish Colonization Association under the auspices of Baron de Hirsch. By 1914 probably around 85,000 Jews had settled, and owned about 2 per cent of the land. Some estimates, however, based on 1922 census figures argue that the number was considerably lower. Certainly, however, in 1914, the Jews did not make up more than 10 per cent of the population of Palestine.[17]

The area in which the new Jewish colonists settled was populated by a people commonly known as 'Arabs'. In the second century BC Arab tribes moved out of Arabia and settled in modern Syria and Iraq. But it was really only with the rise of Islam in the seventh century that the Arab culture and language spread with the Arab conquest of Syria, Iraq, Persia, Egypt, the North African coast and finally Spain. With this flowering of civilization the meaning of 'Arab' changed from that of bedouin, or nomadic tribesmen of Arabia, to refer to all those peoples who spoke the arabic language and had intermixed their blood with Arabs. In some circles the old meaning lasted. 'Arab' is not necessarily co-extensive with Islam, the Muslim religion, and there are examples of Christian Arabs as well as non-Arabic Muslims. The Muslim world, too, divided between those who accepted the 'orthodox' successors, or 'caliphs', to Muhammad, the Sunnis who make up the great majority of adherents, and those who believed that Ali, Muhammad's son-in-law, was the true successor and who formed the minority, the Shias, many of whom live in modern Iran. Islam demands toleration of Jews and Christians as possessors of divine revelation. And just as Jerusalem had become a holy city for Jews and Christians, it became a place of special reverence for the Muslims. Towards the end of the seventh century, in the middle of the stone platform on which the Jewish temple had once stood, the Arabs built a mosque known as the Dome of the Rock. Next to it, on the same sacred platform, was the mosque al Aqsa: from there, the Muslims believe, Muhammad rode on his magic steed to heaven. Together with Mecca, Muhammad's birthplace, and Medina, Jerusalem became one of the three most holy places of Islam. With the disintegration of the Arab Empire Palestine suffered subjection to the Seljuk Turks, the medieval invasions from Christian Europe known as the Crusades, then further subjection to the Mameluke dynasty in Egypt until it was conquered in 1517 by the Ottoman Turks. With the expansion of European trade routes the power of the Ottoman Empire slowly declined, and in the aftermath of the Napoleonic Wars Russia, Britain, France and other European powers tried to manipulate Turkey, the 'sick man of Europe'. Britain appeared concerned to maintain the integrity of the Ottoman Empire and so safeguard the route to the Indian Ocean, a lifeline of empire. But the British government, under the influence of Victorian religious morality, was prepared to interfere to attempt to improve the position of the 'oppressed' Ottoman subjects. The need to maintain stability in the region even led to a British occupation of Egypt in 1882, and by 1898, as in 1840, Britain was willing to go to war with France to ensure this. The Arabs that the Jewish settlers encountered were products of the disintegrating Ottoman Empire.[18]

In the last quarter of the nineteenth century, under Abdul Hamid II, the empire was divided into *vilayet* or provinces, and subdivided into *sanjak* or counties. Some counties were created as separate administrative units known as independent *sanjak*. This was the case in Jerusalem. Large areas of Arabia were only loosely under Turkish power, particularly the principalities ruled by the families of Ibn Saud and Ibn Rashid in the interior. On the southern and eastern coasts Britain was paramount: it occupied Aden and had treaty relationships with the Arab rulers of the Persian Gulf sheikhdoms. In the Ottoman regions there was increasing antagonism from the Arab subjects towards Turkish rule. As one traveller reported in the 1880s: everywhere he encountered a hatred of the Turks, and the Arabs seemed gradually to be thinking of concerted action to get rid of the oppressor. The traveller saw, in the distance, a rising Arab movement. This growing Arab national consciousness has been traced to a literary revival in Syria in the 1850s and 1860s: newly established societies began to study Arab history, literature and culture of the golden age of the Arab Empire. It could be seen as a sort of spiritual renaissance. But this had political overtones, and one authority has argued that at a meeting of the Syrian Scientific Society, the Arab national movement uttered its first cry: a poem was read praising the achievements of the Arab race, the splendours of Arab literature and inciting the Arabs to go to their own past for inspiration. The foundation of the Syrian Protestant College in 1866, under American auspices, probably stimulated this activity.

Growing dissatisfaction with the despotism of Abdul Hamid II increased Arab national awareness. The Young Turk movement was also formed, and from 1889 it recruited supporters from students at military colleges. In 1895 a group of young Turks in Constantinople called themselves the Committee of Union and Progress. Some serving officers, in 1906, began to form themselves into revolutionary cells, and in 1908 there was mutiny in the Turkish armed forces. The Sultan promulgated a Constitution based on the representation of all the provinces. But Arab hopes for autonomous provinces enabling the development of Arab culture were frustrated. Agitation continued in the open with the Arab Literary Club in Constantinople, and also with the formation of several secret societies, the most important of which was Al-Fatah. From Damascus it aimed at independence. The Committee of Union and Progress, standing for centralization, opposed these groups, and in February 1914 Arab feeling against the Turks hardened with the trial of one of the leaders of a secret society, Aziz al-Masri. The first Arab National Congress was held in Paris in 1913. It was concerned with the likely chaos in the Arab provinces brought about through Turkish thwarting of Arab aspirations; there was also the danger of European intervention. A resolution of 21 June, forwarded to Sir Edward Grey, the British Foreign Secretary, demanded that the Arabs should be able to exercise their political rights and play an effective role in the administration of the Empire. Decentralized governments should be established in the Arab provinces.[19] This was only an Arab awakening; it was not yet a 'national movement'. The Arabs, whose numbers were virtually double those of the Turks, usually put their tribal loyalties first.[20]

The Arabs in Palestine were conscious of this awakening. In the early 1880s there were reports from the British consulate of sympathies for their fellows struggling for their race against Ottoman domination and misrule. But by 1891 some Arabs in Palestine were conscious of another threat to their aspirations: the increasing flow of Jewish settlers. They started to demand an end to Jewish immigration and land purchases. In the late 1890s Arabs warned the Zionist movement that its programme was not feasible: there were 650,000 Arabs in Palestine who were already clashing with the Jewish colonists. Because of the administrative structure of the Ottoman Empire knowledge of the Zionist programme spread to the Arabs outside Palestine. It is evident that the Arabs distinguished between the 'Ottoman' Jew and the 'foreign' Jew, only the former deserving equal rights in a decentralized administration. They also knew the difference between Jew and Zionist. Between 1909 and 1914 nationalist opposition in Palestine to Zionism grew: there were fears that if the Jews conquered Palestine the territorial unity of the Arab world would be shattered and the Arab cause weakened. Some nationalists, however, were prepared to work for an agreement with the Zionists, but Arabs were not prepared to support arguments in favour of Zionism for its own sake. Indeed, from 1909, Arabs took effective action against the Zionists, and ensured the passing of restrictive legislation. Arabs outside Palestine were involved in this, and by 1914 there was an awareness that Zionism had to be considered in relation to the wider Arab cause as well as to local conditions in Palestine. Zionism was not responsible for the Arab awakening, but from an early stage it appeared as a threat.[21] The growing dispute between the Arabs and the Zionists, however, was a local one and focused on land. In the first decade of the twentieth century the Middle East became increasingly an area of Great-Power rivalry. The growing German challenge forced Britain to divide its Middle Eastern interests with rivals: in 1904 Britain agreed to the French having a free hand in Morocco in exchange for the same in Egypt; in 1907 Britain and Russia divided Persia into spheres of influence. The map of Europe had been fought out in Africa; the same now happened in the Middle East. This was the age of imperialism and local aspirations were not thought particularly significant.[22]

REFERENCES

1.   Marcel Proust, trans. C. K. Scott Moncrieff, *The Sweet Cheat Gone* (London 1941), p. 219.
2.   For an account of the Dreyfus affair in relation to anti-Semitism see Hannah Arendt, *The Origins of Totalitarianism*, 2nd edn (New York 1958), pp. 3–120; *L'Affaire Dreyfus*, France 1899, directed by Georges Méliès; *Dreyfus*, Great Britain 1931, directed by F. W. Kraemar starring Cedric Hardwicke; *The Life of Emile Zola*, United States 1937, directed by William Dieterle starring Paul Muni; *I Accuse*, United States 1958, directed by and starring José Ferrer.
3.   Neville J. Mandel, *The Arabs and Zionism before World War I* (Berkeley 1976), pp. xix–xx.
4.   Histories of anti-Semitism include: Leon Poliakov, *The History of Anti-Semitism*, 3 vols (London 1966–75); Ernest L. Abel, *The Roots of Anti-Semitism* (London 1975); Leonard Schroeter, *The Last Exodus* (Seattle 1979); James Parkes, *The Jew in the Medieval Community* (London 1938); Jacob Katz, *Out of the Ghetto. The Social Background of Jewish Emancipation, 1770–1870* (Cambridge, Mass. 1973); Jean Laloum, *La France Anti-sémite de Darquier de Pellepoix* (Paris 1968). For specialized studies see Peter G. J. Pulzer, *The Rise of Political Anti-Semitism in Germany and Austria* (New York 1964); Colin Holmes, *Anti-Semitism in British Society, 1976–1939* (London 1979); Paul Lendvai, *Anti-Semitism in Eastern Europe* (London 1971). Short summaries can be found in Martin Gilbert, *Exile and Return. The Emergence of Jewish Statehood* (London 1978), pp. 26–43; Walter Laqueur, *A History of Zionism* (London 1972), pp. 3–39; Harold Wilson, *The Chariot of Israel, Britain, America and the State of Israel* (London 1981), pp. 8–11. Excerpts from a summary of Pinsker's *Auto-Emancipation* can be found in Arthur Hertzberg (Ed.), *The Zionist Idea* (Connecticut 1970), pp. 178–98. There is an English edition of *Auto-Emancipation* included in B. Natangahu (Ed.), *Road to Freedom* (New York 1944). A philosophical discussion of the links between the composer, Richard Wagner, the philosopher, Friedrich Nietzsche and anti-Semitism can be found in J. L. Talmon, *Israel Among the Nations*

(London 1970), pp. 50–67.

5. David Vital, *The Origins of Zionism* (Oxford 1975), p. xvi. Vital argues that 'Palestine' was a Roman invention which fell into disuse until the arrival of the British.

6. Histories of the Jewish people include: Werner Keller, *Diaspora. The Post-Biblical History of the Jews* (London 1971); Roland de Vaux, *The Early History of Israel*, 2 vols (London 1978); John M. Allegro, *The Chosen People* (London 1971); H. H. Ben-Sasson (Ed.), *A History of the Jewish People* (London 1976); Solomon Grayzel, *A History of the Jews* (New York 1968); Heinrich Gratz, *History of the Jews*, 6 vols (Philadelphia 1898). There is a convenient summary of the history of the Jews in *Cmd 5479, Palestine Royal Commission Report* (July 1937), pp. 2–15; see also Gilbert, op. cit., pp. 3–25; Wilson, op. cit., pp. 1–11; and the political case made in Berl Locker, *A Stiff-Necked People, Palestine in Jewish History* (London 1946).

7. See Hertzberg, op. cit., *passim*, for a collection of these writings; Vital, *Origins of Zionism*, pp. 23–229; Laqueur, op. cit., pp. 40–83; for a consideration of these ideas in a recent context see Harold Fisch, *The Zionist Revolution. A New Perspective* (London 1978); for the case made by some Arab writers that the roots of Zionism can be found in the designs of imperialism in early-nineteenth-century Europe see A. W. Kayyali (Ed.), *Zionism, Imperialism and Racism* (London 1979), esp. pp. 9–105.

8. Raphael Patai (Ed.), trans. Harry Zohn, *The Complete Diaries of Theodor Herzl*, 5 vols (New York 1960), pp. 88–9; Desmond Stewart, *Theodor Herzl* (London 1974), pp. 71–2, 169, 188–92.

9. There are various English translations of Theodor Herzl, *The Jewish State*, trans. S. d'Avigdor (London 1967); a revised version by Ben Halpern and Moshe Kohn is in Hertzberg, op. cit., pp. 204–26.

10. Vital, *Origins of Zionism*, pp. 354–70; Laqueur, op. cit., pp. 160–1; Stewart, op. cit., pp. 292–3.

11. R. Patai, op. cit., pp. 1, 294, 344; Richard P. Stevens (Ed.), *Zionism and Palestine before the Mandate* (Beirut 1972), pp. 12–15; Julian Amery, *Life of Joseph Chamberlain* (London 1951), Vol. IV, pp. 256–61; Denis Judd, *Balfour and the British Empire* (London 1968), p. 99.

12. Marvin Lowenthal (Ed.), *The Diaries of Theodor Herzl* (New York 1956), pp. 370–83; *FO 78* (Public Record Office, London), 5479, contains the British documents of the Anglo-Zionist negotiations on Sinai; R. Patai, op. cit., pp. 1432 and 1458–60; see also, Frank Hardie and Irwin Hermann, *Britain and Zion, the Fateful Entanglement* (Belfast 1980), pp. 6–8.

13. Amery, op. cit., Vol. IV, pp. 262–7; *FO 2* (Public Record Office, London), 785, contains the British documents on the East African discussions; R. Patai, op. cit., pp. 1, 473–5; Stewart, op. cit., pp. 327–9; Hardie and Hermann, op. cit., pp. 9–15; R. Patai, op. cit., p. 581; a map of the East Africa settlement areas is printed in Stewart, op. cit., facing p. 205. Besides Stewart, biographers of Herzl include Alex Bein, *Theodor Herzl, A Biography* (London 1957); Israel Cohen, *Theodor Herzl, Founder of Political Zionism* (New York 1959); Jacob de Haas, *Theodor Herzl, A Biographical Study*, 2 vols (New York 1927); Josef

Fraenkel, *Theodor Herzl, A Biography* (London 1946); Josef Patai, trans. Francis Magyar, *Star over Jordan, the Life of Theodore Herzl* (New York 1946); Amos Elon, *Herzl* (London 1975); see also David Vital, *Zionism: the Formative Years* (Oxford 1982), esp. pp. 95–271.

14. Leon Simon, *Ahad ha-am. Asher Ginzberg; a biography* (Philadelphia 1960), p. 193.

15. For an account of Weizmann's early life see Chaim Weizmann, *Trial and Error* (London 1949), pp. 11–174; see generally, Paul Goodman (Ed.), *Chaim Weizmann, A Tribute on his Seventieth Birthday* (London 1945); Dan Leon and Yehuda Adin, *Chaim Weizmann, Statesman of the Jewish Renaissance* (Jerusalem 1974); Meyer W. Weisgal and Joel Carmichael, *Chaim Weizmann – a Biography by Several Hands* (London, 1962); Meyer W. Weisgal, *Chaim Weizmann – Scientist Builder of the Jewish Commonwealth* (New York 1944); for an account of the Manchester School based on information from Lord Sieff see Jon Kimche, *Palestine or Israel* (London 1973), pp. 93–158.

16. *United Kingdom Parliamentary Debates House of Commons*, 149, col. 155, 10 July 1905; Sydney H. Zebel, *Balfour. A Political Biography* (Cambridge 1973), 238–40; K. Young, *Arthur James Balfour* (London 1963), p. 388; Judd, op. cit., pp. 99–100; Blanche E. C. Dugdale, *Arthur James Balfour*, Vol. I (London 1936), pp. 433–6; Hardie and Hermann, op. cit., pp. 79–80; Weizmann, op. cit., pp. 142–5.

17. Isaiah Berlin, 'The biographical facts', in Leon and Adin, op. cit., pp. 33–92 at p. 51; Weizmann, op. cit., pp. 156–71; Bernard Wasserstein, *The British in Palestine. The Mandatory Government and the Arab–Jewish Conflict 1917–1929* (London 1978), p. 5; for an account of the Jewish settlements see Simon Schama, *Two Rothschilds and the Land of Israel* (London 1978); Mandel, op. cit., esp. pp. 1–31 and 229; A. L. Tibawi, *Anglo-Arab Relations and the Question of Palestine 1914–1921* (London 1977), pp. 15–27.

18. William Yale, *The Near East. A Modern History* (Ann Arbor 1958), pp. 3–144; Peter Mansfield, *The Ottoman Empire and its Successors* (London 1973), pp. 1–13; John Bagot Glubb, *Britain and the Arabs, A Study of Fifty Years, 1908 to 1958* (London 1959), pp. 19–46; Jon Kimche, *The Second Arab Awakening* (London 1970), pp. 9–16; A. H. Hourani, *Great Britain and the Arab World* (London undated), pp. 8–10; see also J. Carmichael, *The Shaping of the Arabs* (London 1967); B. Lewis, *The Emergence of Modern Turkey* (London 1968); Thomas W. Arnold, *The Caliphate 623–1924* (London 1965).

19. *British Documents on the Origins of the War, 1898–1914*, Vol. X, pp. 824–6, esp. FO 29037/29037/13/44, Carnegie to Grey, No. 339, 24 June 1913 and Enclosure of Resolutions voted at the Arab congress.

20. George Antonius, *The Arab Awakening. The Story of the Arab National Movement* (London 1938), pp. 13–125; a summary of critiques of Antonius can be found in George E. Kirk, *A Short History of the Middle East from the Rise of Islam to Modern Times*, 7th edn (London 1964), pp. 308–19; Glubb, op. cit., pp. 49–54; Mansfield, op. cit., pp. 14–33; Zeine N. Zeine, *Arab-Turkish Relations and the Emergence of Arab Nationalism* (Beirut 1958); *The Struggle for Arab Independence* (Beirut 1960); *The Emergence of Arab Nationalism* (Beirut 1966); Sylvia G. Haim,

Arab Nationalism: An Anthology (Berkeley 1962); Albert Hourani, *Arabic Thought in the Liberal Age, 1789–1939* (London 1962).
21. A.W. Kayyali, *Palestine. A Modern History* (London 1978), p. 15 quoting documents in the Public Record Office London in, *FO 226, FO 195*, 1477; Tibawi, op. cit., pp. 18–19; Mandel, op. cit., *passim.*
22. Elizabeth Monroe, *Britain's Moment in the Middle East*, 2nd edn (London 1981), pp. 11–21; R. Robinson, J. Gallagher with A. Denny, *Africa and the Victorians* (London 1965).

TWO PLEDGES AND THE ORIGINS OF A CONFLICT

Before the outbreak of the First World War it appears that Germany hoped for an accommodation with Britain over the disintegrating Ottoman Empire. In 1903 Germany had secured the concession for the building of the Baghdad Railway; Britain had shown a readiness to compromise over this and over Kuwait. By 1912 Britain was even prepared to allow for increasing French influence: an understanding – not known even to all members of the Cabinet – was reached about the disposition of the British fleet in the North Sea and the Atlantic, and the French in the Mediterranean. The French could have seen this as leading to future opportunities in Syria, and in 1913 negotiations over the Ottoman loan and the Baghdad Railway assured the French presence in Syria and Lebanon while arousing the suspicions of the local population. Indeed, in May 1913, the Kaiser thought that Britain and France were already squabbling as to which one would take over Palestine and Syria. By the end of July 1914, however, the Kaiser was prepared to launch a *jihad* or holy war against Britain: he assured the ruler of Afghanistan of his desire for the Muslim nations to be independent, and of the continuation of the common interests of Germany and the Muslims after war; General Liman von Sanders was commanded to stay on in Constantinople to promote feeling against Britain; a team was formed under Max von Oppenheim to arrange subversion in Muslim countries and it worked in close alliance with German Zionists. Germany hoped to sabotage, or annex, the Anglo-Persian oilfields. Contact was also made with Hussein Ibn 'Ali, the Sherif of Mecca. As custodian of the holy places and a lineal descendant of Muhammad, Hussein was thought to have great influence. He agreed to aid German propaganda, and also to other unspecified operations in the area he controlled. For this Hussein was paid by the Germans till at least June 1915. As a reinsurance policy the Germans also contacted Ibn Saud, the Sherif's main rival. But Arabia in the end seemed peripheral, and there was the difficulty that the Turkish authorities did not like the encouragement of subversion among their Arab subjects. For the first few years of the war most of the world Zionist movement

wanted Germany to win. German diplomats were prepared to inter-
cede with the Turks over the Jews in Palestine, and in November 1915
Zionist pressure secured a directive to consuls that the German
government was well disposed towards Jewish aspirations in Palestine.
Berlin, however, refused to make any official declaration supporting
Zionism, and in August 1917 Djemal Pasha, the Turkish commander
in Palestine, told Zionists in Germany that he was hostile to the idea of
a Jewish Palestine as he had to consider Arab feelings.[1]

Before 1914, with an eye on the route to India, Britain had an
interest in the stability of the Ottoman Empire. But, as early as 1909, a
subcommittee of the Committee of Imperial Defence suggested that, if
there were war with Turkey, Arab feeling against Turkey could be
cultivated to balance any Turkish propaganda promoting Muslim sentiment. Forces could also be landed at Haifa, and British strategy
would require communications and intelligence networks in the land
east of Sinai, in effect Palestine.[2] In 1910 Lord Kitchener visited
Constantinople, and noted the German take-over. His experiences in
India and the Sudan had awakened him to the political importance of
Islam. Germany's position in the Ottoman Empire appeared to
threaten Britain's position in the Persian Gulf and India. The Committee of Imperial Defence ordered reconnaissance operations in the
Lebanon, Palestine and the Sinai–Negeb area. Around 1912 a dele-
gation of Syrian Muslims visited Kitchener, then consul-general in
Cairo, and petitioned Britain to annex Syria to Egypt and to grant
Syria an independent administration. About the same time members
of the Arab secret societies approached the British consul-general in
Beirut with the request that Britain assist the Arabs in their struggle
against the Turks. These advances were tactfully received.[3] Then, at
the time when Britain was campaigning in favour of Aziz al-Masri,
Kitchener was approached on 5 February 1914 by Ibn al-Hussein
Abdullah, the son of the Sherif of Mecca, on his father's behalf: there
was trouble with the new Turkish governor in the Hejaz; should the
Arab tribes in the area fight for the Sherif against Turkey would
Britain stop reinforcements being sent that could prevent the Arabs
from exercising their rights in their own country around the holy
places? Kitchener's reply was seemingly negative.[4]

On 18 March Sir Lewis Mallet reported from Constantinople that it
was impossible to say what prospect there was for a united Arab
movement. Any sherif of Mecca could put himself at the head of an
Arab movement, and his alleged descent from Muhammad could be an
asset. The present Sherif, however, would have difficulty in that he
had been seen as acting for the Turkish government in his squabbles
with Ibn Saud and Idris. But a combination of the Sherif, Ibn Saud who
had shown his independence from the Turks, and Seyyid Talib from
Basra could result in unrest, particularly if these leaders combined in
constitutional agitation for devolution or autonomy, or even in a

separatist movement. Mallet thought that the Arabs looked to the British for sympathy, and if they achieved independence, protection; Arab officers in the Turkish army had even enquired as to the British attitude. Arab success could mean that the caliphate, the seat of the chief civil and religious leader of Islam, would pass out of Turkish hands. Europe would be faced with the partition of the Turkish Empire, and there could be repercussions in Muslim India over any prolonged struggle over the caliphate.[5] In April Abdullah was in Cairo again, and this time sent for Ronald Storrs, the acting Oriental Secretary. On 18 April Storrs learnt that the Arabs would before long achieve 'complete unity'; Abdullah wanted an agreement from Britain to maintain the status quo in the Arabian Peninsula and to eliminate Turkish aggression. The next day, on instructions from Kitchener, Storrs explained that Abdullah could not expect any encouragement from the British government. Britain's only interest in Arabia was the safety of Indian pilgrims. Kitchener observed, however, that the Arabs were 'much excited'.[6]

After the outbreak of war Sir Edward Grey, the Secretary of State for Foreign Affairs, on 1 September, instructed that when Turkey joined Germany Britain should immediately encourage and support the Arabs to take over Arabia. After initial soundings a note drafted by Kitchener, and approved by Grey, was prepared for transmission to Abdullah: for Arab help in the war Britain would guarantee that no internal intervention took place in Arabia, and would assist the Arabs to resist external aggression. This was transmitted to Cairo on 31 October. Kitchener referred to the 'Arab nation'; Storrs in the version passed on to Abdullah spoke only of Arabs 'in general', though there is confusion over what the Arabic version could have conveyed. Abdullah replied that he took this letter as a basis for action.[7] Turkey became Germany's ally in the war on 31 October 1914. Kitchener was Secretary of State for War. At a meeting of the newly formed War Council on 25 November 1914 mention was made of the 1909 recommendation that an attack on Egypt could be met by a landing at Haifa. Instead troops were concentrated in Egypt to counter a possible attack on the Suez Canal. An expeditionary force of the Indian army occupied Basra in southern Mesopotamia and in February 1915 Lord Hardinge, the Viceroy of India, promised that Turkish rule would not be restored in its old form.

Grey and the Cabinet were concerned about the French and Russian attitudes: Russia might want Constantinople, and France, Syria. On 10 March 1915 the War Council discussed these countries' rival claims to the Christian holy places in Jerusalem.[8] On 23 March Grey learnt that M. Delcassé thought that Britain and France should embark on informal discussions, either verbally or through private letters, about their requirements in Asia Minor. The Cabinet had not considered British desiderata, but Grey told M. Cambon that Britain had already stipulated that when the Ottoman Empire collapsed there had to be, in the interests of Islam, an independent Muslim political unit somewhere else. Its centre would be the Muslim holy places, and it would include Arabia. Britain and France would have to settle what else should be incorporated. It had not been decided whether Mesopotamia would be included in this independent Muslim state, or whether Britain should promote its own claim in that region.[9]

On 18 December 1914 Britain announced a protectorate over Egypt, and Sir Henry McMahon, a product of Sandhurst who had served the government of India, was appointed to the new post of High Commissioner. Another military man, Sir Reginald Wingate, was Governor-General of the Sudan. He passed on to Grey the interest in some Sudanese quarters over the British message that an Arab of true race might assume the caliphate at Mecca or Medina. As a result of this Grey authorized McMahon, should he think it desirable, to let it be known that Britain would make it an essential condition of any peace that the Arabian Peninsula and the Muslim holy places would remain under the control of an 'independent Sovereign Moslem state'. At that time the territory to be included could not be defined. The caliphate question was to be decided by Muslims without interference. The Shia holy places, mainly in Iraq, required separate treatment, and Grey said that he had worded the British promise so as not to commit Britain.[10] With McMahon's authority a leaflet was distributed in the Hejaz to this effect with the assurance of no annexation and independence from all foreign control. In the Foreign Office, George R. Clerk observed that this was open to a wide interpretation and went further than anything authorized.[11]

It is not clear whether British officials intended the Muslim holy places in Jerusalem to be covered by their guarantee. Weizmann had other ideas about the future of that city, and by the end of 1914 he was forging contacts with important people in British political life. He converted C. P. Scott, the editor of the *Manchester Guardian*, to Zionism. On 3 December 1914, through Scott, Weizmann met David Lloyd George who as a young man had acted as legal adviser to the Zionists over the East African scheme, and Herbert Samuel, a Cabinet minister and a Jew who had abandoned his religion though he retained his links with the Jewish community. Samuel mentioned a memorandum he was preparing about a Jewish state in Palestine. Later, in January 1915, through an introduction from Lord Rothschild, Weizmann met Lord Bertie, the British ambassador in Paris. Bertie was not impressed with the scheme outlined to form an Israelite state in Palestine, preferably under the protection of Britain. Bertie was sceptical of the reaction of the Pope, Italy and Catholic France with its hatred of the Jews. The Prime Minister, H. H. Asquith, recorded at the end of January 1915 that he was not attracted by Samuel's draft memorandum on the future of Palestine: it seemed to suggest that race was everything and read like an updated edition of Disraeli's *Tancred*. Asquith did not like this proposed addition to Britain's responsibilities, and the planting of 3 or 4 million European Jews in a barren land was not practical. In March, Samuel sent a revised version: it would be too costly and dangerous for the Zionist movement to establish an autonomous Jewish state in Palestine immediately; rather there should be a British protectorate that could be a safeguard to Egypt. Britain should assist the Jews through immigration preferences and land purchases to become the majority, and achieve self-government. The inclusion of Palestine within the Empire would enhance British prestige and win the favour of Jews throughout the world, particularly the 2 million settled in the United States. The Protestant world also had a deep-rooted sympathy with the fulfilment of the prophecy that the Hebrews would have restored to them the land of their inheritance. Asquith remained sceptical, and noted that Kitchener had a poor opinion of Palestine and favoured instead the port of Alexandretta, Britain leaving the Jews and the holy places alone. The Prime Minister thought that the only protagonist of the Samuel scheme was Lloyd George: this was not through a concern for the Jews but because Lloyd George, with a background of fundamentalist Welsh Christianity, did not want the Christian holy places to go to agnostic, atheist France. This was probably an exaggeration by Asquith.[12]

Asquith, himself, betrayed a latent anti-Semitism: in March 1915 he described the Jews as a tribe: scattered and unattractive. But it seems that the most specific opposition at this time was formulated by Edwin Montagu, the son of a Jewish banker and later to be Secretary of State for India and husband to Asquith's young lady friend, Venetia Stanley: on 16 March Montagu recorded that it would be disastrous to establish a Jewish state under British protection. Montagu, who had been assimilated, argued that there was no longer a homogeneous Jewish race and suggested that if the Jewish peoples stopped asking for special favours, Zionism would die.[13] Samuel also saw Grey several times but, judging from his policy, the Foreign Secretary was not impressed.[14] In any case a War Council meeting on 19 March revealed divisions between Kitchener and Indian government opinion on the eastern question, with Grey anxious to keep Britain out of further territorial complications.

Asquith set up an interdepartmental committee, the Committee on Asiatic Turkey, to discuss British desiderata. Established on 8 April 1915 it was chaired by Sir Maurice de Bunsen, a sixty-three-year-old former ambassador to Vienna, and had as its secretary Maurice Hankey who was in his thirties. The most active member, however, was Mark Sykes, also in his thirties. Sykes, a devout Roman Catholic who had had an unconventional education during which he had travelled widely in the Middle East without acquiring a knowledge of Arabic, showed proconsular ambitions, and, through the advocacy of

Oswald Fitzgerald, Kitchener's personal secretary, had managed to be attached to the War Office. Sykes was Kitchener's personal representative on the de Bunsen committee. Early on the committee decided that Britain's interests could not be served by the status quo, and Sykes advocated a scheme of partition, or, alternatively, of spheres of interest with a British Mediterranean port at Haifa and a railway link with British Mesopotamia. These schemes were dismissed as unacceptable. Sykes then devised one of devolution, dividing the Ottoman Empire into five provinces with Britain being able to secure influence in the Asian ones. It was this which the committee finally recommended on 30 June. British desiderata included the fulfilment of the pledges already given to the Gulf and the Arab sheikhs, and, generally, of the assurances to the Sherif of Mecca and the Arabs. Palestine was considered a special case which could eventually be settled with the other powers: a self-determining Palestinian people could prove to be a neutral guardian of the holy places in Jerusalem.[15]

Sykes was sent east to sound British officials about their reaction to the de Bunsen report. In Cairo he saw Storrs who had been a fellow undergraduate at Cambridge and with whom he shared an inadequate knowledge of Arabic. Storrs introduced Sykes to Gilbert Clayton, the Chief of Military Intelligence, and a former member of Wingate's staff in the Sudan. Sykes approved of Clayton's devout Roman Catholicism. Both Clayton and Storrs apparently influenced Sykes who formed a close relationship with them; the mood of these officials in Cairo favoured Hussein as having political power over the Arabs. From there, on 14 July, Sykes suggested to London that if France would forgo its claims in Syria, then Mesopotamia, Syria and Palestine could fall under the government of the Sultan of Egypt and the spiritual dominion of the Sherif of Mecca. That would mean that they would be controlled from Britain. McMahon's response to de Bunsen was to favour partition, with Haifa going to Britain, and Palestine being included in the dominions of the Sultan of Egypt. That would give Jerusalem a nominal Muslim ruler while the local self-administration could be adapted to meet international interests. The officer in command in Egypt, General Sir John Maxwell, disagreed: he favoured devolution. Mesopotamia and Palestine could be under British protection with the Sherif of Mecca as nominal suzerain.[16]

On 14 July Hussein sent a messenger to Cairo with a note. It arrived five weeks later. McMahon's initial reaction was favourable. Storrs, who did the translation, was not so impressed. Hussein explained that the Arabs had decided to regain their freedom; they hoped for British assistance. Emphasizing the identity of British and Arab interests, the Sherif proposed a defensive and conditionally offensive alliance. The terms included British recognition (acknowledgement) of the independence of the Arab countries from Mersina and along the latitude of 37 degrees to the Persian frontier in the north, in the east by the Gulf of

Basra, on the south by the Indian Ocean with the exception of Aden, and on the west by the Red Sea and the Mediterranean up to Mersina. Storrs noted that the Sherif had no mandate from other potentates, knew that he was demanding more than he could expect and that the boundaries should be reserved for subsequent discussion. These points were taken up by McMahon in his advice to the Foreign Office: the Sherif had no mandate beyond Hejaz; and though his pretensions were exaggerated it would be difficult to negotiate in detail without discouraging him. McMahon suggested a reply acknowledging gratification at the identity of British and Arab interests, but pointing out that boundary discussions were premature during the war, and noting with regret that some Arabs were still working with Turks and Germans. After initial approval of this reply, Grey endorsed George R. Clerk's suggestion that 'discuss' replace 'negotiate'.

Austen Chamberlain, the Secretary of State for India, had earlier expressed reservations about approaches to Hussein: only diplomatic assistance should be given; material assistance could conflict with British obligations to maintain the independence of other Arab chiefs. The Arabs should be left to manage their own affairs, and Britain should avoid an adventurous policy in the interior. The terms proposed by the Sherif seemed to Chamberlain to have been dictated by extreme Pan-Arab aspirations. On 30 August McMahon replied to Hussein: it would be premature to discuss details of frontiers in the heat of war.[17]

Hussein, in a note dated 9 September complaining of British ambiguity, asked for a statement of British policy and an indication of what action the Arabs should take. In Cairo, Clayton and Maxwell used the apparent testimony of an Arab officer, Faruki, to promote the idea of an Arab revolt, and the need to act quickly lest the Arabs turn to Germany. McMahon, influenced by Clayton, on 20 October urged action. In the Foreign Office Clerk suggested that Britain accept the establishment of an Arab state, and start discussions to determine the boundaries. But the Permanent Under-Secretary, Sir Arthur Nicolson, pointing to rivalries among the Arabs, supported only an interim reply. Grey authorized McMahon to give assurances of Arab independence and boundary discussions, but, in the event of something more precise being required, McMahon could give that. Grey, however, did urge circumspection. McMahon's letter of 24 October was consequently cautious, and perhaps deliberately obscure. He suggested that the two districts of Mersina and Alexandretta, and portions of Syria to the west of the districts of Damascus, Homs, Hama and Aleppo could not be said to be purely Arab and should therefore be excluded. Britain's existing treaties with Arab chiefs could not be prejudiced, and Britain was not free to act in those areas which would harm the interests of its ally, France. The Arabs should recognize Britain's established position in the *vilayets* of Baghdad and Basra which necessitated special administrative arrangements. It was also understood that the Arabs would employ only British advisers. There was subsequent confusion as to the area covered by the districts of Damascus, Homs and Aleppo, and Hussein could have been misled by the Arabic translation. This argument, however, focused on the position of Palestine which does not appear to have been an issue uppermost in the minds of either the British or Arab negotiators.[18]

Grey authorized what McMahon wrote. Perhaps the Foreign Secretary was particularly influenced by the arguments of Wingate and his message of 7 September 1915 that in the prevailing confusion over the future government of Syria, Mesopotamia and even the Arabian Peninsula – regions in which British actions and political arrangements would be criticized by Muslims all over the world – he was increasingly drawn to an attempted solution on Pan-Arabian lines. Wingate suffered no delusion about the political difficulties in the way, or about 'the elusive character of Arabian political conceptions', but he thought that it was not impossible that in the future a federation of semi-independent Arab states could exist under European guidance and supervision, linked together by racial and linguistic bonds, owing spiritual allegiance to a single Arab primate, and looking to Britain as patron and protector.[19]

The subsequent negotiations with the Sherif were complicated by the British withdrawal from Gallipoli, and conversations with the French. The French thought that they would have to be consulted about the boundaries of Syria. Accordingly, on Grey's authorization, McMahon wrote to the Sherif on 13 December to explain that, as French interests were involved, reservations about the *vilayets* of Aleppo and Beirut required further consideration. To dispel Hussein's hesitations, reference was made to Arab independence from Turkish domination, but it was pointed out that the strength and permanence of the agreement depended on Hussein's ability to unite the Arab peoples, and the efficacy of the measures the Arabs would take to aid the joint cause. Hussein insisted that the issue of Beirut and the northern coast would be returned to after the war, but said that the Arabs would keep to their resolve to revolt against the Turks. Britain agreed to examine the matter of the *vilayet* of Baghdad at the peace, but only mentioned the friendship between Britain and France in relation to the northern territories.[20] This seemed to satisfy the Sherif: in a letter dated 18 February he spoke of the 'required understanding and intimacy' being attained. Several Foreign and India Office officials minuted their disquiet.[21]

British reservations about French interests derived from the considerations of an interdepartmental committee, chaired by Nicolson, which started negotiations with the first secretary of the French embassy in London, François Georges-Picot, a suave former consul at Beirut, on 23 November 1915. Picot demanded Syria, and Palestine apart from the holy places, for France. When Sykes returned from his eastern tour gauging reaction to the de Bunsen report, he spoke to the War Committee on 16 December: he argued that an Egyptian offensive against the Turks would win the Arabs for the Allied cause. Though Hussein and his followers liked Britain, they were frightened of the French, and so reluctant to join the fight against the Turks. Sykes was conscious of France's traditional position in the Middle East, probably through the influence of a French Dominican, Father Jaussen, whom Sykes had met in Cairo. Sykes warned that the Arabs should not be encouraged at the expense of good relations with France. After this he was invited to attend Nicolson's committee on 21 December. At that meeting Picot offered modified French desiderata: France was willing to accommodate the Arabs lest they went over to the enemy, and so proposed that the envisaged Arab state be divided into British and French commercial spheres of influence. The British sphere would be based on Mesopotamia, the French on Syria. France would also cede a British port in Palestine in exchange for Mosul. Special arrangements would be necessary for Jerusalem. Nicolson asked Sykes to draft a memorandum with Picot outlining the requirements of the parties. Using the maps he had prepared for the de Bunsen committee, Sykes negotiated an arrangement which secured French acceptance of the Arab 'confederation' under the nominal leadership of the Sherif of Mecca, of most of Palestine under an 'international administration' with an acknowledgement that world Jewry had 'a conscientious and sentimental interest in the future of the country', and that Jerusalem also contained the holiest Muslim shrine outside Mecca, and of a British land link between Palestine and Mesopotamia. In his correspondence with McMahon the Sherif had acknowledged the need for British advisers.

The Sykes–Picot plan, however, envisaged an Arab confederation in which France would have economic priority in the north and Britain in the south. Furthermore, in an area along the Syrian coast, France, and at the head of the Persian Gulf, Britain, could establish such direct or indirect administration as they desired. Britain took the ports of Haifa and Acre in Palestine, and Mosul fell within the French region of economic priority as did Homs, Hama, Aleppo and Damascus. Foreign and India Office reaction was not altogether favourable. In particular, Arthur Hirtzel of the India Office pointed to the sacrifice of Mosul and the French desire to exploit the oil deposits there. But the War Office liked the idea of a wedge of French territory between the area of British influence and Russia. In any case Nicolson saw an escape clause: should the Arab scheme fail Britain and France could make new claims. The Sykes–Picot plan was accepted at an inter-departmental meeting on 4 February, but it was pointed out to the French that the British sacrifice was dependent on the Arabs fulfilling the conditions. France agreed, but Grey insisted on Russian consent.

Sykes volunteered to accompany Picot to Petrograd, and before leaving learnt Samuel's views on the need for a British protectorate over Palestine to promote Jewish aspirations. In Russia, Sykes was impressed with the power of Zionism, and he and Picot discussed how the Allies could secure Zionist support. But the Foreign Office did not like the suggestion of a chartered Jewish company in Palestine. Samuel introduced Sykes to the rabbi, Moses Gaster, and Sykes's attitude to the Jews changed from one of suspicion to admiration. Picot, however, was not impressed by Gaster. Grey also considered the proposals of a Jewish, but anti-Zionist journalist, Lucien Wolf, for securing political rights and facilities for immigration and colonization in Palestine and, in time, management of internal affairs. Possibly disturbed by reports from the ambassador in Washington, Sir Cecil Spring-Rice, about Zionist sympathy in the United States for Germany, Grey overrode Nicolson's warnings that the Zionists were possibly in a minority, and that in any case Britain could not advocate another scheme at a time when it was proposing an international administration for Palestine.

Lord Robert Cecil, the Under-Secretary of State at the Foreign Office, also pointed to the international power of the Jews. The scheme was not pursued: Russia did not object but the French had doubts. The discussions in Petrograd led to France and Russia adjusting their territorial difficulties, and exchanges of letters between the three countries, May to October 1916, made the Sykes–Picot agreement official. Grey, as he told the War Committee on 23 March 1916, doubted whether anything would come of these territorial arrangements or the Arab rising on which they depended. In any case British officials took care to ensure that there were no contradictions between the assurances to Hussein and the Sykes–Picot agreement. Britain insisted that French interests would have to be taken into account, and only mentioned the hope of Anglo-French friendship as a means of settling the matter after the war.[22]

On 10 June 1916 Hussein raised the Arab revolt. By the end of September forces of Arab tribesmen had captured Mecca, Jedda and Taif, but Medina remained in Turkish control. The momentum of the revolt seemed uncertain. In Cairo, following pressure from Sykes in December 1915, an Arab bureau had been formed headed by D. G. Hogarth, an Oxford orientalist, assisted by Clayton, Storrs and Kinahan Cornwallis. T. E. Lawrence was attached to the bureau in January 1916. Small, long-haired and untidy, a shared interest in classics led to his befriending Storrs. In October 1916 Storrs secured permission to take Lawrence as a companion on a mission to Jedda to reorganize the Arab revolt.

T. E. Lawrence became a legend. After the war an American journalist, Lowell Thomas, helped to create a myth with a widely seen lantern slide show. In 1962 the British film director, David Lean, released *Lawrence of Arabia*, a film which rapidly acquired a status comparable to that of *Gone with the Wind* two decades previously; Lean did not attempt a definitive picture of Lawrence, for the film was structured so as to present Lawrence only through other people's eyes. Even the female Russian agent in John le Carré's *Tinker, Tailor, Soldier, Spy* wanted to think of her British confessor as 'Colonel Lawrence'. Arguably the best-known Englishman of the twentieth century, if anything, Lawrence's fascination has been enhanced by revelations about his personal life. In a sense the legend and myth have become the reality. Whether Lawrence contributed significantly to the Arab revolt, or indeed whether that was only a sideshow, is almost irrelevant. It was through Lawrence of Arabia that Westerners learnt that Arabs did exist. Perhaps there is even an element of truth in Robert Bolt's script for the film when Feisal is depicted as saying, in a burning Damascus, that Lawrence gave the Arabs something of inestimable value, the concept of being Arab. If this is so, Lawrence achieved what the Arab secret societies had failed to do.

Lawrence said that his main motive in Arabia was personal. His account of the revolt, *Seven Pillars of Wisdom*, confirms this. And, as he explained in the introduction, the book was not a history of the Arab movement, but of himself in it. The emphasis on his role, he ceded, was unfair to his British colleagues. Indeed *Seven Pillars of Wisdom* does not pretend to be academic history; it should rather be compared to Leo Tolstoy's *War and Peace* or Paul Scott's *The Raj Quartet*. Lawrence's 'history' can be found in his published despatches and the collection of articles he wrote after the war. *Seven Pillars of Wisdom* is a great work in the tradition of quest literature, comparable to Herman Melville's *Moby Dick*. It is evident that Lawrence has fictionalized many of the episodes, perhaps to convey an inner truth, if only to himself. But it does offer a key to Lawrence's motives.

Lawrence dedicated *Seven Pillars* to 'S.A.':

> I loved you, so I drew these tides of men into my
>   hands and wrote my will across the sky in stars
> To gain you Freedom, . . .

A person? A place? People? Places? It is deliberately enigmatic. But it is known that in 1912 Lawrence discovered the poet Algernon Charles Swinburne and the significance of pain. Around that time it seems that he allowed himself to share a beating with the young Arab he loved, Dahoum, near the banks of the Taurus River. The Turks presumably thought that the Oxford graduate, dressed in his friend's clothes, was an Arab, and a possible deserter. For Lawrence this was a formative experience. Something like it is described by Ernest Raymond in his novel of the First World War, *Tell England*: the friendship between Rupert Ray and Edgar Doe is cemented at public school when they are caned together: 'It was rather fun being whacked side by side, being twins.' Lawrence fictionalized his experience in *Seven Pillars* with

Daud who is allowed to share his friend Farraj's beating.

During the revolt Lawrence formed a bond like that between the biblical David and Jonathan with another Arab, Sherif Ali. It is possible that the Deraa incident in *Seven Pillars* – in which Lawrence described himself being beaten and raped for the benefit of a Turkish bey – was based on something similar that Lawrence arranged for himself to undergo at Azrak with the assistance of Sherif Ali. Perhaps Lawrence, at this time, can be best understood in terms of the relationship between the pilot and the little prince in Antoine de Saint-Exupéry's *The Little Prince*. Indeed Lawrence, in his life, anticipated the philosophy which Saint-Exupéry later developed as resistentialism. After the end of the war Lawrence attended beating parties in Chelsea, and arranged similar rituals with at least two members of the armed services until the time of his death. Perhaps he underwent what Marcel Proust, Jean-Paul Sartre, Jean Genet and Andre Malraux enunciated as sado-masochism and objective love. Those ideas were later popularized in the cinema with films like *Girl on a Motorcycle* and Bertolucci's *Last Tango in Paris*. The dedication in *Seven Pillars* could have been to Dahoum, apparently known as Saleem Ahmed, or to Sherif Ali, or possibly to both and an ideal which these two men came to represent.

The Arab revolt, and Lawrence's role in it, cannot be considered in terms of blind impersonal forces. Rather it has to be seen in the light of a man trying to resolve his own personal contradictions on the map of Arabia. Lawrence arrived in Jedda on 16 October 1916. He left Damascus two years later. From those two years a legend emerged. On 19 October 1916 Lawrence, together with Storrs and Aziz al-Masri, travelled towards Rabegh. From al-Masri Lawrence learnt guerrilla tactics. The Arab revolt needed a leader. Lawrence rejected the obvious claimant, Abdullah, as he imprudently wanted Christian soldiers in the Hejaz. Abdullah's liking for handsome young men possibly also disturbed Lawrence. At Rabegh Lawrence met, and rejected, two of Hussein's other sons. Lawrence then travelled painfully on camel back to Bir Abbas to see Hussein's other son, Feisal. On the way he caught his first sight of Sherif Ali. To Lawrence Feisal, arrayed in white, looked both noble and tragic. He was chosen. Feisal could also speak English. Returning via Khartoum, Lawrence won over Wingate who shortly afterwards replaced McMahon as head of the Arab bureau. Lawrence did the same with his British colleagues in Cairo. By early December Lawrence was acting as Feisal's political officer at Yenbo. In March 1917 Lawrence was instructed to implement a British strategy, advanced under pressure from the French who feared Hussein's growing power: the Turks were to be left in Medina lest they strengthened their Palestine front, but their railway line to the north was to be damaged to prevent a Turkish evacuation there. It was also thought necessary to capture Aqaba, an object of Anglo-French rivalry. This was done from the land side: Feisal, Lawrence and Auda abu Tayi, the desert leader, have all claimed that they thought of the idea. It is also possible that at this time Lawrence went off in search of Dahoum.

Conveying the news of the capture of Aqaba to Cairo, Lawrence met the new commander of the Egyptian Expeditionary Force, General Edmund Allenby, and it was this rather dull professional soldier who master-minded the Arabian campaign. Lawrence had suggested that the Arabs in Syria could be useful in an attack on Palestine. Either this, or his own classical reading, impressed Allenby, and Lawrence was given the support he asked for. Aqaba was well supplied. Lawrence persuaded Feisal, engaged in attacking the Turkish railway, to allow the northern Arab army to come under Allenby's control. Lawrence also secured the compliance of Hussein, but the Sherif whose suspicions had been aroused by visits from Sykes and Picot, told Lawrence that he had refused French annexation of the Lebanon or Beirut. After the war Lawrence implied that he, himself, had not been honest in his dealings, but there is little to indicate that that was how he felt at the time. At the beginning of November 1917 Allenby took Gaza. With Balfour's statement favouring a Jewish national home in Palestine, Allenby was under pressure to capture Jerusalem by Christmas, and eliminate Turkey from the war. To do this Allenby needed Lawrence's help to recruit Arabs, and to cut off the Turkish retreat by dynamiting a railway viaduct near Deraa. Lawrence was assisted on this expedition by Sherif Ali, and an Algerian, Abdel Kader, who saw the Arab movement in strictly nationalist terms and whose easy relationship with Ali aroused Lawrence's jealousy. The viaduct was not blown up. Lawrence seems to have experienced a sense of guilt comparable to that of the artist in Ingmar Bergman's film, *The Hour of the Wolf*. He needed to experience punishment and expiation. Seemingly Ali, athletic, outstandingly attractive and loved by Lawrence complied during their time together at Azrak. This Lawrence later fictionalized as the Deraa incident. Lawrence's failure limited the wider implications of Allenby's entry into Jerusalem on 11 December 1917.

On 9 December Lawrence met Colonel Richard Meinertzhagen. Meinertzhagen recorded that a beautiful apparition appeared, and he enquired whether it was a boy or a girl. Lawrence told him of his loathing of the French, of his fears that the French could interfere with his dream of an Arab empire in Arabia, Mesopotamia, Syria and Palestine. Meinertzhagen reminded Lawrence of Zionism, and Lawrence promised Palestine as a self-governing province under Arab sovereignty.

With the Bolshevik take-over in Russia, the Arabs learnt the terms of the Sykes–Picot agreement. Attention moved to the western front, and it was not until September 1918 that Arabia became important again with the move on Damascus. Lawrence, either upset by Dahoum's death, or distressed to discover that Ali was not present but instead a convert to Kader's nationalist cause, advanced to Damascus with great cruelty. There Lawrence, after being threatened by Kadar's dagger, managed to oust an administration loyal to Hussein and an independent Arab state, and replaced it with one headed by Nuri el Said who could promote British interests. Allenby arrived, and announced that Feisal would rule inland Syria with the help of the French. Lawrence would have, as a counterpart, a French liaison officer. Feisal, perhaps forgetting the later correspondence from McMahon to his father about French interests, objected that he could only accept British assistance. Lawrence told Allenby that he had not informed Feisal that the French would have a protectorate over Syria. Feisal withdrew. Lawrence refused to work with a Frenchman, and left for England.[23]

During the early stages of the Arab revolt, in December 1916, Lloyd George replaced Asquith as Prime Minister. Leopold Amery was appointed secretary to the Committee on Territorial Change. Amery was convinced by Sykes of the importance of Zionism for Britain's strategic requirements. This view was shared by William Ormsby-Gore who, while working with the Arab bureau in Cairo, had been influenced by the Zionist, Aaron Aaronsohn. In March 1917 Ormsby-Gore joined the War Secretariat. A memorandum by Amery of 11 March reflected this preoccupation: Amery argued that the objective of British policy was security, and this necessitated the retention by Britain of German East Africa, Palestine and Mesopotamia and the German Pacific colonies. Lloyd George managed foreign policy through his War Cabinet. Of the five original members Bonar Law and Arthur Henderson looked at domestic affairs; George Curzon, Lord President of the Council, and Alfred Milner managed foreign policy; Curzon had been Viceroy in India; Milner had served as Governor and High Commissioner in South Africa. Both these men were great imperialists. They were later joined by Jan Christiaan Smuts, who had been a republican general during the Second Anglo-Boer War. This tended to give British policy an imperial slant, and, from the Cabinet's point of view though not that of the War Office, to shift emphasis from the western to the eastern theatre. A subcommittee on territorial desiderata, chaired by Curzon and including Robert Cecil, Austen Chamberlain and Smuts, emphasized the importance of communications in any settlement. Smuts took a profound interest in Palestine. He argued for British control of Palestine to protect Egypt and communications with the East. The subcommittee agreed, and recommended revision of the Sykes–Picot agreement to give Britain exclusive control over Palestine. On 25 April 1917 the Imperial War Cabinet discussed the 'impossible' provision of the Sykes–Picot agreement about the 'internationalization' of Palestine. Lloyd George explained that the French had been cold over his suggestion at the conference at Saint-Jean-de-Maurienne that Palestine come under British control. On 1 May, however, the Imperial War Cabinet heard from Curzon that his subcommittee had been unanimous in recommending that the broad consideration of imperial security made it desirable for Britain to keep German East Africa, and Palestine and Mesopotamia.[24]

Zionists in Britain capitalized on this imperial thinking. The Manchester group, inspired by R. W. Seton-Watson's article suggesting a Jewish state in Palestine as an Allied war aim, enlisted the assistance of journalist Herbert Sidebotham who, with the connivance of Scott, published an editorial article in the *Manchester Guardian* on 22 November 1915 along similar lines. A British Palestine Committee was formed in April 1916 made up of Sidebotham, Harry Sacher, Israel M. Sieff and Simon Marks. Under the guidance of Weizmann, the committee related Zionist aspirations to the British war effort, particularly in its journal, *Palestine*. The first issue on 26 January 1917 spoke of a new British dominion in Palestine. This upset Sykes who was worried about the French, and also the advocacy of a Jewish legion by Jabonitsky. Sykes argued his case with Zionist leaders on 7 and 10 February, meeting them without official sanction. Sieff was convinced that Sykes had reached an agreement with the Arabs, and considered Jewish political aspirations in Palestine as secondary. A memorandum by Nahum Sokolow, the Executive Chairman of the Zionist International Committee, also worried Sykes: it seemed that, apart from the holy places, the Zionists intended to colonize the whole of Palestine. That would, again, upset France. Sykes suggested to Picot that the United States should act as protector. From the Foreign Office Arthur J. Balfour mentioned to Weizmann the possibility of an Anglo-American protectorate.[25]

By April 1917 Zionism had achieved a new status in British political thinking. Not only was Palestine necessary for the security of empire, but it was thought that Zionist sympathies for the Allied cause could help the war effort. Zionists in Russia could stop that country's drift out of the war; in the United States Zionists could speed up the American contribution following the declaration of war on 3 April. The United States, in particular, had a large and influential Jewish population. Centred on the east coast it numbered around 4 million. Originally the Jewish settlers had concentrated on becoming American, and Zionism had had little appeal. Between 1914 and 1918, however, the movement's enrolled membership increased from 5,000 to 150,000. The Zionist Organization of America was founded in 1918. The movement's early leaders included the young Rabbi Stephen Wise, Louis Brandeis who by 1917 was the first Jew to have been appointed to the Supreme Court, and Felix Frankfurter from the Harvard Law School. It was largely through the efforts of Ormsby-Gore, private secretary to Milner and married to Robert Cecil's niece, and Cecil who, during Balfour's absence in the United States as Foreign Secretary, that the importance of Zionist sympathies was brought before the British Cabinet. By this time both Cecil and Ormsby-Gore were Zionist converts. Ormsby-Gore emphasized the importance of propaganda: in his *Eastern Report* of 26 April he suggested that Zionism could secure the support of Russian Jews from the Allies. But despite efforts by Sykes, this view was undermined by the British ambassador in Russia. Weizmann hoped for a resolution from a Jewish conference in Petrograd welcoming a Zionist Palestine under British trusteeship and supported by a British declaration in favour of Zionism. Cecil took this plan to Milner, explaining that it was supported by Ormsby-Gore, but it was criticized by Claude Montefiore and nothing came of it anyway. Sykes, Ormsby-Gore and Cecil concentrated on the American angle. Through Weizmann, Sykes arranged for Balfour, while he was in the United States, to meet Brandeis. These conversations apparently convinced Balfour that it was acceptable for him, as Foreign Secretary, openly to endorse Zionism.

In London Cecil authorized propaganda instigated by Sykes and Ormsby-Gore, with the assistance of Aaronsohn, about alleged Turkish anti-Semitic outrages. They also played on the fear that Germany could use the Zionist movement. This was used over the American proposal to approach Turkey for a separate peace. That initiative, originating from Henry Morgenthau, a former American ambassador to Constantinople, appeared to entail a solution for Palestine other than the Zionist one. Ormsby-Gore argued that this could lead to a Zionist shift towards Germany. Weizmann elaborated in correspondence with the Foreign Office. He offered to use his personal influence with Morgenthau, accompanied by Frankfurter, to stop the American mission. Weizmann also continued to ask the British government for a statement supporting Zionism. Ronald Graham of the Foreign Office, a Zionist sympathizer, also urged this on Balfour, pointing to French support for Zionism. Lord Rothschild, regarded as the head of the Jewish community in Britain, asked Balfour to see Weizmann and himself. The three men met on 19 June, and Balfour asked for a draft of Zionist aspirations. Shortly afterwards Weizmann, in Gibraltar, impressed on Morgenthau and Frankfurter that Britain felt there could be no peace with Turkey unless Palestine, Syria, Armenia and Mesopotamia were detached from the Ottoman Empire.[26]

In Weizmann's absence Harry Sacher, a member of the British Palestine Committee, and Sokolow worked on the Zionist draft. They disagreed. Lord Rothschild handed Balfour a draft approved by the Political Committee on 18 July. This envisaged recognition of Palestine as the national home of the Jewish people and of the Zionist organization. Sacher persuaded the Labour Party to endorse the return of the Jewish people to Palestine: the party's manifesto even included the phrase 'Jewish Palestine'. A favourable reply was drafted for the War Cabinet's approval. This was partly dictated by fears of Russian withdrawal from the war, and the reluctance of Jewish businessmen to support President Woodrow Wilson's call for support for the War Loan. The reply was revised, particularly by Milner. Milner approved of an autonomous Jewish community in Palestine under a British protectorate, but not of an independent Jewish state. In the Jewish zone Britain would also have to insist on fair treatment for Christians and Muslims. Milner eliminated 'national' and made 'the' home merely 'an' home. The Jewish minister, Montagu, opposed the whole idea. In a memorandum called 'The anti-Semitism of the present government', dated 23 August, he dismissed Zionism as 'a mischievous political creed untenable by any patriotic citizen of the United Kingdom'. The Jews were not a nation, and a national home would make them aliens in the countries in which they lived. The editors of the *Morning Post* and others supported Zionism because they wanted Jews to leave Britain. Though not intentionally anti-Semitic, British policy would 'prove a rallying ground for anti-semites in every country in the world'. He objected to the proposals for a Jewish regiment on similar grounds. Lloyd George and Balfour were not present when the War Cabinet discussed the memorandum on 3 September. It seems that Montagu was isolated. Cecil insisted that the Allies needed Zionist support: the Zionists were particularly strong in the United States, and it was important that nothing should be done to risk a breach with them. The War Cabinet asked Cecil to find out how Wilson viewed London's proposed declaration of sympathy with the Zionists, and then to inform the American government.[27]

Wilson, acting on the advice of Colonel Edward M. House, was cautious: there could be a statement of sympathy provided it did not convey a real commitment. This was used by Montagu to suggest that Palestine could be a place of 'refuge' for Jews. Graham was annoyed with the attitude of certain rich Jews who feared they would be asked to leave Britain and cultivate farms in Palestine. Weizmann tried to see Lloyd George, and also to change Wilson's attitude. Weizmann contacted Brandeis who saw the President. Balfour also asked Lord Rothschild to urge American Zionists to lobby Wilson. Graham, in a note to Lord Hardinge, pointed once again to propaganda urging German protection for a Jewish settlement in Palestine, and how useful Zionists in Russia and the United States could be. On 3 October Lord Rothschild and Weizmann asked Balfour to consider the Zionist case in the light of British imperial interests: a favourable British declaration would enable them to counteract the demoralizing influence of the enemy press. Just before the War Cabinet met on 4 October, Milner and Amery worked on the British draft. Milner, possibly influenced by warnings from Gertrude Bell, the Assistant

Political Officer in Baghdad, that neither Arabs nor Muslims would accept Jewish authority, insisted on guarantees for the existing non-Jewish communities in Palestine. With that, he allowed 'national' to creep back. Milner recorded in his diary that the Cabinet meeting was 'a tiresome and time-wasting sitting largely concerned with Zionism'. Balfour stated the case for the Zionists: the danger of German sympathies; a sympathetic declaration by France; Wilson approved of the Zionist movement. Montagu was angry: how could he negotiate with the peoples of India if the British government announced that his national home was in Turkish territory. Curzon, the Lord President, enquired how it was intended to move the Muslims from Palestine, and to introduce Jews. Following this, at Balfour's request, Wilson was shown the Milner–Amery draft and agreed to it, but insisted that his approval should not be mentioned. Soundings of Jewish opinion in Britain suggested considerable support for Zionist aspirations, but when Graham learnt that Curzon was preparing a memorandum counselling delay, the Assistant Under-Secretary reinforced Balfour in his earlier arguments with a briefing on developments. At a meeting of the War Cabinet on 25 October, Curzon explained his concern about the nature of the British commitment. Palestine could only support a small population and the 500,000 native Muslims would not be content 'either to be expropriated for Jewish immigrants, or to act merely as hewers of wood and drawers of water'. Sykes, with his apparent expertise in Middle Eastern affairs, took it upon himself to refute Curzon's arguments. In a memorandum of 30 October, Sykes claimed that the barrenness of Palestine was a consequence of neglect: the Arabs were a 'naturally idle and indolent race'. With proper support the population of Palestine could be doubled in seven years.

On 31 October Balfour, using arguments provided by Graham and Sykes, addressed the War Cabinet. A declaration in favour of Zionism would help propaganda in Russia and the United States. Scientific development could enable Palestine to sustain a larger population. By 'national home' Balfour understood some form of British, American and other protectorate enabling Jews to build up 'a real centre of national culture and focus of national life'. That did not necessarily involve the early establishment of an independent Jewish state 'which was a matter for gradual development in accordance with the ordinary laws of political evolution'. By a strange logic Balfour argued that this would eliminate any danger of the Jews having a double allegiance or non-national outlook. Curzon objected. His information was that Palestine could not be developed in this way. It was necessary to retain the Muslim and Christian holy places in Jerusalem and Bethlehem. That would mean that the Jewish people could not have a political capital in Palestine. Some expression of sympathy with Jewish aspirations could help British propaganda, but this would have to be carefully worded. The War Cabinet authorized Balfour to make a declaration of sympathy with Zionist aims:

> His Majesty's Government views with favour the establishment in Palestine of a national home for the Jewish people, and will use its best endeavours to facilitate the achievement of this object, it being clearly understood that nothing shall be done which may prejudice the civil and religious rights of existing non-Jewish communities in Palestine, or the rights and political status enjoyed by Jews in any other country.

Graham urged immediate publication, and on 2 November a letter was sent from Balfour to Lord Rothschild. The same day Graham met Weizmann, Sokolow, Aaronsohn and Sykes to arrange the requisite propaganda.[28]

Initially Weizmann appears to have been disappointed. Indeed the declaration that finally emerged, after Milner's careful alterations, just offered a national home, presumably only in part of Palestine, and one which would not prejudice the existing 90 per cent of the population. Despite Curzon's repeated warnings, the declaration was open to manipulation. Zionists for over twenty years had discussed the nuances of the meanings of commonwealth, national home and state. Some, like Weizmann, were prepared to give one interpretation to one listener, and another elsewhere. For most, the objective was a Zionist state, though it was recognized that that might have to be obscured for tactical reasons. And the British Zionists excelled at tactics. The Manchester School converted newspapermen and Cabinet ministers. It worked on Foreign Office officials and military personnel. By October 1917 most of the key people concerned with Middle Eastern affairs in the War Cabinet and its secretariat, in the Foreign Office, and even in the military and intelligence services, were either convinced Zionists or Zionist sympathizers. It is not clear whether Lloyd George admired the Zionists or even liked Jews, but he thought they would be useful in his eastern policy, and it was the Prime Minister himself who, under pressure from Weizmann, placed the Zionist declaration on the Cabinet agenda. Milner, though possibly sympathetic, was a great liberal imperialist as had been shown by his concern for the non-white races in Southern Africa a decade earlier. He and Curzon were particularly conscious of the position of the Arabs, but, even so, over 90 per cent of the population of Palestine was referred to negatively as the 'existing non-Jewish communities'. Smuts was a Zionist, and later it was a cause he preached with passion. Smuts was a Dutch Reform Calvinist. Like the Jews his religion was that of the Old Testament. Like the Jews Smuts's people, the Afrikaners, had also been chosen and led across the desert: they had trekked into the interior of South Africa when the British placed slaves on an equal footing with Whites. Smuts had been offered the command of the Palestine campaign, but refused as it seemed that it would not be a first-class campaign. He was an ambitious man and an astute opportunist: 'slim Jannie'. But even at a time when his fellow Afrikaners did not like the Jews Smuts remained a Zionist; part of a development in Israel was named after him. One of the last people to see Balfour before he died was Weizmann, but it is possible that Balfour suffered from a latent anti-Semitism. The secretaries to the War Cabinet, Ormsby-Gore and Amery, were Zionist sympathizers, as was Philip Kerr, Lloyd George's personal secretary. But most significant of all were the activities in the Foreign Office of Sykes, Cecil and Graham. At crucial times they arranged for suitable information to be passed on, selected propaganda material and, with apparent expertise, undermined counter-arguments whether from the India Office or British representatives in the Arab world.[29]

REFERENCES

1. Jon Kimche, *The Second Arab Awakening* (London 1970), pp. 17–40; Fritz Fischer, *Germany's Aims in the First World War* (London 1967), pp. 3–50; Marian Jackson (trans.), *War of Illusions: German Policies from 1911 to 1914* (London 1975), esp. pp. 205–7, 330–54; Walter Laqueur, *A History of Zionism* (London 1972), pp. 172–8; William I. Shorrock, *French Imperialism in the Middle East, the Failure of Policy in Syria and Lebanon 1900–1914* (Madison 1976), pp. 65–169; Briton Cooper Busch, *Britain and the Persian Gulf 1894–1914* (Berkeley 1967), pp. 357–69; K. A. Hamilton, 'An attempt to form an Anglo-French "Industrial Entente" ', *Middle Eastern Studies, XI* (1975), 45–73; 'Great Britain and France 1905–11', 'Great Britain and France 1911–1914' in F. H. Hinsley (Ed.), *British Foreign Policy under Sir Edward Grey* (Cambridge 1977), pp. 113–32, 324–41.

2. *Cab 16* (Public Record Office, London), 12; Frank Hardie and Irwin Hermann, *Britain and Zion, the Fateful Entanglement* (Belfast 1980), p. 19.

3. *British Documents on the Origins of the War, 1898–1914* (hereafter cited as *BDOW*), Vol. X, pp. 824–5, George H. Cassar, *Kitchener: Architect of Victory* (London 1977), pp. 220–1; Jukka Nevakivi, 'Lord Kitchener and the partition of the Ottoman Empire, 1915–1916' in K. Bourne and D. C. Watt (Eds), *Studies in International History* (London 1967), pp. 317–18.

4. *BDOW 1898–1914*, Vol. X (2), p. 827, FO 6672/6672/14/44, No. 22, Kitchener to Grey, Secret, 6 February 1914 received 14 February 1914 (available in *FO 371*, 2130, which also contains other pertinent correspondence), pp. 831–2, Abdullah's account of conversation with Kitchener.

5. *BDOW 1899–1914*, Vol. X (2), pp. 827–30, FO 13871/4588/14/44, No. 193, Mallet to Grey, 18 March 1914 received 30 March 1914 and Enclosure and Minutes.

6. Ibid., p. 831, Kitchener to Sir W. Tyrrell, 26 April 1914; *FO 371*, 1973,

87396, Enclosure, Note by Storrs, 19 April 1914.

7. Relevant documentation can be found in *FO 371*, 2139, esp. 65589/ 44923; 1973, esp. 87396.

8. *Cab 42*, 2/14, Meeting of War Council, 10 March 1915.

9. *FO 371*, 2486, f. 2, 34982, Grey to Sir F. Bertie (Paris), 23 March 1915.

10. Ibid., f. 7, 44598, Grey to McMahon, Confidential, Telegram No. 173, 14 April 1915.

11. Ibid., ff. 43–6, 34982/87023, McMahon to Grey, Telegram No. 306, 30 June 1915.

12. C. P. Scott in T. Wilson (Ed.), *Scott Journal, Political Diaries 1911–1928* (New York 1970), p. 113, Diary, 27 Nov. 1914; Chaim Weizmann, *Trial and Error* (London 1949), pp. 192–3; Lady Algernon Gordon Lennox, (Ed.), *The Diary of Lord Bertie of Thame 1914–1918*, Vol. I (London 1924), pp. 105–6, Diary, 25 Jan. 1915; H. H. Asquith, *Memories and Reflections*, Vol. II (London 1928), pp. 59–60, Diary, 28 Jan. 1915; pp. 66–7; Diary, 13 March 1915; John Bowle, *Viscount Samuel* (London 1957), pp. 170–8; Viscount Samuel, *Memoirs* (London 1945), pp. 39–44; *FO 800* (Public Record Office, London), 100 Memorandum by Samuel on the Future of Palestine, 22 Jan. 1915; *Cab 37*, 123/43; 126/1; Michael G. Fry, *Lloyd George and Foreign Policy, The Education of a Statesman: 1890–1916* (Montreal 1977), pp. 260–1.

13. Martin Gilbert, *Exile and Return. The Emergence of Jewish Statehood* (London 1978), pp. 83–4 quoting Memorandum by Montagu, 16 March 1915, in the *Lloyd George Papers*; Hardie and Hermann, op. cit., pp. 80–3; Stephen Koss, *Asquith* (London 1976), p. 126.

14. Keith Robbins, *Sir Edward Grey, a Biography of Lord Grey of Fallodon* (London 1971), pp. 310–11.

15. *Cab 27*, 1, Report of the Committee on Asiatic Turkey, 30 June 1915; this volume also contains important memoranda by Sykes; Roger Adelson, *Mark Sykes, Portrait of an Amateur* (London 1975), pp. 180–5; Marian Kent, 'Asiatic Turkey, 1914–1916' in Hinsley, op. cit., pp. 443–4; the Bunsen Committee maps, drawn by Sykes, are reproduced in Hardie and Hermann, op. cit., pp. 116–17; Christopher Sykes, *Two Studies in Virtue* (London 1953), pp. 109–235; Nevakivi, 'Lord Kitchener and the partition of the Ottoman Empire', pp. 325–6.

16. *FO 371*, 2490, 108253, No. 12, Sykes to Charles Callwell, Director-General of Military Operations, 14 July 1915; No. 14, 14 July 1915; 1476, 106764, No. 11, Sykes to Callwell, 12 July 1915; Elie Kedourie, 'Sir Mark Sykes and Palestine', *Arabic Political Memoirs and Other Studies* (London 1974), pp. 236–42; 'Cairo and Khartoum on the Arab question, 1915–1918', *The Chatham House Version and other Middle Eastern Studies* (London 1970), pp. 13–32; Adelson, op. cit., pp. 187–8.

17. *FO 371*, 2486, ff. 39–40, 84355/34982 J. W. Holderness (India Office) to Foreign Office, Secret, 24 June 1915; ff. 43–6, 87023/34982, McMahon to Foreign Office, Telegram No. 306, 30 June 1915 and Minutes; ff. 99–102, 117236/34982, McMahon to Foreign Office, Telegram No. 450, Secret, 22 Aug. 1915, Minute by Grey; ff. 103–9, 118580/34982, Minute by Clerk, 25 Aug. 1915; Minute by Grey, undated; Sir A. Hirtzel (India Office) to Foreign Office, 24 Aug. 1915; ff. 124–45, 125293/34982, McMahon to Grey, No. 94, Secret, 26 Aug. 1915; Hussein to Storrs, 14

July 1915; Statement of Messenger, Alexandria, 18 Aug. 1915; Note by Storrs, 19 Aug. 1915; McMahon to Hussein, 30 Aug. 1915.

18. *FO 371*, 2486, 152901/34982, McMahon to Foreign Office, Telegram No. 623, 18 Oct. 1915; 153045/34982, McMahon to Grey, Telegram 18 Oct. 1915; Minutes by Clerk and Nicolson; 54122/34986, McMahon to Foreign Office, Telegram No. 627, 20 Oct. 1915; 155203/34982, Grey to McMahon, Telegram No. 796, 20 Oct. 1915; McMahon to Hussein, 24 Oct. 1915.

19. Ibid., f. 183, 138500/34982, Wingate to Grey, 7 Sept. 1915.

20. Ibid., 181834/34982, Grey to McMahon, Telegram No. 961, 10 Dec. 1915; 198266/34982, McMahon to Grey, No. 172, Secret, 14 Dec. 1915 and Enclosures; 2771, 16451, McMahon to Foreign Office, Telegram No. 70, 26 Jan. 1916.

21. Ibid., 2767, 40645/938, McMahon to Foreign Office and Enclosures, 1 March 1916. Besides the copies in the Public Record Office printed versions of the McMahon–Hussein correspondence exist based on both Arabic and English sources. See George Antonius, *The Arab Awakening. The Story of the Arab National Movement* (London 1938), pp. 413–27 for versions based on the Arab sources; Antonius was also consulted about the texts printed in *British Parliamentary Papers*, Vol. XXVII, Cmd. 5957, *Correspondence between Sir Henry McMahon and the Sharif Hussein of Mecca in 1915 and 1916*, 1939; Vol. XIV, Cmd. 5974, *Report of a Committee set up to consider Certain Correspondence between Sir Henry McMahon and the Sharif of Mecca in 1915 and 1916*, 1939. Recent discussions of the material include Isaiah Friedman, 'The McMahon–Hussein correspondence and the question of Palestine', *Journal of Contemporary History*, 5 (1970) 83–122; Correspondence from Toynbee in same volume, pp. 185–201; A. L. Tibawi, *Anglo-Arab Relations and the Question of Palestine 1914–1921* (London 1977), pp. 64–100 is interesting on the Arabic translations; Elie Kedourie, *In the Anglo-Arab Labyrinth* (Cambridge 1976), pp. 65–137 quotes extensively from Foreign and India Office minutes.

22. *FO 371*, 2486, 34982, Foreign Office Note, 27 Nov. 1915 and Minutes; *Cab 42*, 6, 9–10, War Committee Meeting, Secret, 16 Dec. 1915 and evidence of Sykes; *FO 882*, 2, Memorandum on Third Meeting of Nicolson Committee, 21 Dec. 1915; *Cab 42*, 11, Arab Question by Sykes and Picot, 5 Jan. 1916; *FO 371*, 2767, 8117, Hirtzel to Foreign Office, 13 Jan. 1916; 3851, Macdonough to Nicolson, 6 Jan. 1916; War on Turkey File, Meeting of Nicolson Committee, 21 Jan. 1916; 26444, Meeting of Nicolson Committee, 4 Feb. 1916; *Documents on British Foreign Policy 1919–1939* (hereafter cited as *DBFP*), 1st series, Vol. IV, pp. 241–51 (correspondence embodying the Sykes–Picot agreement); pp. 340–9, 132187/2117/44A, Memorandum by Balfour on Syria, Palestine, and Mesopotamia, 11 Aug. 1919; pp. 479–89, 143507/2117/44A, Lloyd George to Clemenceau, 18 Oct. 1919; Shane Leslie, *Sir Mark Sykes: His Life and Letters* (London 1924), pp. 242–3; Adelson, op. cit., pp. 196–209. For the Wolf approach see Robbins, op. cit., pp. 332–3; Isaiah Friedman, *The Question of Palestine, 1914–1918* (London 1973), pp. 48–64; Hardie and Hermann, op. cit., pp. 48–52. For the oil question see Marian Kent, *Oil and Empire, British Policy and Mesopotamian Oil*

1900–1920 (London 1976), pp. 122–4. See also Jukka Nevakivi, *Britain, France and the Arab Middle East 1914–1920* (London 1969), pp. 13–44. For a map illustrating the Sykes–Picot agreement see Hardie and Hermann, op. cit., p. 115.

23. Desmond Stewart, *T. E. Lawrence* (London 1977), esp. pp. 110–12, 137–211, 237–55; Phillip Knightley and Colin Simpson, *The Secret Lives of Lawrence of Arabia* (London 1976), pp. 147–74, 415–41; Ernest Raymond, *Tell England, A Study in a Generation* (London 1928), pp. 38–42; T. E. Lawrence, *Seven Pillars of Wisdom, a Triumph* (London 1962); John Bagot Glubb, *Britain and the Arabs A Study of Fifteen Years, 1908 to 1958* (London 1959), pp. 79–89; Richard Meinertzhagen, *Middle East Diary 1917–1956* (London 1959), pp. 28–30, Diary 10 Dec. 1917; *Lawrence of Arabia*, Great Britain, 1962, directed by David Lean; *Girl on a Motorcycle*, Great Britain, 1968, directed by Jack Cardiff; *Last Tango in Paris*, Italy/France, 1972, directed by Bernado Bertolucci; *Hour of the Wolf*, Sweden, 1968, directed by Ingmar Bergman. Antoine de Saint-Exupéry, *Le Petit Prince* (London, 1958); Curtis Cane, *Antoine de Saint-Exupéry. His Life and Times* (London 1970).

24. *Cab 24*, 10, Note on Possible Terms of Peace by Amery, 11 March 1917; *Cab 21*, 77, Meetings of Subcommittee on Territorial Desiderata, April 1917; *Cab 23*, 2, Imperial War Cabinet, 25 April 1917; 40, Minutes of Imperial War Cabinet, 1 May 1917; Kimche, *Second Arab Awakening*, pp. 52–6; L. S. Amery, *My Political Life*, Vol. II, *War and Peace 1914–1929* (London 1953), pp. 114–15.

25. Jon Kimche, *Palestine or Israel*, (London 1973), pp. 93–123, also quotes pp. 119–20, Sieff to Weizmann, 17 Feb. 1917; Adelson, op. cit., pp. 214–28; Laqueur, op. cit., pp. 181–93.

26. Friedman, *The Question of Palestine*, pp. 63–4, 119–219; Laqueur, op. cit., pp. 190–6; Jon Kimche, *The Unromantics. The Great Powers and the Balfour Declaration* (London 1968), pp. 31–40; Hardie and Hermann, op. cit., pp. 66–74; William A. Yale, 'Ambassador Henry Morgenthau's Special Mission of 1917', *World Politics*, I (April 1949), 308–20. In his memoirs Cecil does not mention his Zionist activities at this time. See Robert Cecil, *All the Way* (London 1941); *A Great Experiment* (London 1941).

27. Friedman, *The Question of Palestine*, pp. 254–61; *Cab 21*, 58, Note by Milner, 18 Aug. 1917; *Cab 24*, 24, GT 1868, Memorandum by Montagu on the anti-Semitism of the Present Government, 23 Aug. 1917, also in *FO 371*, 3083; *Cab 23*, 24, Minutes of War Cabinet, Secret, 3 Sept. 1917.

28. *FO 371*, 3083, 143082, Graham to Harding, 24 Sept. 1917; Rothschild and Weizmann to Balfour, 3 Oct. 1917; 3059, 162432, Hirtzel to Graham, 30 Aug. 1917, Enclosing Memorandum by Gertrude Bell on the Turkish provinces in Asia, Syria, 23 June 1917; *Cab 23*, 4 WC245(18), 4 Oct. 1917; John Marlowe, *Milner, Apostle of Empire* (London 1976), p. 333, quoting Diary, 4 Oct. 1917. Extracts of the soundings of Jewish opinion are printed in Doreen Ingrams (Ed.), *Palestine Papers 1917–1922, Seeds of Conflict* (London 1972), pp. 13–16; *Cab 23*, 4, WC257(12), 25 Oct. 1917; *FO 371*, 3083, 143082, Drummond to Balfour, 30 Oct. 1917, Enclosing Memorandum by Sykes on Palestine, Sykes asked that his memorandum be anonymous; *Cab 23*,

4, WC261(12), 31 Oct. 1917; Friedman, *The Question of Palestine*, pp. 259–81; Gilbert, op. cit., pp. 92–108; see also Leonard Stein, *The Balfour Declaration* (London 1961); D. Z. Gillon, 'The antecedents of the Balfour Declaration', *Middle Eastern Studies*, V (May 1969); Majir Verete, 'The Balfour Declaration and its makers', *Middle Eastern Studies*, Vol. VI (Jan. 1970).

29. H. C. Armstrong, *Grey Steel (J. C. Smuts)* (London 1939), pp. 218–20; W. K. Hancock, *Smuts, The Sanguine Years 1870–1919* (Cambridge 1962), pp. 432–5; W. K. Hancock and Jean van der Poel, *Selections from the Smuts Papers* (Cambridge 1966), pp. 493–5, 523. I am indebted to Dr K. A. Hamilton for pointing out that Harold Wilson presumably means Lord Robert Cecil when he writes Lord Robert Balfour in *The Chariot of Israel, Britain, America and the State of Israel* (London 1981), p. 48 note; Zara Steiner, 'The Foreign Office and the war', in Hinsley, op. cit., pp. 516–31 at p. 528.

Chapter 3

THE DIVISION OF THE MIDDLE EAST AND THE ROOTS OF WAR

Shortly after the Balfour Declaration was issued the new Bolshevik government in Russia publicized the Sykes–Picot agreement. This increased alarm among the Arabs, already nervous over the growth of Zionism which appeared to threaten their interests. From Cairo, Sir Reginald Wingate explained to Hussein that these documents were merely provisional exchanges. On 9 December 1917 General Allenby's forces took Jerusalem. He issued a proclamation that Britain's object was to liberate all peoples oppressed by the Turks and to establish national governments 'deriving authority from the initiative and free will of those people themselves'. In a Foreign Office memorandum dated 19 December, Arnold Toynbee and Lewis Namier, a Jew born in Galicia, observed that objections to Jews being given exclusive political rights in Palestine – this being considered undemocratic to the local populations – were imaginary. Palestine could be held in trust by Britain and the United States until there was a sufficient population to govern it on European lines.[1] Then, on 8 January 1918, President Wilson outlined his Fourteen Points to Congress. The twelfth stated that the Turkish portions of the Ottoman Empire needed sovereignty, but the other nationalities 'should be assured an undoubted security of life and an unmolested opportunity of autonomous development'. The same day D. G. Hogarth, in charge of the Arab bureau in Allenby's headquarters, saw Hussein for the first time. Later Hogarth mentioned a return of the Jews to Palestine and the Sherif observed that he welcomed the Jews to all Arab countries. Hogarth reported that Hussein would not accept an independent Jewish state in Palestine, but he had not been instructed to warn him that such a state was contemplated by Britain.[2]

In London the War Cabinet's Middle East Committee, on 19 January, decided to send a Zionist commission to Palestine: it was necessary to put the Balfour Declaration into practice.[3] Weizmann headed the commission; he was advised by Sykes and Ormsby-Gore. *En route* Weizmann assured Sir Reginald Wingate in the Residency in Cairo that there was complete accord between British and Jewish interests in Palestine. On 25 March General Clayton told Weizmann that support for the Arabs was a war measure: the development of Jewish colonization would be a permanent asset to Palestine. In Palestine Weizmann found that the Arab state of mind made useful negotiations impossible at that time. The Military Governor, Ronald Storrs, speaking 'as a convinced Zionist' thought the commission 'lacked a sense of the dramatic activity': the Balfour Declaration hardly opened for the inhabitants of Palestine 'the beatific vision of a new Heaven and a new Earth'.[4] Major Kinahan Cornwallis, the director of the Arab bureau in Cairo, warned that the frank avowal of Zionist aims had produced 'a considerable revulsion of feelings amongst the Palestinians, who have for the first time come into contact with European Jews of good standing'.[5] On 18 April Clayton wrote to Sykes that while he was personally in favour of Zionism, caution was necessary to bring that policy to a successful conclusion.[6] In June Weizmann saw Feisal near Aqaba. Feisal insisted that, as an Arab, he refused to consider Palestine as a British protectorate, or an area for Jewish colonization.[7] At the time of the Zionism commission seven Arab leaders in Cairo, on 7 May, asked for an assurance that it was the aim of the British government that the Arabs should enjoy complete independence in all the Arab countries which would be formed into a federation like the United States. Sykes drafted the reply. This was not submitted to Balfour. It was ambiguous, full of reservations and was not well received by the Arabs. Arab territories free from Turkish rule or liberated by Arab armies would have governments 'based upon the principle of the consent of the governed'. In those areas still under Turkish rule, northern Iraq and most of Syria, Britain desired that the oppressed peoples should obtain their freedom and independence.[8]

At this time another factor influenced British Middle Eastern policy: oil. In 1916, on the recommendations of Admiral Slade, a start was made to form a British National Oil Company to check the dominance of Royal Dutch-Shell and the American Standard Oil. During July 1918, at the instigation of Sir Reginald Hall, the Admiralty Director of Naval Intelligence, Slade circulated a memorandum on the significance of oilfields in the Middle East. Colonel Sir Maurice Hankey, on 1 August, urged Balfour to read this vitally important paper: oil could take the place of coal in the next war, or would be at least of equal importance. The only potential supply under British control was in Persia and Mesopotamia. Balfour thought that the securing of these oil wells would be imperialistic, but Hankey overcame his resistance,[9] and on 13 August the Foreign Secretary told a conference of dominion prime ministers that it would be unthinkable to allow Iraq to revert to Turkish or Arab rule as Mesopotamia could supply the British Empire with the one source it lacked: oil. Mesopotamia would have to be the exception to the policy that there should be no expansion of the British Empire as a result of the war. The same day

Lloyd George told the conference that he was prepared to surrender British control of Palestine and a German African colony to the United States to secure approval of British control over Mesopotamia.[10] Two days later Curzon told the War Cabinet that he would accept the trusteeship of Palestine being offered to the United States. G. N. Barnes thought that Palestine and Mesopotamia should be Arab states under British guardianship, while Austen Chamberlain argued that the question was one of the security of the British Empire, particularly India and its allies. Both the Prime Minister of New Zealand, W. F. Massey, and Montagu were worried at the effects upon the Muslim population of the British Empire of handing over a mainly Muslim country, Palestine, to the United States, whose ideas on the future of Palestine might be unsympathetic.[11] In October 1918 Toynbee, in the Political Intelligence Department, stated in a memorandum that Britain had pledged to Hussein that Palestine should be 'Arab' and 'independent'. He recommended that whatever the administration of Palestine and the facilities granted to non-Arab elements in the population, it should nominally be included in an Arab confederation.[12]

In the Middle East the Allied forces advanced: Damascus fell on 1 October 1918; Beirut on 8 October; and Aleppo on 26 October. On 30 October Turkey capitulated and signed the Mudros armistice. The Ottoman Empire was finished. Wherever possible Allenby allowed Feisal's troops to take over the administration in the captured cities, but, following objections from France, Feisal's flag was lowered in Beirut. Iraq became an Anglo-Indian administrative unit. The rest was divided between France and Britain: France administered Syria and the Lebanon coastal area from Tyre to Cilicia; Britain the territory that later formed the Palestine mandate.[13]

Friction between Zionists and Arabs grew in the British area with, as Sykes reported, fears that the Zionist objective was an independent Jewish state. Toynbee minuted on 2 December that British policy should be founded on a Palestinian state with Palestinian citizenship for all inhabitants, whether Jewish or non-Jewish. 'This alone seems consistent with Mr Balfour's letter. Hebrew might be made an official language, but the Jewish element should not be allowed to form a state within the state, enjoying greater privileges than the rest of the population.'[14] Clayton warned that anti-Jewish action might be initiated by the Arabs to show opposition to Zionism. He found it pertinent to mention that the administrator's latest reports gave the existing population of Palestine as 512,000 Muslims, 61,000 Christians and 66,000 Jews.[15] Arab notables petitioned Balfour, Wilson and the peace conference at Paris:

> The country is ours and has been so of old. We have lived in it longer than they did, and have worked in it more than they did. Our historical and religious relations with it, we Moslems and Christians, far exceed those of the Jews. Therefore, their claim to their ancient historical rights in the

41

country do not give them the right of appropriating it, in as much as in our historical rights we Arabs cannot justify our claims in Spain, our old home, where our rule and glory flourished for eight centuries and thus gave birth to the modern civilization of Europe.[16]

Against this background, the newly named Eastern Committee met on 5 December 1918. Curzon said that he doubted whether there was anyone who favoured an international administration of Palestine. Nobody wanted France there. He doubted whether American custodianship was a wise idea. The committee had to consider Britain being invited to take charge. Lord Robert Cecil was not enthusiastic: Britain would not get anything out of it and would just have to keep the peace between Arabs and Jews. In reply to Smuts's protest that it would affect Jewish national opinion, 'and nationally they are a great people', Cecil pointed out that they were likely to quarrel with the protecting power.[17] On 16 December the committee adopted appropriate resolutions for the peace conference: either Britain or the United States should act as the representative of the nations in Palestine.[18]

Britain had used 1,400,000 men in the eastern campaign. At the end of the war most of the occupying 1 million troops were British. Britain wanted to revise the Sykes–Picot agreement, but France refused. On 1 December Georges Clemenceau, the French Prime Minister, spoke to Lloyd George in London and apparently agreed to Britain attaching Mosul to Iraq and Palestine being under British control. In December the Eastern Committee decided to support Feisal as a leader of an Arab state centred at Damascus, and to follow the principle of self-determination over Syria. The Foreign Office was worried about the spread of French influence throughout the Arab world, and felt that Palestine was desirable for strategic reasons. It also supported the Sherif, while the India Office backed Ibn Saud. The British position was strengthened by the acceptance of Smuts's mandate scheme at the peace conference: Smuts claimed that areas like Mesopotamia were not ready for self-government, and Palestine with its population problem would have to be administered by an outside power. Syria, however, was almost ready for independence. This meant that France would be restricted, having only limited power in Syria while Britain would have effective control in Mesopotamia and Palestine.[19]

Feisal was chosen by T. E. Lawrence. On his return from Damascus Lawrence told the Eastern Committee that Feisal was pro-British, but that could change if Britain backed French claims in the East. Perhaps influenced by his meetings with Robert Cecil, Lawrence suggested that Feisal wanted British or American Zionists as advisers. Apart from allowing the French Beirut and the Lebanon, Lawrence hoped to 'bif' them out everywhere else and scrap the Sykes–Picot agreement.[20] In Mesopotamia Lawrence wanted Zeid and Abdullah as British nominees. But this was opposed by the British representative there, Sir Percy Cox, and the India Office worried about the effect on Muslims in

India.[21] Lawrence, however, suggested that Feisal should represent Hussein at the peace conference. France did not like this. Feisal was slighted travelling through Paris *en route* to London. In London Feisal saw Balfour and gave him the impression that he was vehemently anti-French. Feisal thought Britain had behaved badly over Beirut. Even Smuts ceded to the Eastern Committee that the Arabs had been in Beirut before the British arrived, but agreed that it went naturally with the Lebanon and had to be given to the French. At the instigation of Lawrence, Feisal also saw Weizmann. Lawrence acted as interpreter, and his inadequate knowledge of Arabic could account for subsequent misunderstandings. Early in January 1919 Feisal signed an agreement with Weizmann for Zionist money and financial advice in return for allowing the Zionists the right to enter Palestine and to settle even beyond its borders. But Feisal changed Weizmann's phrases 'Jewish state' and 'Jewish government' to 'Palestine' and 'Palestinian Government', and added a codicil to the document in effect making all this conditional on the Arabs attaining their independence. This codicil was abbreviated and misleadingly translated by Lawrence who omitted 'independence'.[22]

At this time Curzon understood the Hussein–McMahon correspondence to cover Palestine. He told the Eastern Committee on 5 December 1918 that in October 1915 Palestine was included in the areas Britain pledged should be Arab and independent in the future.[23] This interpretation was confirmed by Sir Lewis Mallet, the head of the Turkish section to the British delegation in Paris, in a minute of 30 January 1919: Britain was committed by implication to the independence of all Arab countries excepting those areas mentioned by McMahon 'from which Palestine was excluded'. Balfour initialled this.[24] But Weizmann in his meeting with Feisal was reported to have spoken of Palestine as a Jewish commonwealth under British trusteeship. Curzon found the dictionary definition of commonwealth to be 'a State', 'a body-politic', 'an independent community', 'a republic'. That, he felt, was what the Zionists wanted with British trusteeship as a screen. Balfour, on 20 January 1919, recorded that, so far as he knew, Weizmann had never claimed a Jewish *'Government'* of Palestine: 'Such a claim is in my opinion certainly inadmissible and personally I do not think we should go further than the original declaration which I made to Lord Rothschild'. Curzon remained convinced that Weizmann contemplated a Jewish state, a Jewish nation, with a subordinate population of Arabs ruled by Jews and with the Jews in possession of the fat of the land, and directing the administration.[25] On 19 February Balfour wrote to Lloyd George about the British position at the peace conference: the weak point of Britain's position was that it rightly declined to accept the principle of self-determination for Palestine; if the inhabitants were consulted they would give an anti-Jewish verdict. The justification was that Palestine was exceptional: the question was one of world importance, and Britain thought the Jews had a historic claim to a home in their ancient land provided that home could be given to them without either dispossessing or oppressing the present inhabitants.[26]

But, in many ways, the rival Arab and Zionist claims became subsumed in a British policy at the peace conference dominated by the French factor. This position was clearly stated by Sir Arthur Hirtzel, the Assistant Under-Secretary for India, in a memorandum of 14 February on the French claims in Syria. He argued that Britain needed an understanding with France which should not be endangered by supporting Arab claims. The United States could withdraw from world affairs. Britain and France might have to face together a revival of German power or the threat of bolshevism. He referred to 'the purely parochial importance of the Arab question' as compared with 'the ecumenical importance of the maintenance of cordial relations with France'. The Arabs had to pay the price for Britain. In 1915 Hirtzel had recorded that the Arabs were no more capable of administering than Red Indians; in 1919 he thought profession of support for Arab self-determination 'make believe'. He supported French claims in Syria. Britain should act as an 'honest broker' between the French and Arabs, telling Feisal that he should come to terms with the French. In effect this was British policy. Milner told Clemenceau that until a Franco-Arab arrangement had been reached British troops would remain in Syria; but Feisal and Clemenceau failed to come to terms.[27]

At Paris Feisal, in the words of Sir James Headlam-Morley, was 'the most dignified figure'.[28] He and Lawrence appeared in Arab dress before the Council of Ten on 6 February 1919. Feisal pleaded for the independence of all the Arab countries. In an interview with a Paris newspaper he specifically mentioned Palestine in this regard; in another one, on 1 March, he said oppressed Jews would be welcome in Palestine provided they submitted to an Islamic authority or a Christian one delegated by the League of Nations. This so disturbed the Zionist delegates that a letter was drawn up by Lawrence, Meinertzhagen, Weizmann and Felix Frankfurter – and attributed to Feisal – to the effect that Feisal found the Zionist proposals moderate and looked forward to mutual co-operation.[29]

Weizmann was the principal Zionist speaker in Paris. When questioned by Robert Lansing, the American Secretary of State, he explained that the Zionists wanted to send 70,000 to 80,000 Jews annually to Palestine. The Zionist Organization did not want an autonomous Jewish government. The hope was that a nationality would gradually be built up to 'make Palestine as Jewish as America is American or England English'. When the Jews formed the large majority, it would be time to establish such a government as would answer to the state of the development of the country and to Jewish ideals. A conference of Zionist leaders, attended by Weizmann, was more specific: it demanded absolute control of immigration into Palestine; official observance of Jewish holidays; immediate control of water rights carrying with it control of the land; Jewish nationalization of all public land and of the surplus land of all private estates exceeding a certain size; complete control of all public works; Jewish supervision of all educational institutions; and use of Hebrew as the main language in all schools. On 25 March Curzon wrote to Balfour that he shuddered at the prospect of Britain having to adjust these ambitions to the interests of the native population.[30]

Lloyd George, following his disagreements with the French, decided that as France was not going to send commissioners to the Middle East to determine the wishes of the inhabitants as to a mandatory power, Britain could not do so either. So two American commissioners, Charles R. Crane and H.C. King, went on their own. They found in Syria opposition to any separation of Syria and Palestine, a preference for an American mandate and failing that a British one, but under no circumstances would Syrians peaceably accept France as the mandatory power. Indeed, even Feisal was no longer prepared to accept a moderate Zionist programme in a Palestine as part of a Syrian state under British trusteeship: his people had been frightened by the wider Zionist aspirations.[31] Crane and King, though they started with a strong disposition in favour of Zionism, concluded that the extreme Zionist programme would have to be greatly modified if the civil and religious rights of the non-Jewish inhabitants of Palestine were to be protected in the terms of the Balfour Declaration. They felt that the Zionists looked forward to a practically complete dispossession of the non-Jewish inhabitants by various forms of purchase.[32]

The findings of the commission were ignored. They were known to Britain, but the Americans did not publish them until 1922. Indeed, in the United States, Justice Louis D. Brandeis, the head of the American Zionist movement, told Balfour that Palestine should be the Jewish homeland, not merely that there be a Jewish homeland there. He assumed that was the commitment of the Balfour Declaration. The Jews there needed economic elbow room, and the future Jewish Palestine had to have control of the land and the natural resources. Balfour agreed, but pointed to the difficulties: the British and French agreement of November 1918 to consult the people of the East about their future; and in Palestine 'we are dealing not with the wishes of an existing community but are consciously seeking to re-constitute a new community and definitely building for a numerical majority in the future'. On 11 August 1919 Balfour wrote to Curzon that the four Great Powers were committed to Zionism: 'And Zionism, be it right or wrong, good or bad, is rooted in age-long traditions, in present needs, in future hopes, of far profounder import than the desires and prejudices of the 700,000 Arabs who now inhabit that ancient land.'[33] Feisal perhaps astutely observed that Britain was giving the impression that it had 'sold the Arabs to suit the exigencies of politics in Europe'.[34]

Key policy-makers in Britain became increasingly concerned over the deterioration in Anglo-French relations, and the Cabinet decided that Britain should help France while at the same time remembering the commitments to the Arabs. There was the worry that the dispute over Syria could threaten co-operation with France in Europe. With the withdrawal of British troops, Britain allowed France to occupy Cilicia, Armenia and Syria. Feisal felt betrayed by Britain. He had to come to terms with the French, and late in 1919 he returned from Paris with a draft secret agreement providing for a French mandate over Syria and a separate Lebanon. Feisal would govern an Arab state with the help of French advisers. On 21 December 1919 France and Britain signed an agreement on oil rights: France would get a 25 per cent share of the Turkish Petroleum Company which was placed under British control. France agreed to Britain's building two pipelines, and also a railway to transport oil from Mesopotamia and Persia through the French area in the Middle East to the Mediterranean.[35] In February 1920, at the Conference of London, France accepted the British view of the historic frontiers of Palestine stretching from Dan to Beersheba; Britain agreed to the boundary wanted by France between Syria and Turkey. Then, in March, the Syrians reacted to the proposed agreement with France: an elected assembly in Damascus proclaimed Feisal King of the sovereign independent state of Syria which included Palestine, Lebanon and Transjordan. From Cairo Allenby, fearing that France might drag Britain into war against the Arabs, urged that the powers acknowledge the sovereignty of Feisal over an Arab nation or confederation embracing Syria, Palestine and Mesopotamia, the administration of Syria being 'secured' to France, and that of Palestine and Mesopotamia to Britain.[36] Feisal refused to go to Europe unless the independence of the Arabs were recognized.

It was against this background of rival interests that the conference at San Remo, in April 1920, decided the future of the Middle East. By then Britain had decided that Mesopotamian oil resources were sufficient to pay for the administration of that country. France and Britain reached an agreement on oil similar to the one of December 1919.[37] It was decided that the form of the mandates should be decided first by Britain and France, and then submitted to the League of Nations. The mandates for Syria and the Lebanon were allotted to France, and those for Palestine and Mesopotamia to Britain. The mandatory power in Palestine was to implement the Balfour Declaration. An independent decision of the Supreme Council declared Britain as the mandatory power in Palestine.[38]

In Syria there were attacks on French positions. France with 90,000 troops, largely North African Arabs and Black Senegalese, responded and took Damascus on 25 July. Feisal went to Italy and then to London. Winston Churchill, the new Secretary of State for the

Colonies, told the Imperial Conference in 1921 that this spectacle had been painful to British opinion, but Britain's strong ties with France had had to prevail. France enlarged the Lebanon with its Maronite Catholics and other Christian sects to secure a small Christian majority that could not be maintained because of the high Muslim birth-rate. This enlargement was at the expense of Syria.[39]

Meanwhile Britain was drafting the terms of its mandate over Palestine. Curzon, then Foreign Secretary, objected to the phrase 'development of a self-governing Commonwealth': that was a 'euphemism for a Jewish State, the very thing they accept and that we disallow'. On 20 March 1920 he minuted:

> The Zionists are after a Jewish State with the Arabs as hewers of wood and drawers of water.
>
> So are many British sympathizers with the Zionists.
>
> Whether you use the word Commonwealth or State that is what it will be taken to mean.
>
> That is not my view. I want the Arabs to have a chance and I don't want a Hebrew State. . . .
>
> Here is a country with 580,000 Arabs and 30,000 or is it 60,000 Jews (by no means all Zionists). Acting upon the noble principles of self-determination and ending with a splendid appeal to the League of Nations, we then proceed to draw up a document which reeks of Judaism in every paragraph and is an avowed constitution for a Jewish State.
>
> Even the poor Arabs are only allowed to look through the keyhole as a non-Jewish community.
>
> It is quite clear that this mandate has been drawn up by someone reeling under the fumes of Zionism. If we are all to submit to that intoxicant, this draft is all right.[40]

In effect the draft of the British mandate was prepared by the Zionists in Paris, and accepted by the British officials, Forbes Adams and Robert Vansittart. After objections, Hubert Young, working with Adams, made minor amendments to the Zionist draft, but the substance remained unaltered. The French Foreign Secretary, Philippe Berthelot, and Prime Minister, Alexandre Millerand, were alarmed by it: they thought it 'much too judaized and judaizing'.[41] Curzon had told Weizmann that he could not allow the phrase 'recognizing the historical connection of the Jewish people with Palestine', but in Paris Vansittart inserted this. Curzon minuted: 'It is certain to be made the basis of all sorts of claims in the future. I do not myself recognize that the connection of the Jews with Palestine, which terminated 1,200 years ago, gives them any claim whatsoever.' In the end Curzon had to accept similar phrasing.[42]

In Palestine itself, on 4 April 1920, there were calls for the incorporation of Palestine into the kingdom of Syria. Arab rioters rampaged through the Jewish quarter of Jerusalem. Over the next four days 9 people died and 244 were wounded, the Jews being the principal casualties. The Committee of Inquiry found that the Zionist Commission had provoked Arab hostility, and usurped functions proper to the government. Weizmann, concerned over the pogroms in the Ukraine and the death of 60,000 Jews there, wanted immigration restrictions relaxed to allow more Jews into Palestine and also land for them to settle. The military administration in Palestine was replaced by a civilian one under Herbert Samuel. Lloyd George appointed a man who, though a non-practising Jew, had become an ardent spokesman for the Zionist cause. Although Samuel never joined a Zionist organization, he had collaborated closely with Weizmann during 1918 and 1919, argued the Zionist case with Feisal and Allenby, and lobbied the Zionist cause in Paris at the peace conference. Allenby and senior British officers in Egypt and Palestine objected to the appointment. Samuel chose as his civil secretary Wyndham Deedes, a known sympathizer with Zionism and a close friend of Weizmann. Although Samuel's administration in Palestine appeared favourable to the Zionists, he did appoint known opponents of Zionism to senior positions.[43]

At the beginning of 1921 Palestine and Mesopotamia became the concern of the Colonial Office under Winston Churchill.[44] Churchill had organized a new Middle East Department, and he persuaded T. E. Lawrence to join as adviser on Arab affairs. Together they effectively worked out British policy in the area before the conference at Cairo in March 1921.[45] The Cabinet confirmed Churchill as overall director of British policy in Arabia, Iraq and Palestine. Curzon accepted this.

In June 1920, following the destruction of the Arab dream of a free Arab confederacy under Feisal with the announcement of the mandate system, a rebellion had broken out in Iraq. British authority there broke down. Quelling the revolt cost £40m. and 2,000 casualties. A. T. Wilson who headed the civil administration recommended that Feisal should head an Arab administration there. At a dinner in London, Lawrence and Lord Winterton persuaded Feisal to accept the kingdom of Iraq. From the meeting of the principal British administrators and military officers in the Middle East, held at Cairo in March, Churchill reported to Lloyd George a unanimous view in favour of selecting Feisal. On 22 March the Cabinet accepted Churchill's proposal, and approved arrangements to stage an election. Churchill could not wait for a demand for Feisal from Mesopotamia, wanted by Lloyd George who was worried about French reaction. Instead the Colonial Secretary accepted a procedure devised by Sir Percy Cox, his secretary Gertrude Bell and Lawrence. In a referendum 96 per cent of those who voted favoured Feisal. He became King of Iraq in August 1921.[46]

While the conference was sitting in Cairo, Abdullah, Hussein's third son, marched into Amman, the main city of Transjordan with the apparent intention of liberating Syria and restoring Feisal as its ruler. France urged Britain to get rid of Abdullah. Churchill was worried that

Transjordan could become a base for anti-Zionist activities. Lawrence, however, suggested that if there were a just policy in Transjordan opposition to Zionism would decrease in four to five years. If Abdullah were appointed ruler he could persuade him to check anti-Zionism. Lawrence envisaged a ruler of Transjordan who would not be too powerful, and hence would have to rely on the British government to stay in office. Churchill endorsed this idea, provided Abdullah prevented anti-French and anti-Zionist propaganda in Transjordan. Abdullah might regard British policy more sympathetically if Britain reached a general understanding with his family: his brother would be appointed to the throne of Iraq, a subsidy would be paid to Hussein and there would have to be a guarantee to restrain Ibn Saud. On 21 March Lawrence met Abdullah at Salt and urged his support for installing Feisal in Iraq and threatened the danger of Ibn Saud reaching Mecca. In Jerusalem Churchill, Samuel and Lawrence persuaded Abdullah to accept their proposals. Samuel assured Abdullah that there was no question of setting up a Jewish government in Palestine. Following this, Article 25 was introduced into the Palestine mandate: this entitled Britain to 'postpone or withhold' application of certain unsuitable provisions, and to provide local administration for Transjordan. Zionist leaders were informed of this on 25 April and accepted the distinction between Palestine and Transjordan without comment. The French did not like this creation of a separate dependency. On 7 February 1922 Churchill recorded that it was undesirable, at that time, to move Transjordan towards closer assimilation into Palestine. The Council of the League received a British memorandum on Article 25 on 16 September 1922: the provisions pertaining to Zionism would not be applicable to Transjordan, defined as all territory lying to the east of a line drawn from a point 2 miles (3 km) west of Aqaba up the centre of the Wadi Araba, Dead Sea and Jordan River to its junction with the River Yarmuk, and thence up the centre of that river to the Syrian frontier. The council endorsed the memorandum. In December 1922 Britain recognized the independent constitutional government in Transjordan under the Emir Abdullah. A second agreement in 1928 confirmed Britain's authority by virtue of the mandate in affairs affecting international obligations. For the first time Palestine was defined in the new restricted sense as the area west of the Jordan. This lasted until 1946 when a treaty of alliance recognized Transjordan as a fully independent state with Abdullah as its sovereign ruler.[47]

Having established Abdullah in Transjordan, Britain still had to cope with Ibn Saud and Hussein. For over a year Britain had encouraged Ibn Saud to attack the Shammar, the rulers of northern Nejd. But a projected road and air route between Palestine and Iraq necessitated the friendship of the Shammar, so the Cairo Conference recommended that Ibn Saud be given a subsidy of £100,000 a year. It would be paid by monthly instalments, dependent on the fulfilment of certain conditions. The conference also recommended that Hussein be paid a similar subsidy. But Hussein had first to ratify the Treaty of Versailles, including the mandatory principle and the disposal of the Arab countries. Lawrence and the Middle East Department prepared a treaty for Hussein to sign, and on 8 July 1921 Lawrence sailed for Jedda. For two months Hussein insisted that Britain should withdraw from Palestine and 'leave the question to the nation'. Curzon then ordered Lawrence to Transjordan to keep Abdullah on the throne there, and the Colonial Office tried other tactics – unsuccessfully. Hussein empowered Abdullah to negotiate for him, and on 9 December Abdullah signed an agreement with Lawrence. Hussein refused to ratify it. In 1924 Ibn Saud and the Wahabis invaded the Hejaz and captured Mecca. Hussein abdicated in favour of his eldest son Ali and went into exile. But Medina and Jedda surrendered, and in January 1926 Ibn Saud became King of the Hejaz. In the Treaty of Jedda of 1927 Britain acknowledged this. In 1932 Ibn Saud took the title of King of Saudi Arabia.[48]

The Cairo Conference was mainly concerned with Iraq and Transjordan. Discussion on Palestine centred on the creation and financing of a defence force. Afterwards, Churchill travelled to Jerusalem: he heard Arab demands for the abolition of the principle of a national home for the Jews and the creation of a national government elected by those resident in Palestine before the war. But the Colonial Secretary argued that the national home would be good for the Jews, the British Empire and the Arabs who dwelt in Palestine.[49] Planting a tree on the site of the Hebrew university on Mount Scopus, Churchill said that personally his heart was full of sympathy for Zionism. But he mentioned Britain's double promise and the assurance that the non-Jewish inhabitants should not suffer as a consequence of the national home.[50] At a time of agitation over Churchill's visit the old Mufti of Jerusalem died. The government declared Haj Amin, an outspoken opponent of the Jewish national home who had been charged with incitement to violence in the April 1920 riots, elected. Later, with Samuel's approval, Haj Amin became President of the newly created Supreme Muslim Council and effective head of the Muslim community in Palestine.

An illegal May Day procession by Jewish communists in Tel Aviv led to clashes with Jewish socialists and Arab riots in Jaffa: 27 Jews and 3 Arabs were killed that day. The Haganah, the Jewish army, intervened with administration support, but Arab attacks continued and martial law was proclaimed. By 7 May 47 Jews and 48 Arabs had died. Samuel tried conciliation: he suspended Jewish immigration. The Va'ad Leumi, the National Council of the Jews of Palestine, threatened to resign. General William Congreve, the commander of British forces in the Middle East, criticized Samuel for trying to enforce the policy of the Jewish national home on a majority who hated it and intended to fight. Churchill immediately invited the Air Ministry to assume responsibility for the defence of Palestine. An Arab delegation went to London, but was told by Churchill on 22 August 1921 that Britain meant to carry out the Balfour Declaration. Negotiations between the delegation and the Colonial Office made no progress. In May 1922 Samuel visited England and drew up a statement of policy, accepted by Churchill and the Cabinet. It was then published in a White Paper in June and approved by the House of Commons.[51]

This document formed the basis of British policy in Palestine for almost a decade. On the one hand it attempted to reassure the Arabs: Britain had never contemplated the disappearance or the subordination of the Arab population, language or culture in Palestine. The Balfour Declaration did not envisage that Palestine as a whole would be converted into a Jewish national home. It said that such a home should be founded in Palestine. The Zionist Commission in Palestine did not have any share in the general administration of the country. The development of the Jewish national home in Palestine did not mean the imposition of Jewish nationality upon the inhabitants of Palestine as a whole, but the further development of the existing Jewish community, with the assistance of Jews in other parts of the world, so that it could become a centre in which Jewish people as a whole could take an interest. To enable the Jewish community in Palestine to develop it was essential that it should be known that it was in Palestine as of right and not on sufferance. The White Paper said that was the interpretation the British government placed on the Balfour Declaration.[52] The Zionists formally accepted this document. The Arab delegation rejected it and returned to Palestine.

At the time of the publication of the White Paper, Parliament discussed Zionism in relation to the Rutenberg scheme which would give Zionists control over the development of resources for the production of electricity in Palestine. It would also dispossess Arabs of land. On 21 June Lord Islington moved a motion in the House of Lords that the Palestine mandate was unacceptable as it was opposed to the sentiments and wishes of the great majority of the people of Palestine. Though challenged by Balfour, Islington carried the House by 60 votes to 29. Churchill, however, defended the Rutenberg concession in the House of Commons. That House endorsed the Colonial Secretary's policy by 292 votes to 35.[53]

On 22 July the League of Nations approved the Palestine mandate.[54] Britain assumed a responsibility it had deliberately sought, partly to curtail French interests in the Middle East, partly to satisfy the Zionist aspirations of a section of the Establishment. Effectively, however, the decision had already been taken at the San Remo Conference that Palestine would constitute a distinct exception to the Wilsonian principle of self-determination. It could be seen as a move by the Great Powers to impose a settlement on an area of significance for their strategic interests. If this endangered the rights of the local inhabitants that was a price to be paid. Alternatively, it is possible to view the League of Nations decision as making possible Herzl's dream of a Zionist state and a refuge for persecuted Jews. The British White Paper of 1922 was a shrewd compromise: while suggesting continued support for Zionism it sought to reassure the Arabs and stated that Palestine would not constitute *the* national home, but merely *a* national home for the Jews with no subordination of the Arab population.

The year 1922, as well as being notable for an evolution of a British policy that attempted to balance the conflicting interests in Palestine, also saw formal independence being conceded to Egypt and the abandonment of Kitchener's 1914 paternalistic experiment of a pro- tectorate. By the end of 1917 Sir Reginald Wingate, the High Com- missioner, had detected a mood of truculence among the Egyptian ministers which developed a year later into demands for complete autonomy. Nationalist feelings focused around Sa'd Zaghlul, a former judge who had held ministerial office with Cromer's approval. He led a group of notables which later emerged into the Wafd or 'Delegation' Party.[55] Wingate urged a liberal programme, and at the beginning of 1919 Balfour agreed to receive Egyptian ministers in March. Curzon questioned the need for concessions to the Egyptians, and when Sir Milne Cheetham, Wingate's deputy, suggested Zaghlul and his friends be deported, Curzon agreed. Disturbances ensued throughout Egypt in March, and Allenby replaced Wingate. Allenby secured the release of Zaghlul and his party, and Lloyd George suggested a commission under Milner to inquire into the future of the protectorate. In December 1919 the Milner mission arrived in Egypt. The proconsul concluded that Egyptian policy had to be subordinated to the wider British interests in the Middle East and India, and this analysis formed the background of the treaty of alliance that maintained British strategic control of, and influence in, Egypt. In the middle of 1920 the Milner mission and Zaghlul conferred in London, and by the middle of August reached agreement. Though Egypt would become an independent constitutional monarchy it would be bound by a treaty of alliance with Britain. Britain would be allowed to station troops in Egypt, and the British High Commissioner would remain pre-eminent in Cairo. Milner felt this would give Britain a strong foothold in Egypt, a vital link in the chain of empire. Churchill did not like the agreement, nor did Montagu. Indeed, the creation of the Middle Eastern Department under Churchill probably led Curzon, fearing Churchill's programme of stability and retrenchment, to open negotiation with the Egyptian nationalists. These could not really progress because they took place against the background of debates on the Irish question.

Zaghlul organized a political crisis in Egypt, and on 8 January 1922 the Residency in Cairo accepted a deal whereby an Egyptian ministry would be formed provided Britain recognized Egyptian independence. Curzon risked Churchill's wrath, and supported Allenby in Cabinet, initially unsuccessfully. Allenby threatened resignation. Lloyd George forced the matter through Cabinet, and by the 1922 Declaration Britain pledged itself only to intervene in the affairs of Egypt if the imperial interest or that of foreign communities necessitated it. Egypt could conduct its own foreign policy provided it did not clash with Britain's international interests.[56]

The Sultan in Egypt became King Faud I. A parliamentary constitution was introduced, but the King retained considerable powers. The Wafd came to power, but it tended to be dominated by landowners, and its leading politicians battled with the other main political forces in Egypt – the King and the ultimate authority of Britain.[57]

The period from the time of Allenby's entry into Jerusalem in December 1917 to his stand over the 1922 Declaration on Egypt saw the division of the Middle East among the European powers. It resembled the scramble for Africa in the 1890s. The powers pursued their own interests at the expense of any ideas of self-determination. Even Woodrow Wilson, in many ways the initiator and proponent of this philosophy, found exceptions to it as was evidenced in the American disregard for the report of the King–Crane Commission. Domestic factors and the emerging Zionist lobby, headed by respected personalities, played an increasingly important role in the politics of the United States. Many Western officials still thought the Arabs incapable of administration or self-government. Some evidenced a racial superiority and scorn, others the sort of benevolence towards the lesser breeds beneath the law shown by Rudyard Kipling in his poem 'White Man's Burden', written in the late 1890s to urge the United States to undertake imperial responsibilities and annex Cuba. The defeat of Germany and Turkey and the collapse of the Tsar, suddenly made Britain, with its 1 million occupying troops, the dominant power in an area stretching from India to Constantinople, from the Caspian Sea to the Indian Ocean. The acquisition of this vast new empire had not been planned. It was rather unexpected. Initially there had been strategic considerations influenced by the opening of the Suez Canal and the need to safeguard the route to India, and this was followed by the significance of oil when the British navy moved over to oil-fired ships in the early years of the twentieth century. But the results of the military campaigns in the Middle East of the First World War could not have been foreseen. Britain organized its vast new empire with the confidence of a nineteenth-century imperialistic power. There were limitations. Some British officials distrusted France. But a future had to be considered where the United States might withdraw from world responsibilities, and Britain and France alone would have to face either Germany or Russia. France had to be accommodated, but preferably not in a way that would endanger the British imperial interest. Even if Britain's imperial strength was only a façade, it at least had to appear a reality.

British policy in the Middle East was decided not just by the Cabinet, but by military officers and permanent officials. It was a handful of men, and a few women, who decided boundaries and laid the foundations of new states. Many came from upper-class backgrounds, and had been through a public school system designed to enable both the exercising of authority and an understanding of the suffering that being under that authority might entail. Others, like Mark Sykes, had had a more Bohemian education. Many like Lawrence, Curzon and Milner had lived in the Middle East. This was a time of proconsuls and personal rule. Men were chosen, not elected. Individual friendships, hatreds and rivalries determined the destiny of the Arabs and the Zionists.

Individuals with power could be influenced. The Zionists knew this, and chose their men carefully. But, from 1919, Zionist influence in London, and particularly in the Foreign Office, lessened. Many of their converts became disillusioned as they realized that what was being pursued was a Zionist state in Palestine. In February 1919 Robert Cecil recorded his misgivings over the British pro-Zionist policy. Ronald Graham found that he was no longer a 'hot partisan': Weizmann had sold Britain a 'pip'. Ormsby-Gore, in February 1919, found political Zionism an 'embarrassment'. Even Sykes had doubts. In Curzon's Foreign Office many of the officials dealing with Palestine opposed Zionism, as did the Foreign Secretary.[58] But the Zionists still managed to influence the right people at the right time, as was shown by Vansittart's activities in Paris. Effectively, they drafted the British mandate for Palestine. Curzon only secured minor modifications. When control of Palestine shifted to the Colonial Office, Churchill, though sympathetic to the Zionist cause, came under the influence of Lawrence of Arabia and showed an awareness of Arab fears. This was reflected in the White Paper of 1922 which stressed that the Balfour Declaration merely envisaged a Jewish homeland in Palestine, and no subordination of the Arabs to Zionism.

The seeds of the Arab–Israeli conflict, however, were sown at the San Remo Conference. French and British mandates were imposed unceremoniously on reluctant Arab populations, and Palestine was specifically excluded from the principle of self-determination. The Western powers carved up an area in their own imperial and domestic interests. The Arabs had little say. Lawrence was often seen as their spokesman. He had personal difficulties. After establishing Feisal in Iraq, Abdullah in Transjordan and attempting to settle with Hussein, he seems to have felt that his debt to the Arabs had been paid.

Lawrence left the Arabs behind, and embarked upon his own personal resistentialist odyssey.

REFERENCES

1. *FO 371*, 3054, Memorandum by Toynbee and Namier, 19 Dec. 1917.
2. *FO 882*, 7, ff. 236–50; 13, ff. 35–40.
3. *Cab 27*, 23, 19 Jan. 1918.
4. *FO 371*, 3398, Weizmann to Ormsby-Gore, 16 April 1918; Storrs to Foreign Office, 22 April 1918.
5. Ibid., 3394, Memorandum by Cornwallis, 20 April 1918.
6. *Clayton Papers* (University of Durham), Clayton to Sykes, 18 April 1918. Quoted by Jon Kimche, *Palestine or Israel* (London 1973), p. 45.
7. *FO 882*, 14, Memorandum by P. C. Joyce, 5 June 1918; Memorandum by Walrond, July 1918.
8. *FO 371*, 3380, ff. 557–72.
9. Stephen Roskill, *Hankey, Man of Secrets*, Vol. I, *1877–1918* (London 1970), pp. 586–7.
10. *Cab 23*, 43, Imperial War Cabinet Minutes, 13 Aug. 1918; W. H. Rothwell, 'Mesopotamia in British war aims, 1914–1918', *Historical Journal*, XIII (1970), 273–94 at 290.
11. *Cab 23*, 7, War Cabinet Minutes, 15 Aug. 1918.
12. *FO 800*, 221, Memorandum by Toynbee, Oct. 1918.
13. Peter Mansfield, *The Ottoman Empire and its Successors* (London 1973), pp. 45–6.
14. *FO 371*, 3398, Sykes to Ormsby-Gore, Nov. 1918, Minute by Toynbee, 2 Dec. 1918.
15. Ibid., 3386, Clayton to Foreign Office, 6 Dec. 1918.
16. Ibid., 4153, Arab Petitions.
17. *Cab 27*, 24, Minutes of Eastern Committee, 5 Dec. 1918.
18. Ibid., Minutes of Eastern Committee, 5 Dec. 1918.
19. Michael L. Dockrill and J. Douglas Goold, *Peace without Promise, Britain and the Peace Conference, 1919–23* (London 1981), pp. 143–50.
20. *Cab 27*, 24, 29 Oct. 1918; 36, Report by Lawrence to War Office, 4 Nov. 1918.
21. Ibid., 37, Baghdad to India Office, 20 Nov. 1918.
22. For an account based on Weizmann's record see Philip Knightley and Colin Simpson, *The Secret Lives of Lawrence of Arabia* (London 1971), pp. 139–41; for an account based on Feisal's correspondence see A. L. Tibawi, *Anglo-Arab Relations and the Question of Palestine 1914–1921* (London 1977), pp. 330–4; *FO 608*, 98.
23. *Cab 27*, 24, Minutes of Eastern Committee, 5 Dec. 1918.
24. *FO 608*, 98, f. 247, Minute by Mallet, 30 Jan. 1919.
25. *FO 371*, 4153, Minute by Graham, 25 Jan. 1919; Curzon to Graham, 26 Jan. 1919; *FO 800*, 215, Balfour to Curzon, 20 Jan. 1919; Curzon to Balfour, 26 Jan. 1919.
26. *FO 371*, 4179, Balfour to Lloyd George (extract), 19 Feb. 1919.

27. *Milner Collection* (Public Record Office, London), *PRO 30*, 30/10, Memorandum by Hirtzel on France's claim to Syria, 14 Feb. 1919.
28. James Headlam-Morley, Agnes Headlam-Morley et al. (Eds), *A Memoir of the Paris Peace Conference, 1919* (London 1972), p. 30.
29. Desmond Stewart, *T. E. Lawrence* (London 1979), pp. 222–3; Tibawi, op. cit., pp. 343–9; Richard Meinertzhagen, *Middle East Diary 1917– 1956* (London 1959), pp. 14–15; Arnold Toynbee, *Acquaintances* (Oxford 1967), pp. 182–3; *FO 608*, 92; Zeine N. Zeine, *The Struggle for Arab Independence. Western Diplomacy and the Rise and Fall of Feisal's Kingdom in Syria* (Beirut 1960), pp. 65–83.
30. Martin Gilbert, *Exile and Return. The Emergence of Jewish Statehood* (London 1978), pp. 117–21; Dockrill and Goold, op. cit., pp. 158–62.
31. *Documents on British Foreign Policy 1919–1939*, (hereafter cited as *DBFP*), 1st series, Vol. IV, pp. 311–13, French to Curzon, Telegram, 10 July 1919.
32. For Report see *Foreign Relations of the United States, Peace Conference 1919*, Vol. 12, pp. 751–863; see also H. N. Howard, *The King–Crane Commission* (Beirut 1963), *passim*.
33. *FO 800*, 217, Interview between Balfour and Brandeis; *FO 371*, 4183, Balfour to Curzon, 11 Aug. 1919.
34. *DBFP*, 1st series, Vol. IV, pp. 290–2, Appendix B, Clayton to Curzon, 23 July 1919. In August Balfour minuted: 'I am an ardent Zionist.' (Ibid., pp. 329–30, Curzon to Balfour, 5 Aug. 1919; Minute by Balfour.)
35. Ibid., Vol. IV, pp. 114–16, Memorandum of Agreement between Greenwood and Berenger, 21 Dec. 1919.
36. Ibid., Vol. XIII, p. 231, Allenby to Curzon, Telegram, 18 March 1920.
37. Ibid., Vol. VIII, pp. 9–19, Notes of Meeting of British, French and Italian Delegations at San Remo on 18 April 1920, 24 April 1920.
38. Ibid., pp. 251–2, Curzon to Hardinge, Telegram, 26 April 1920.
39. Mansfield, *Ottoman Empire and its Successors*, pp. 54–5.
40. *FO 371*, 5199, f. 6 ff. Minute by Curzon, March 1920; Minutes by Curzon, 20 March 1920.
41. Ibid., 5244, Vansittart to Young, 21 June 1920.
42. Ibid., 5245, Minute by Curzon, 6 Aug. 1920; Minute by J. A. C. Tilley, 10 Sept. 1920; 5248, Memorandum by Curzon for Cabinet, 30 Nov. 1920.
43. Bernard Wasserstein, *The British in Palestine. The Mandatory Government and the Arab–Jewish Conflict 1917–1929* (London 1978), pp. 34–88.
44. *DBFP*, 1st series, Vol. XIII, p. 428, Curzon to Samuel, 7 Jan. 1921.
45. Aaron S. Klieman, *Foundations of British Policy in the Arab World: The Cairo Conference of 1921* (Baltimore 1970), p. 248.
46. *FO 686*, 85; *AIR 8* (Public Record Office, London), 37; Knightley and Simpson, op. cit., pp. 165–8; John Darwin, *Britain, Egypt and the Middle East. Imperial Policy in the Aftermath of War 1918–1922* (London 1981), pp. 191–207, 215–23.
47. Knightley and Simpson, op. cit., pp. 168–71; Klieman, op. cit., pp. 205–35.
48. *FO 686*, 93; *AIR 8*, 37; Knightley and Simpson, op. cit., pp. 171–7; Mansfield, *Ottoman Empire and its Successors*, pp. 58–9.
49. Martin Gilbert, *Winston Churchill*, Vol. IV (London 1975), pp. 564–9.

50. Ibid., pp. 570–1, 574, 597.
51. Wasserstein, op. cit., pp. 89–118.
52. *British Parliamentary Papers, Cmd. 1700, Correspondence with the Palestine Arab Delegation and the Zionist Organization.*
53. *United Kingdom Parliamentary Debates House of Lords*, 50, cols. 994–1019, 21 June 1922, *House of Commons*, 156, cols. 332–5, 4 July 1922.
54. Copy of text in Doreen Ingrams, *Palestine Papers 1917–1922* (London 1972), pp. 177–83.
55. See Elie Kedourie, 'Sa'd Zaghlul and British', *The Chatham House Version and other Middle-Eastern Studies* (London 1970), pp. 82–159.
56. Darwin, op. cit., pp. 49–137; Peter Mansfield, *The British in Egypt* (London 1971), p. 220.
57. Elie Kedourie, 'The genesis of the Egyptian Constitution of 1923', *The Chatham House Version*, pp. 160–76; Mansfield, *Ottoman Empire and its Successors*, pp. 62–3.
58. Wasserstein, op. cit., p. 55.

Chapter 4

BRITISH PARAMOUNTCY OVER ARABS AND ZIONISTS

British paramountcy in the Middle East prevailed until the beginning of the Second World War, and arguably lasted till its conclusion. The Russians had no real opportunity to penetrate the area. The French were preoccupied with problems in Syria and did not interfere with the British mandates. Some Americans were worried that Britain was securing control of too large a share of the world's potential oil resources, and American commercial interests were established in Saudi Arabia, but at that time these did not seriously challenge British predominance. To some extent Britain controlled the area in the name of the League of Nations and had to make reports to the Mandates Commission. In effect, British paramountcy depended on a relationship between Briton and Arab, one that was perhaps based on illusion or legend, but which nevertheless secured British authority in the area for over two decades. Even before the enigmas surrounding Lawrence of Arabia made the public at large aware of the existence of the Arabs, an élite had acquired a fascination for the Middle East with the publication of works like A. W. Kinglake's *Eothen or Traces of Travel brought Home from the East*, impressions of a tour undertaken in 1834, or Edward Fitzgerald's mistranslation of the *Rubaiyat of Omar Khayyam*, illustrated in a mysterious oriental style by Willy Pogány but reflecting more the influence of Art Nouveau and the Vienna Secession. The English were supposed to have a hunger for wide, empty and forbidden spaces. Arabia fulfilled that need, at least in the imagination. Richard Burton travelled to Mecca in disguise, and left an erotic literature for posterity. Charles Doughty dared to journey as a Christian. Even eccentric women ventured into the desert. Archaeologists and their excavations – be it Paul Emile Botta discovering Nineveh, the exhibition at the Crystal Palace in 1854 of the reliefs at Nimrud brought back by Austen Henry Layard, or Major Henry Creswicke Rawlinson's decipherment of the memorial to King Darius – excited an educated public.[1] A few saw Petra and travelled down the Nile. For many public school products the Middle East remained an area in which they could apply Arnold's principles of discipline and

58

moral leadership.[2] They were able to relate to the Arab leaders who had been chosen. They appreciated their courtesy. The Arab hierarchy responded in return: it sent its sons to Harrow and Sandhurst. A section of the British upper and upper middle classes came to respect and admire the Arabs, and particularly the bedouin. The desert seemed clean. On the whole the British administrative structure established in the Middle East showed at least a façade of equality to the governed. There was a liberal tradition and even an idealism. The social snobberies so prevalent in the Indian subcontinent[3] were largely absent, except in Egypt. Above all, British policy in the Middle East appeared to be flexible, and to respond to local needs.

Another section of the British Establishment, however, was subject to rather different influences. An education based on Old Testament Protestant Christianity, combined in some cases with a guilt over latent anti-Semitism, proved fertile ground for the Zionists. Britain was also the paramount power in Palestine. The rise of Adolf Hitler in Germany, and his persecution of the Jews, forced new difficulties on the country committed to securing a Jewish homeland in Palestine.

Preoccupations in *le Grand Liban*, Syria and the Lebanon, meant that France was never able to present a serious challenge to British paramountcy in the Middle East during the inter-war years. A constitution, drafted in Paris, was imposed on the Lebanon in 1926. It established the principle that seats in parliament and the cabinet should be divided between the Christians and the Muslims, effectively giving the Christians a working majority. The offices of president and prime minister were also allocated on religious grounds. In Syria, the revolt by the Druses in 1925 over local grievances, leading to an alliance with nationalists in Damascus, resulted in a constitution in 1930 establishing a parliamentary republic, with France retaining control over foreign affairs and security, but that was suspended from 1932 to 1937. Late in 1936, following a series of independent treaties in the British Middle East, France negotiated similar agreements with Syria and the Lebanon, but these were never ratified by the French government as the Popular Front fell. Fear of the coming war meant that France was concerned over the loyalty of its Arab population in North Africa: that could be inspired by other examples to revolt. The prospect of war also led to France's agreeing to the incorporation of the 'Syrian' *sanjak* of Alexandretta into Turkey, a move resented by Syrian nationalists which left a bitter legacy. France sometimes attempted to impose its language and culture, something the Christians in the Lebanon continued to accept, but which was not liked by Arabic speakers. The administrative structure, however, was efficient, and Lebanese commerce flourished, even if the profits were often repatriated to the metropolitan state.[4]

The area of greatest British control was Transjordan, though there were only between six and eight Britons in the country. Colonel Henry

Cox replaced H. St Jean Philby as British Resident in 1924, and remained there until 1939. A man of considerable administrative capacity, Cox presided at a time when Abdullah recognized Transjordan's total dependence on Britain. Two Britons – Colonel F. G. Peake who trained the villagers in self-defence, and General John Glubb who was largely responsible for the bedouin whom he saw as the corner-stone of the whole state – pacified Transjordan with the Arab Legion, protected it from the Wahhabi warriors and fashioned it into a unified state.[5]

In the Sudan British authority was also almost absolute. From 1899 that country had been governed as an Anglo-Egyptian Condominium, though, with the establishment of the protectorate over Egypt, British control was extended. In 1924 extreme Egyptian nationalists, using the methods of Sinn Fein adopted in 1919, murdered Sir Lee Stack, the Governor-General of the Sudan and Commander-in-Chief (Sirdar) of the Egyptian army in a street in Cairo. Britain forced the evacuation of the Egyptian army from the Sudan, and a new Sudan force under British control was established in 1925. In effect, the Sudan was governed by a devoted British Civil Service. Egypt tried to re-establish its former position through negotiation, but it was only with the Anglo-Egyptian Treaty of Friendship and Alliance of 1936 that the Condominium Agreement of 1899 was reaffirmed, and even then Britain remained formally the predominant power, with Egypt having only a share in the higher administrative and judicial posts of the Sudan government.[6]

The murder of Stack led to the fall of Zaghlul in Egypt. Allenby's subsequent resolute action meant that he was replaced by Lord Lloyd, a Tory who insisted on maintaining key British officials. When Labour came to office in 1929 Sir Percy Lorraine took over, but he could not reach an agreement with Nahas Pasha, the new head of the Wafd, which in any case was ousted from power by King Faud in 1931. It was only really with Mussolini's occupation of Abyssinia in 1935, and his expansionist policies in the Mediterranean, that Britain started to negotiate a new treaty to safeguard its position in Egypt. An uprising, similar to the riots of 1919, necessitated this new approach. With the growing menace in Europe, Britain could not afford to be preoccupied with quelling revolutions in areas of strategic significance. Sir Miles Lampson, who became the British ambassador in Cairo, was the principal architect of the consolidation of Britain's position. Working with Nahas Pasha, he tried to check the excesses of the young King Farouk. The Anglo-Egyptian treaty of 1936, in effect, did not lessen Britain's power or prestige in Egypt. Although British occupation formally came to an end, British troops remained in the country, though provision was made for their gradual withdrawal to the Suez Canal Zone and Sinai, and a limit of 10,000 land forces and 400 air personnel. In the event of war Britain had the right of reoccupation and the unrestricted use of Egyptian roads, ports and airports. It was in domestic affairs that Egyptians enjoyed some new freedoms. Lampson's discreet policy at least allowed the Egyptians a feeling of independence, even though the reality was British paramountcy.[7]

In contrast to Egypt, Iraq formally achieved an independence with the signing of the Anglo-Iraqi treaty on 30 June 1930. The treaty, however, bound Iraq to have 'full and frank consultations with Great Britain in all matters of foreign policy'. Iraq was not a homogeneous country: possibly Britain wanted to avoid any obligation to maintain the peace between the various feuding elements. Iraq had achieved a substantial degree of independence in 1925, but even then nationalist activities in the new parliament had endangered British policy. A principal British concern had been to secure the accession of Mosul to Iraq, and to prevent Turkey from occupying an area that could then leave the British Middle East with a northern frontier that could not be defended. Potential oil resources in Mosul were a factor, though not a dominant one. Washington, however, accused Britain of trying to assume control of the oil resources of Mesopotamia. This was resolved in 1929 with a private agreement between the British owners of the Turkish Petroleum Company, the French Compagnie des Pétroles, and two American companies, Standard Oil of New Jersey and Socony-Vacuum to form the Iraq Petroleum Company. After major discoveries in 1927, with the opening of the pipeline from Kirkup to the Mediterranean, Iraq became by the mid-1930s the second largest oil producer in the Middle East.[8] On 21 November 1925 the Permanent Court of International Justice awarded Mosul to Iraq, and with it came Kurds, Turcomans and Assyrians, making one-quarter of the population of the new state non-Arab. The Arabs in Iraq were themselves divided: there was a Shia majority, and a politically dominant Sunni minority. The bedouin also feuded among themselves. To secure Iraq's admission to the League of Nations in 1932, Britain had to persuade some members of the League that Iraq was able to maintain its independence. Feisal died in 1933. His heir, Ghazi, encouraged factionalism, and in 1936 army officers seized power in the first of a series of military coups that dominated the life of the state. It was a group of officers known as 'The Seven' which secured power in 1938 for Nuri el Said, Feisal's former chief of staff. This pro-British civilian dominated Iraq for twenty years, and tried to secure British interests there. On Ghazi's death in 1939 it was The Seven and Nuri Said who appointed the Regent of the Crown Prince Feisal. In return it was British support in 1937 which ensured that the question of navigation rights on the Shatt al-Arab River between Iraq and Iran went in Iraq's favour. But Iraq was a fragmented country, and the nationalists resented Britain. Italy and Germany were both active in Baghdad and there was considerable Italian, German and Japanese commercial penetration. Nuri Said felt the German minister, Dr Grobba, did more than anyone else to damage the Anglo-Iraq relationship. As an independent country Iraq also became a refuge for disaffected elements from Syria and Palestine. The Mufti of Jerusalem arrived in Baghdad in October 1939.[9]

Iraq's neighbour Iran (Persia) was important to Britain because of its oil production. Before the Second World War the Americans were Britain's principal source of oil. In 1938 57 per cent of Britain's oil came from there. But 22 per cent originated in the Middle East, and of that 18 per cent was supplied by Iran. Iran's leader, Reza Shah, disliked foreigners. When the royalties from the Anglo-Persian Oil Company fell in 1932 with the world economic crisis, he unilaterally cancelled the concession. Britain took Reza Shah to the League of Nations in 1933, but in the end he emerged with a more advantageous agreement. In Kuwait, later Britain's principal supplier of oil, there were disagreements between American and British companies between 1932 and 1933 over concession applications, but in the end the two companies applied jointly for a concession. In the Persian Gulf the British government was prepared to support the applications of the Iraq Petroleum Company for concessions: but this proved unnecessary and the rulers of the smaller sheikhdoms signed in 1938. In Saudi Arabia the Iraq Petroleum Company was unsuccessful: in 1933 Ibn Saud granted a concession to Standard Oil of California. In 1944 the Texas Oil Company, Standard Oil of New Jersey and Socony-Vacuum joined Standard Oil of California to form the Arabian-American Oil Company (Aramco) in 1944. Similarly, American concessionaries secured rights in Bahrain.[10]

Elsewhere in Arabia, Britain felt threatened by the Yemen, bordering on the Aden protectorate which had signed a forty-year peace and friendship treaty with London in 1934. Through the efforts of Harold Ingrams, an administrative structure was devised of an eastern and western division. This protected Aden colony, and its port which had become a bunkering station and a vital link in the structure of the British Empire. Throughout the region precise boundaries were not defined.[11]

With the exception of Saudi Arabia and the Yemen, the Arabian Peninsula and the Persian Gulf were under direct or indirect British control. Britain was the paramount power in the Middle East. The Americans had educational and missionary interests, particularly in Egypt and the Lebanon, and private oil companies with considerable concessions, but these never effectively challenged British suzerainty. France might have wanted to do this, but was prevented by its preoccupations with le Grand Liban. On the whole Britain had good relations with the old Arab ruling élite it had largely chosen. At times British policy might have seemed paternalist, but it was flexible. Britain ensured comparative stability in the area for over two decades. At a time of nationalist stirrings in parts of the Empire, Britain needed to maintain at least a façade of imperial strength. With hindsight, it is possible to exaggerate the importance of commercial interests and particularly oil. During the inter-war years the Middle East was, perhaps, regarded more as of strategic importance as a link securing the communications of the British Empire. Among the new generation of Arabs emerging, a more resentful view of British paramountcy could be discerned. In 1935 Gamal Abdel Nasser took part in a high school demonstration demanding an end to British interference. Iraqi nationalists detested the Iraq Petroleum Company, and what seemed to them British tutelage. But the growing focus of resentment was British policy in Palestine. As the mandatory power Britain was seen as being responsible for Zionist immigration and Arab oppression. An emerging Arab nationalism found focus in resentment at what seemed a British imposition of an alien population. Hitler's persecution of the Jews and the flood of refugees exacerbated the situation. More than ever the politics of the Middle East became determined by the interests of the Great Powers, rather than local considerations. Britain as the paramount power over Zionists and Arabs was the legatee.

There was comparative calm in Palestine after Churchill's White Paper of 1922. Arab fears of a Zionist take-over lessened. Jewish immigration continued, but after reaching a peak of 34,386 in 1924, it dropped to 3,034 in 1927, and with the economic depression more Jews left than entered the country. Most Jews preferred to go to the United States. In 1921 it is estimated that 119,036 Jews entered the United States, whereas only 8,294 went to Palestine. In 1924 the Americans imposed a quota system for immigrants, and the number of Jews arriving fell to 10,292 in 1925. But in the last few years of the decade approximately three times as many Jews left for the United States as entered Palestine.[12] Between 1919 and 1931 the Jewish population of Palestine grew from around 60,000 to 175,000, an increase from 8 to 17.7 per cent of the total population. To the Arabs, the Zionist problem often seemed a numbers game. Some Zionists regarded the Arab problem in the same way, but between 1923 and 1929 the Yishuv (the Jewish community in Palestine) concentrated on its own internal matters, and the Arabs adopted a conciliatory attitude towards the British administration – though concerned about Jewish labour's opposition to the employment of Arab workers in Jewish-owned enterprises.[13]

Then on 28 September 1928, Yom Kippur, the Jewish Day of Atonement, the police removed by force a screen illegally placed near the 'Wailing Wall' to separate Jewish men and women at prayer. To the Jews the Western Wall, the lower courses of the outer wall of Herod's temple, was a sacred sanctuary and a reminder of past glory. To the Arabs it was part of Haram esh-Sherif, where Muhammad had tethered his horse after his journey from Mecca to Jerusalem, while he ascended to the seventh heaven. Jews throughout the world objected to the British action, taken after a complaint from the Supreme Muslim Council in Jerusalem. The Mufti tried to establish Muslim rights and the Jews were deliberately antagonized by building works and noise. The Va'ad Leumi demanded that the administration expropriate the wall for the Jews. On 14 August 1929 6,000 Jews demonstrated in Tel Aviv shouting, 'The wall is ours.' The next day 300 youths raised the Jewish flag at the wall, and sang the Jewish national anthem. On 16 August Muslims burnt pages of Jewish prayer books, and on the next day, the birthday of Muhammad, there was a minor brawl between Jews and Arabs in Jerusalem in which a Jew died. On Friday 23 August riots broke out in Jerusalem, spreading to other parts of Palestine. British troops were called in, and the Haganah was deployed. In Hebron a community of non-Zionist Jews was wiped out; though a committee concluded their books had not been mutilated, in Jaffa the Jews attacked the Arabs and killed 7 of their number. 113 Jews and 116 Arabs died in a week of violence. Complicity of the Mufti was never proved.[14]

The High Commissioner, Sir John Chancellor, urged a move in British policy away from Zionism. A commission of inquiry under Sir Walter Shaw examined the reasons for Arab unrest, and reported in March 1930 that Zionist demands on immigration had aroused Arab apprehension about Jewish political domination. Shaw thought the Zionist demands a breach of the principle, accepted by the Zionist Organization in 1922, that immigration should be regulated by the economic capacity of Palestine to absorb new arrivals.[15] An Arab delegation, including the Mufti, went to London and saw the Prime Minister, Ramsay MacDonald, and Lord Passfield, the Colonial Secretary. Its demands included the prohibition of land sales from Arabs to non-Arabs, a halt to Jewish immigration and national parliamentary government in terms of the League covenant. Britain sent Sir John Hope Simpson to Palestine to investigate the land question. He reported that the amount of cultivated land in Palestine was considerably less than the estimates of the Zionists and the Commissioner of Lands. This land was not even sufficient to provide the Arab population with a decent livelihood. Pending development, there was no more room for Jewish settlers. This report formed the basis of the 1930 Passfield White Paper[16] which intimated immigration restrictions.

Zionist influence on British policy had lessened during the 1920s. It now reasserted itself. Lewis Namier, effectively an employee of the Zionist executive, on the evening of 17 October took the White Paper to Weizmann. The following day Baffy Dugdale, Balfour's niece, contacted the Conservative politician, Leo Amery. Namier used the Prime Minister's son, Malcolm MacDonald, to get through to 10 Downing Street. On 6 November Ramsay MacDonald proposed a meeting between the Zionists and a Cabinet subcommittee, chaired by Arthur Henderson, assisted, at Weizmann's request, by Malcolm

MacDonald. The Zionists mounted an orchestrated campaign, and there were anti-British demonstrations throughout the Jewish world. The national consensus on Palestine was shaken in the House of Commons and Anglo-American relations appeared strained. The government felt threatened. The Anglo-Zionist conference finished its work in January 1931. Using as a basis a memorandum provided by Leonard Stein, it drafted the letter MacDonald officially sent to Weizmann on 13 February 1931.[17] In what the Arabs dubbed the 'Black Letter' MacDonald reaffirmed Britain's intention to stand by the mandate, viewed as an obligation to world Jewry, to uphold the policy of the Jewish national home by further land settlement and immigration, and to condone the Zionist insistence on Jewish labour for work on Jewish enterprises.[18]

In Palestine the Arab executive announced that it was looking to the Arab and Muslim worlds for help as it no longer had confidence in Britain. On 18 September 1931 a conference of Arab activists resolved to concentrate on 'independence within Arab unity'. In December the Mufti inaugurated the General Islamic Congress in Jerusalem: it announced the central importance of Palestine to the Muslim world and denounced Zionism and British policies. An Arab Independence Party was established in 1932. The increase in Jewish immigration led to Arab riots in September and October 1933; largely directed against the mandatory power. Zionist purchases meant an increase in landless Arabs. In 1935 Sir Arthur Wauchope, the High Commissioner, reported that one-fifth of Arab villagers had no land, and Arab unemployment was growing in the towns. Later he advised that the 60,000 Jewish immigrants who had entered Palestine were beyond the absorptive capacity of the country. A Muslim leader, Quassam, inspired by the duty of *Jihad* (holy war), led twenty-five men in an unsuccessful revolt against Britain and Zionism. He became a martyr and Arab hostility increased.[19]

On 30 January 1933 Adolf Hitler became Chancellor of Germany. Persecution of Jews increased. In August the Zionist Congress in Prague demanded that the Jewish national home be built up as speedily and on as large a scale as possible. On 15 September 1935 the Nuremberg laws effectively barred Jews from German society.[20] Increasingly, Palestine seemed a haven. The number of Jewish immigrants from Germany rose from 353 in 1932 to 5,392 in 1933. Jewish immigration overall rose dramatically: 9,553 in 1932, 30,327 the following year, 42,359 in 1934 and reached a peak of 61,844 in 1935. The Colonial Secretary, Sir Philip Cunliffe Lister, warned the Cabinet on 28 March 1934 that Arabs and Jews were diametrically opposed on the subject of immigration, and criticized the Jewish Agency policy of employing only Jewish labour. The Zionists, however, in their publicity linked the need for Jewish immigration into Palestine with the Nazi persecution.[21]

Britain offered representative government to Palestine. In December 1935 the Arabs would have fourteen seats and the Jews eight on a legislative council. Both parties rejected the idea, and in any case the Zionist lobby achieved its defeat in parliament in March 1936. In April the various Arab groups in Palestine formed the Arab Higher Committee under the Mufti. Alarmed by information that the Zionists were smuggling in arms, and disturbed by the increasing Jewish immigration, they ordered a general strike. This followed disturbances in Tel Aviv and Jaffa. Weizmann antagonized the Arabs with a speech in Tel Aviv on 23 April by calling the Arab–Zionist struggle one between the forces of the desert and destruction on the one side, and the forces of civilization and building on the other. There were 600 arrests, non-payment of taxes was advocated by the Arabs, and when the government on 18 May announced a schedule of 4,500 Jewish immigrants for the next six months, defiance grew. That same day a royal commission was announced to investigate the reasons for unrest, but it would not leave for Palestine until order had been restored. Military reinforcements arrived from Egypt and Malta and disorders increased. The Colonial Office, under Ormsby-Gore, discussed cantonization as a solution. Britain tried to use Abdullah of Transjordan and Nuri el Said, Foreign Minister of Iraq, as intermediaries. On 19 June, in the House of Commons, speakers emphasized the strategic value of Palestine; some equated British interests with the success of Zionism. Clement Attlee wanted a special session of Parliament. Then the Cabinet, on 2 September, decided to crush Arab resistance, and an announcement was made that an additional division of troops was being sent to Palestine. By 22 September British troops in Palestine numbered 20,000. After visitations from a delegation of the Arab Higher Committee, Ibn Saud, Abdullah and King Ghazi of Iraq appealed for the strike to be called off. That marked the end of the rebellion which killed 38 Britons, 80 Jews and 145 Arabs. The refusal to stop immigration left the Arabs with the impression that Britain was committed to a pro-Zionist policy.

The Zionists had not liked the idea of a commission. Weizmann thought that the Colonial Office under its secretary, J. H. Thomas, wanted to use the commission to reduce Jewish immigration. Thomas's replacement, Ormsby-Gore, was considered weak, and unable to resist the supposed pro-Arab tendencies of the Foreign Office. But Labour leaders, including Attlee, advised the Zionists not to boycott the commission. Headed by Earl Peel it left for Palestine on 5 November 1936. At the same time Orsmby-Gore announced there would be no suspension of immigration during the commission's investigations. The Arabs initially refused to give evidence. When they did, they asserted that McMahon's pledge to Hussein included Palestine, therefore the Balfour Declaration and the mandate were invalid. They demanded independence. The Zionists opposed this as it would mean a Palestinian state. The Foreign Office view was largely determined by the Arabist, George Rendel, who made private soundings in the Middle East early in 1937, Anthony Eden, preoccupied with Europe, accepted Rendel's arguments. Rendel warned that Ibn Saud could turn to Italy, driven in despair by British policy in Palestine. The same might happen in Iraq, and Transjordan could follow. Lampson had warned Rendel that Egypt would do the same. But the Christians in the Lebanon welcomed Weizmann and the idea of a Jewish state.[22]

The Cabinet received the Peel Commission report in June 1937. It recommended that Palestine be divided into three parts: an Arab state; a Jewish state; and then certain areas of strategic or religious importance that would remain under a British mandate. As the Jewish state would include the best land, the report recommended that it should pay an annual subvention to the Arab state. Ormsby-Gore endorsed the report. The Foreign Office objected. Eden told the Cabinet it would mean a Jewish state with unviable frontiers, alongside an Arab state with no outlet to the sea. Abdullah, as head of the Arab state, could arouse Iraq and Ibn Saud. The Zionists were uncertain: initially, Ben-Gurion, a Yishuv leader, opposed the idea, but then changed his mind and submitted to Weizmann. The Prime Minister of Iraq called for the opposition of Palestinian Arabs; Britain was embarrassed by Iraq's attitude in the League of Nations. British prestige in the Middle East seemed threatened. Reports from British representatives there warned of conflagration if partition were implemented. A battle developed between the Foreign and Colonial Offices.

In September 1937 a Pan-Arab congress in Syria claimed Palestine as part of the Arab homeland. Arabs everywhere were bound to defend Palestine. A Jewish state could be a foreign base against the Arab world. That same month Lieutenant-General Archibald Wavell was appointed General Officer Commanding Palestine. After the assassination of Yelland Andrews, the District Commissioner of Galilee, the Arab Higher Committee was declared illegal and the Mufti was deprived of his offices and escaped to the Lebanon. In October there were serious disturbances and the Iraq Petroleum Company's pipeline was damaged.

Rendel made Foreign Office policy. He considered the Middle East an organic whole: incidents in one area could affect the rest. Arab disunity, he warned, obscured a growing nationalism. The only way to square the British wartime pledge to the Arabs with the Balfour Declaration would be to assume a Jewish national home as a centre of Jewish civilization. The Jewish population of Palestine would have to be limited. It was decided that a new 'technical' commission would go to Palestine. Ormsby-Gore argued that Britain had already accepted partition. Rendel countered that this was overridden by the implications for Europe of a Middle East aligned with Britain's enemies. The matter was settled on 8 December 1937. Neville Chamberlain, the

Prime Minister, supported the Foreign Office. It was open to the 'technical' commission to represent that partition would be unworkable. The commission, under Sir John Woodhead, was seen by the Colonial Office as a Foreign Office creation. Ormsby-Gore resigned, disillusioned with both Jews and Arabs. Malcolm MacDonald became Colonial Secretary in May 1938. Despite his earlier sympathies with Zionism, a few weeks in office convinced him that the British interest lay elsewhere. Canvassed by Ben-Gurion and Weizmann, he also had to handle Zionist sympathizers in Parliament. An Arabic scholar with service in the Sudan, Harold MacMichael, replaced Wauchope as High Commissioner, and Lieutenant-General Robert Haining took over from Wavell. Palestine was in a state of rebellion. Captain Orde Wingate, a proponent of Zionism, led 'special night squads' of mixed British and Zionist units against the rebels and to protect the Iraq Petroleum Company's pipeline. His methods were ruthless and to the Arabs this appeared as an alliance between Britain and the Zionists. At the time of the Munich crisis civil government had virtually collapsed in Palestine.[23]

The Mufti, though no longer physically present in Palestine, was regarded as the Arab leader. He was suspected of leanings towards Germany. Indeed Peel's report had alarmed Berlin. A Jewish state could consolidate Jewish political influence. Germany moved towards supporting the Arab cause. The Arabs felt unable to compete with the Zionist lobbies in Western capitals. Nazi Germany with its attitude towards Jews was an obvious ally for securing Palestine as an Arab state. Driven out of Palestine, the Mufti remained in the Lebanon till shortly after the outbreak of the Second World War. Frightened about their own position in the Middle East, the French would not give in to British representations to expel him. Besides the Mufti and his entourage, there did not seem to be any representative Arab leaders. Malcolm MacDonald felt reluctant about inviting the Mufti to London. With the Munich crisis Britain wanted to restore friendly relations with the Arabs: Iraq with its oil and communications would be important in war, and Egypt could be an area of battle. In the event of war the friendship of the United States was vital: MacDonald was conscious of the power of the Zionist lobby there. Haining and MacMichael replied that one postponement of partition and the complete cessation of immigration would bring peace to Palestine.[24] On 19 September Weizmann, Ben-Gurion and Baffy Dugdale learnt from MacDonald that fearing Germany, Italy and the Arabs, Britain intended to abandon partition. MacDonald told the Cabinet on 19 October that partition was not the right solution. On 9 November the Woodhead commissioners' report was published. It ruled out partition as the two states envisaged would not be economically viable and would entail large-scale movements of population. Britain proposed a conference in London of Arab and Jewish leaders, together with representatives from the independent Arab states.

The Zionists were kept appraised of Cabinet opinion by Walter Elliot, the Minister of Health. The Jewish Agency resolved that if it could not buy land in Palestine, it would get it in other ways; if arms were forbidden the Haganah would be trained unofficially; if immigration were reduced illegal immigrants would have to be brought in. This was tantamount to a declaration of war on Britain.

The London Round Table Conference opened on 7 February 1939. The Arabs refused to speak to the Zionists. Chamberlain saw them both separately. In January 1939 the Cabinet had approved the policy outlined by MacDonald: Palestine would be neither a Jewish nor an Arab state. Self-governing institutions would be encouraged and the state moved towards independence with an Arab majority. At the end of 1938 the Jews made up 29 per cent of the population of Palestine. Jewish immigration was to be severely curtailed, and suspended after ten years, unless the Arabs of Palestine consented to it. But even that was not enough for the Foreign Office. Some officials were particularly influenced by the appearance of George Antonius's *The Arab Awakening*, a scholarly presentation of the Palestinian Arabs' case. Antonius pointed out that it was morally outrageous to make the Arabs in Palestine bear the burden of Hitler's persecutions. The persecution of one people could not be justified to relieve that of another. MacDonald's policy was what Britain had in mind in its talks with the Arabs and Jews. The Zionists were alarmed, and tried unsuccessfully to involve the United States. Arab opinion was elated by rumours of an agreement on the lines of the Anglo-Iraq treaty. The Zionists reacted with their new tactics: on 27 February thirty-eight Arabs died in a series of bomb explosions throughout Palestine. On 8 March Lord Halifax, the Foreign Secretary, and MacDonald reported that the conference had achieved nothing. To win Arab friendship, Britain needed to decide the final number of Jewish immigrants. Chamberlain, conscious of American opinion, urged as large a figure as possible, close to 100,000. In consultation with the Arabs a figure of 75,000 was agreed over the next five years. Elliot leaked this to Baffy Dugdale and Weizmann, who again tried unsuccessfully for American intervention. On 13 May Weizmann accused MacDonald of betraying the Jews.[25] The Colonial Secretary, however, favoured immediate publication of a White Paper outlining the new British policy. As he told the Cabinet committee on 20 April, this was necessary to secure the benevolent neutrality of the Arabs in the coming war. Chamberlain supported him: if Britain had to offend one side, it was preferable to offend the Jews rather than the Arabs.[26]

The White Paper was published in London on 17 May 1939. It was not British policy that Palestine should become a Jewish state. And London could not accept that the McMahon correspondence formed a just basis for the claim that Palestine should be converted into an Arab state. Britain wanted an independent Palestine with Arabs and Jews sharing authority in government in a way that secured their essential interests. This was to be established within ten years. It would have treaty relations with Britain to meet the commercial and strategic interests of both countries. Over the following five years, 75,000 Jewish immigrants would be allowed into Palestine and after that immigration would be subject to Arab consent. In some areas no transfer of Arab land would be permitted; in others it would be restricted. There was no Jewish veto over the establishment of an independent state in Palestine.[27]

As Europe moved towards war British paramountcy in the Middle East was challenged by events in the Palestine mandate. On 5 July 1937 the Committee of Imperial Defence resolved that in the event of war it was essential to keep control of Egypt and the Middle East.[28] In February 1938, the Cabinet decided to establish a holding force to keep Egypt until battles in the Far East and Europe had been won. The Middle East Reserve Brigade moved to Palestine late in 1938 and stayed there until July 1939 when it was transferred to the Canal Zone.[29] British policy in Palestine undermined good relations with the Arab states and British predominance in the Middle East. In January 1939 a subcommittee of the Committee of Imperial Defence pointed to the strong feeling of the Arab states over British policy in Palestine. It assumed that if war broke out measures would be taken 'to bring about a complete appeasement of Arab opinion in Palestine and in neighbouring countries'.[30] From Cairo, Lampson advised that unless Jewish immigration ceased Britain might have to fight the Arabs as well as the Germans and Italians. He went further: the Arabs regarded a Jewish state as an even greater danger.[31] Lord Zetland, the Secretary of State for India, warned that Muslim opinion in India was roused over what was happening to the Palestinian Arabs.[32] With the coming war Britain also had to consider a difficult and seemingly illogical public opinion in the United States. Rather than producing an anti-German reaction, Hitler's pogrom against the Jews after Munich led to a 'strong anti-British atmosphere' in the United States. Because of the immigration quotas the United States took few refugees. It expected Britain to do everything. Chamberlain, hoping for American co-operation in Europe and the Far East, had to do something. Britain took vast numbers of refugees, and to soften the impact of the 1939 White Paper in the United States, published simultaneously a programme to settle the refugees in British Guiana.[33]

In the early 1930s the Zionist lobby had secured a sympathetic British policy. International circumstances changed that. The Middle East was unlikely to be a secure base in time of rebellion. The British Empire contained many millions of Muslim subjects. They were concerned over Jewish immigration into Palestine, and opposed vehemently the creation of a Jewish state which they regarded as a base for foreign influence in the Arab world. Britain was still the paramount power. The local dispute in Palestine over numbers and land was subsumed by overall imperial interests. These dictated the conciliatory policy towards the Arabs reflected in the White Paper of 1939.

REFERENCES

1. See C. W. Ceram, *Gods, Graves and Scholars, The Story of Archaeology* (London 1952), pp. 207–317.
2. John Bagot Glubb, *Britain and the Arabs. A Study of Fifty Years 1908 to 1958* (London 1959), pp. 220–32.
3. For an outstanding analysis of the British structure in India see Paul Scott, *The Raj Quartet* (London 1966–75), *passim*.
4. Stephen Hemsley Longrigg, *Syria and Lebanon under French Mandate* (London 1958); A. L. Tibawi, *A Modern History of Syria including Lebanon and Palestine* (London 1969), pp. 338–64; Glubb, op. cit., pp. 103–19; Peter Mansfield, *The Arabs* (London 1978), pp. 237–40.
5. Nasser H. Aruri, *Jordan: A Study in Political Development (1921–1965)* (The Hague 1972), pp. 15–32; P. J. Vatikiotis, *Politics and the Military in Jordan. A Study of the Arab Legion 1927–1957* (London 1967), pp. 57–74; Philip P. Graves (Ed.), *Memoirs of King Abdullah of Trans-jordan* (London 1950), pp. 212–28; Glubb, op. cit., pp. 163–75; H. St J. B. Philby, *Arabian Jubilee* (London 1952), p. 197; Elizabeth Monroe, *Philby of Arabia* (London 1973), p. 135.
6. L. A. Fabunmi, *The Sudan in Anglo-Egyptian Relations. A Case Study in Power Politics 1800–1956* (London 1960), pp. 41–114, 400.
7. Laila Morsy, 'British Policy and the Nationalist Movement in Egypt 1935–1939' (Ph.D. Thesis: University College of Wales, Aberystwyth 1976); John Marlowe, *Anglo-Egyptian Relations 1800–1953* (London 1954), pp. 260–313; P. J. Vatakiotis, *The Modern History of Egypt* (London 1969), pp. 239–91.
8. George W. Stocking, *Middle East Oil* (London 1970), pp. 50–3; C. J. Edmonds, *Kurds, Turks and Arabs* (London 1957), p. 398.
9. Majid Khadduri, *Independent Iraq 1932–1958*, 2nd edn (London 1960), pp. 34–158; Elie Kedourie, 'The kingdom of Iraq: a retrospect', *The Chatham House Version and other Middle-Eastern Studies* (London 1970), pp. 236–85; Stephen Hemsley Longrigg, *Iraq 1900 to 1950. A Political, Social and Economic History* (London 1953), pp. 134–297; Lord Birdwood, *Nuri As-Said. A Study in Arab Leadership* (London 1959), pp. 154–72; Abid A. Al-Marayati, *A Diplomatic History of Modern Iraq* (New York 1961), pp. 47–73; Harry C. Sinderson, *Ten Thousand and One Nights. Memories of Iraq's Sherifan Dynasty* (London 1973), pp. 156–72; Philip Willard Ireland, *Iraq. A Study in Political Development* (New York 1970), pp. 406–53; Khadim Hashim Niama, 'Anglo-Iraqi Relations during the Mandate' (Ph.D. Thesis: University College of Wales, Aberystwyth 1974).
10. Elizabeth Monroe, *Britain's Moment in the Middle East 1914–1971*, 2nd

edn (London 1981), pp. 95–115; Mansfield, op. cit., pp. 240–3; Glubb, op. cit., pp. 213–14; Rouhollah K. Ramazani, *The Foreign Policy of Iran 1500–1941* (Charlottesville 1966), pp. 242–57; Donald Hawley, *The Trucial States* (London 1970), pp. 170–2; J. B. Kelly, *Eastern Arabian Frontiers* (London 1964), pp. 117–38; David Holden and Richard Johns, *The House of Saud* (London 1981), pp. 78–122; Stocking, op. cit., pp. 66–90; Geoffrey Jones, *The State and the Emergence of the British Oil Industry* (London 1981), pp. 141–252; Michael J. Hogan, *Informal Entente. The Private Structure of Cooperation in Anglo-American Economic Diplomacy 1918–1928* (Columbia 1977), pp. 159–226.

11.   Mansfield, op. cit., p. 243; Manfred W. Wenner, *Modern Yemen 1918–1966* (Baltimore 1967) pp. 141–71.

12.   Bernard Wasserstein, *The British in Palestine. The Mandatory Government and the Arab–Jewish Conflict, 1917–1929* (London 1978), p. 160.

13.   Neil Caplan, *Palestine Jewry and the Arab Question 1917–1925* (London 1978) pp. 194–203; A. W. Kayyali, *Palestine. A Modern History* (London 1978), pp. 130–7.

14.   *British Parliamentary Papers, Cmd. 3530, Report of the Committee on the Palestine Disturbance of August 1929*, 1930; Wasserstein, op. cit., pp. 215–35; Kayyali, op. cit., pp. 138–51.

15.   *Cmd. 3530.*

16.   *Cmd. 3686, Palestine. Report on Immigration, Land Settlement and Development by Sir John Hope Simpson*, 1930; *Cmd. 3692, Palestine Statement of Policy by His Majesty's Government in the United Kingdom 1930.*

17.   Norman Rose, *Lewis Namier and Zionism* (Oxford 1980), pp. 47–53; N. A. Rose, *The Gentle Zionists. A Study in Anglo-Zionist Diplomacy, 1929–1939* (London 1973), pp. 49–50; Alan R. Taylor, *Prelude to Israel. An Analysis of Zionist Diplomacy 1897–1947* (London 1961), p. 51.

18.   MacDonald to Weizmann, 13 Feb. 1931, in Walter Laqueur (Ed.), *The Israel–Arab Reader*, 3rd edn (New York 1976), pp. 50–6.

19.   Kayyali, op. cit., pp. 162–83.

20.   The predicament of the Jew in German society at this time was captured by Christopher Isherwood in *Goodbye to Berlin* (London 1939); *Mr. Norris changes Trains* (London 1935); and *Christopher and his Kind 1929–1939* (London 1977). Even Evelyn Waugh treated it in passing in *Brideshead Revisited* (London 1945). Isherwood's and Waugh's works later appeared as stage plays, widely acclaimed films – *Cabaret*, United States 1972, directed by Bob Fosse – and television blockbusters.

21.   Martin Gilbert, *Exile and Return. The Emergence of Jewish Statehood*, pp. 157–64; Nicholas Bethell, *The Palestine Triangle. The Struggle between the British, the Jews and the Arabs 1935–48* (London 1979), p. 25.

22.   Kayyali, op. cit., pp. 187–207; Michael J. Cohen, *Palestine: Retreat from the Mandate. The Making of British Policy, 1936–45* (London 1978), pp. 10–65; Bethell, op. cit., pp. 25–30; Jon Kimche, *The Second Arab Awakening* (London 1970), pp. 160–1.

23.   *Cmd. 5479, Palestine Royal Commission Report*, 1937; Cohen, op. cit., pp. 28–41; Kayyali, op. cit., pp. 207–14.

24.   *CO 733*, 367, MacDonald to MacMichael, 24 Sept. 1938; MacMichael to

MacDonald, 25 Sept. 1938.
25. *Cmd. 5634, Policy in Palestine*, 1938; *Cmd. 5854, Palestine Partition Commission Report*, 1938; Kayyali, op. cit., pp. 215–21; Bethell, op. cit., pp. 39–75; Cohen, op. cit., pp. 41–9, 66–87.
26. *FO 371, 23234*, Minutes of Meeting of Cabinet Committee on Palestine, 20 April 1939.
27. *Cmd. 5957, Correspondence between Sir Henry McMahon and the Sherif Hussein of Mecca, July 1915–March 1916*, 1939; *Cmd. 5964, Statements Made on Behalf of His Majesty's Government during the Year 1918 in Regard to the Future Status of Certain Parts of the Ottoman Empire*, 1939; *Cmd. 5974, Report of a Committee Set Up to Consider Correspondence between Sir Henry McMahon and the Sherif of Mecca in 1915 and 1916*, 1939; *Cmd. 6019, Palestine Statement of Policy*, 1939.
28. *Cab 24*, 270, CP 185, Minutes of Meeting of Committee of Imperial Defence, 5 July 1937.
29. *Cab 23*, 92, 23 Feb. 1938; 99, 24 May 1939.
30. *Cab 51*, 11, ME(O)292, 24 Jan. 1939.
31. *Prem 1*, Lampson to MacDonald, 2 Sept. 1938.
32. *Cab 23*, 96, 2 Nov. 1939.
33. Ritchie Ovendale, *'Appeasement' and the English Speaking World. Britain, the United States, the Dominions and the Policy of 'Appeasement' 1937–1939* (Cardiff 1975), pp. 194–6; 251–2.

Chapter 5

THE UNITED STATES AND THE JEWISH STATE MOVEMENT

The White Paper of 1939, followed by the British attitude to a Jewish army during the early stages of the Second World War, led the Zionists to change their tactics. Instead of concentrating on the mandatory power, Britain, they focused on the United States. They threatened electoral punishment through the Zionist vote if the American administration failed to support a Jewish state. It was thought that the United States could force Britain to hand Palestine over to the Zionists. In the mandate itself the Zionists used new methods. A policy of attrition was waged against the administration. Violence and terrorism were aimed at wearing down British morale. Britain, rather than the Arabs, became the principal enemy. Palestine became an area of Anglo-American controversy at the time of the emergence of the Cold War. To Britain, it seemed that the United States was prepared to sacrifice British strategic interests, and indeed those of the West, on the altar of American domestic politics. There was thus a new factor in the equation of Great-Power interests and local squabbles over land. In the years leading to the creation of the state of Israel it was the most important.

Although informed of it at the time, it was not until 1922 that the United States officially endorsed the Balfour Declaration. And then Congress emphasized that nothing should be done to prejudice the civil and religious rights of Christians and all other non-Jewish communities in Palestine. By a separate Anglo-American convention of 1925 American consent was seen as necessary to modifications in the mandate affecting American interests.[1] At the time of the Arab revolt in 1936 an official American party, including Senator Warren Austin, went to Palestine. Austin suggested that the arm of the mandatory should be strengthened: Britain had a difficult and delicate task.[2] Until 1942 the United States considered the Middle East a British responsibility. In March 1943, however, a presidential committee under Senator Harry S. Truman reported that future American demand for oil was likely to be in excess of domestic production. Possibly, the United States was providing a disproportionate share of the Allies' oil;

Britain was achieving this to further its own imperial interests.[3] James F. Byrnes warned President Franklin D. Roosevelt that public discussion of the economic rivalry between Britain and the United States in the Middle East could give rise to 'strong and dangerous anti-British feeling'.[4] Private American oil interests prevented any agreement between Britain and the United States.[5]

Roosevelt became involved in the Palestine issue in 1943. Concern over the security of the Middle East led the State Department to advise that the Arab world needed to be kept pacified. In May, Roosevelt promised Ibn Saud that 'no decisions altering the basic situation of Palestine should be reached without full consultation with both Arabs and Jews'.[6] By this time, however, Zionist tactics had changed. In May 1942 at the American Zionist Conference which took place in the Biltmore Hotel in New York, Weizmann's programme of demanding a 'Jewish commonwealth' in the whole of western Palestine was adopted. After the war millions of refugees would want to settle there. But Weizmann himself, with his 'gradualist' tactics, was effectively removed from the leadership shortly afterwards. David Ben-Gurion, the leader of the Mapai Party in Palestine, replaced him. Ben-Gurion advocated an activist programme: the United States should be stimulated into supporting a revolutionary change of Palestine policy to which Britain would have to acquiesce.[7] Anthony Eden, the British Foreign Secretary, was alarmed by the Zionist propaganda in the United States that followed this. Britain was asking, unsuccessfully, for common Anglo-American action to alleviate the distress of the persecuted in Europe. Eden wanted to ask Washington to damp down pro-Zionist utterances by public figures: the Arabs would not support an Allied victory if it meant Palestine being handed over to the Jews. Roosevelt was also aware of this, and an Anglo-American statement that the Palestine question should be shelved until the end of the war was drafted.[8] The Prime Minister, Winston Churchill, refused to agree that the 1939 White Paper was the firmly established policy of the British government.[9] In any event the statement was not issued. It was leaked to the Zionists. They employed Ben-Gurion's tactics and barraged officials, principally Henry J. Morgenthau, the Secretary of the Treasury, Henry L. Stimson, the Secretary of War, and Sumner Welles. This left the legacy in the State Department that the American Zionist pressure group could change policy agreed upon as being in the national interest. The British ambassador, Lord Halifax, thought it a sinister indication of the power of pressure groups.[10]

While Britain continued to develop ideas of partition in Palestine, Roosevelt considered trusteeship as a solution. This was prompted by the publication in the *New York Times* of an 'extermination' list of the 1,700,000 people who had died in Nazi concentration camps. Five hundred rabbis petitioned the President for the opening up of Palestine and the countries of the United Nations to Jews. Roosevelt spoke privately of admitting those Jews who could be absorbed into Palestine, and then surrounding the 'Holy Land' with a barbed-wire fence.[11] The Zionists then shifted their attentions from the President to congressmen and other influential leaders. Their most influential organization was the American Palestine Committee formed in 1941, chaired by a Roman Catholic, Robert Wagner, and including in its membership two-thirds of the Senate, 200 members of the House of Representatives and the leaders of both major political parties and labour organizations. In co-operation with the American Zionist Emergency Council it supported the creation of a Jewish army, unrestricted immigration of Jews into Palestine, the revocation of the British White Paper of 1939 and the reconstitution of Palestine as a Jewish commonwealth.[12] Two rabbis, Stephen S. Wise and Abba Hillel Silver, were the co-chairmen of the Zionist Emergency Council. Wise, sympathetic to Britain, was a long-standing friend of Roosevelt and had actively supported his presidential campaigns. Silver, a Republican, was, according to Judge Samuel I. Rosenman, disliked by Roosevelt. Towards the end of 1943 the Zionist Emergency Council lobbied systematically in Washington and throughout the United States.[13]

Britain was worried. Eden urged Cordell Hull, the Secretary of State, to warn the Zionists: their 'strident and provocative' attitude could damage the common war effort.[14] But, on 27 January 1944, resolutions were introduced into the House of Representatives, at the instigation of the American Palestine Committee, proposing that the United States secure free entry for the Jews into Palestine so that the country could ultimately be reconstituted as a free and democratic Jewish commonwealth. London refrained from commenting on a matter of legislation in the United States, but warned that the course envisaged included military obligations: British policy would be influenced by American willingness to control the ensuing situation.[15] On 1 February two members of the American Palestine Committee, Wagner and Robert A. Taft, placed an identical resolution before the Senate. Hull was worried, and contacted the Chief of Staff, General George C. Marshall, about the congressional resolutions 'advocating the establishment of an independent Jewish state in Palestine'. The Arabs could 'play hell' with American oil interests. Marshall agreed: conflict in Palestine would use forces intended for Germany and unrest in the Arab world could interfere with arrangements being made to procure oil for combat.[16] As public hearings on the matter started, Senator Harry S. Truman recorded that 'with Great Britain and Russia absolutely necessary to us in financing the war I don't want to throw any bricks to upset the applecart, although when the right time comes I am willing to help make the fight for a Jewish homeland in Palestine'.[17] Seven Arab states objected. Marshall appeared informally before members of the Foreign Relations Committee of the Senate on 23

February. The memorandum he used explained that the congressional resolutions envisaged a Jewish state as distinct from a homeland. That would increase tension in the Muslim world, throughout the entire Mediterranean area, the Near East, North Africa and further east. Troops would be tied down, and naval and military operations could be seriously affected by the interruption of oil supplies.[18] The resolution was squashed.

At this the Zionist lobby, through the offices of Rosenman and David Niles, the adviser on minority rights and a fellow Zionist, tried to see Roosevelt. The Zionists were in a strong position domestically: 1944 was a presidential election year and the 1942 congressional elections had resulted in an almost equal split between the Republicans and the Democrats. Though the Jewish vote was not great, it was concentrated in three key states: New York, Pennsylvania and Illinois. In 1941 the count of Jews in the United States was 4,641,184, and the figure in the 1948 census was 4,500,000. The Democrats were likely to respond to Zionist pressure; the Republicans, out of office, could freely support the Zionist cause. The Arabs were insignificant domestically. The 1940 census listed 107,420 Arabic-speaking American residents. In 1943 the Office of Strategic Services estimated the number at 104,000, mostly Christians from Syria and the Lebanon.[19] On 9 March Roosevelt did see Wise and Silver and authorized a carefully worded statement which only mentioned a Jewish national home. The President, in his correspondence, showed that he was also concerned for the other persecuted peoples in Europe and Asia.[20]

Foreign Office and State Department officials discussed Palestine in April. Britain felt it could control the situation provided the American Zionists could be kept quiet. Firm action had to be taken against Zionist terrorism in Palestine: seven British policemen had been murdered and there could be attempts to assassinate prominent British officials. The Americans, however, warned that, in an election year, there would be support for Jewish agitation.[21] Zionist pressure started almost immediately. Some of it was based on the premise that the doors of Palestine were closed to the Jews, the children of Israel: this was 'a greater crime against the Jews than any perpetrated by Hitler or his aides against them'.[22] On 27 June, the Republican Party adopted an electoral platform calling for the opening of Palestine to unrestricted immigration for the victims of Nazism, unrestricted Jewish land ownership and Palestine as a free and democratic commonwealth. Hull thought this provided for the creation of a Jewish state.[23] There were fears that the Arabs, suspecting that Britain and the United States had sold out to the Zionists, were turning to Russia.[24] Wise, Silver, Wagner and Rosenman petitioned the President, and, in the end, Roosevelt saw Wise who drafted a statement that, strengthened, Roosevelt authorized Wagner to deliver to the convention of the Zionist Organization of America. In this letter of 15 October 1944

77

Roosevelt promised, if re-elected, to help bring about 'the establish-ment of Palestine as a free and democratic Jewish Commonwealth'. Before that, Roosevelt had used the phrase 'national home'.[25]

The Arabs, aggressively bitter, refused to receive William S. Culbertson and his special American economic mission to the Middle East. Culbertson, in a report of 15 November that helped to determine State Department policy, advised that the Palestine question would remain a serious menace to the peace and security of the Middle East: 'Perhaps the price the United States pays for the privilege to hold its widely publicized views on the Jewish state is worth all it costs. The Mission wishes only to emphasize that the price is considerable and that apparently the American people do not realize how considerable it is.'[26]

British policy at this time was influenced by reports from Sir Kinahan Cornwallis in Iraq and Lord Killearn (formerly Sir Miles Lampson) in Egypt. In February 1944, Cornwallis warned that any 'whittling down' of the 1939 White Paper, and even more, the establishment of a Jewish state, would mean that Britain would lose its influence in the Middle East, and the maintenance of oil and other interests would be endangered. Killearn recommended *force majeure* to compel both sides to accept definite and unlimited British control of the area. Palestine should be retained as a vital link in Britain's defence system.[27] The Foreign Office argued that Britain should retain pre-eminence in the Middle East: if it embarked on partition on its own it would cede that position to the United States. There were worries that the United States intended to usurp Britain's place, especially in Saudi Arabia. The Colonial Office offered modifications of the partition scheme. The report of the Palestine Committee, recommending parti-tion, was regarded by the Foreign Office as unfair to the Arabs.[28]

Then, on 6 November 1944, Lord Moyne, the Minister Resident in the Middle East, was murdered in Cairo by the underground Zionist terrorist group, the Stern gang. Churchill told the House of Commons on 17 November that 'if our dreams for Zionism are to end in the smoke of assassins' pistols and our labours for its future to produce only a new set of gangsters worthy of Nazi Germany, many like myself will have to reconsider the position we have maintained so consistently in the past'. Plans for the future.of Palestine could not be considered in such a climate.[29]

Moyne's murder had no impact on Zionist strategy in the United States. Three days afterwards Wise asked the State Department about the introduction of the Palestine resolution in Congress.[30] The State Department was worried that Roosevelt's letter to Wagner could jeopardize American economic and strategic interests in Saudi Arabia. Russia was showing an interest in the Middle East, and hoped for a foothold on the shores of the Persian Gulf near the West's strategic oilfields. Russia could take a sweeping pro-Arab position and the Arabs could turn to Moscow. Alternatively, Britain's position with the Arabs could be strengthened at the expense of that of the United States.[31] Wallace Murray warned that 'ill-considered statements made in the United States for political purposes' had indirectly contributed to the prevailing insecurity 'by giving encouragement, albeit unwittingly, to the more extreme Zionist elements such as the assassins of Lord Moyne represent'. These elements, particularly the Irgun and the Stern gang, were in their training and methods 'essentially totalitarian', and would stop at nothing to overthrow the British administration.[32] Roosevelt informed Wise and Wagner that, following the Moyne murder, a resurrection of the Palestine resolution would be inappropriate. But the Zionist lobby contrived to get it discussed in the Senate and House committees. Roosevelt, influenced by a petition from Cairo, warned Wagner on 3 December that there were 70 million Muslims waiting to cut the throats of the possible 1 million Jews who wanted to go to Palestine the day they landed. Everyone knew what American hopes were: 'if we talk about them too much we will hurt fulfilment'.[33] The Zionist activists split, and, after the Acting Secretary of State Edward Stettinius had appeared before it and warned about likely Arab reaction and that a resolution might affect the conference with Stalin and Churchill, the Senate committee decided to take no action. Wise became sole chairman of the American Zionist Emergency Council.[34]

By the end of 1944 the Zionists were implementing new tactics. On the one hand there was the terrorism of the Irgun and the Stern gang. On the other, the United States became the focus of their political activities. The Zionist groups in the United States were small and divided, but they aroused a public agitation out of all proportion to their size. Using the publicity of the holocaust they aroused widespread sympathy. What they asked for was designed to appeal to Americans. In a country where anti-Semitism was widespread and took the insidious form of preventing Jews from living in certain residential areas, joining certain country clubs and societies, congressmen did not have to worry about urging the immigration of Jews to Palestine.[35] It would mean fewer Jews entering the United States. American immigration laws which restricted the entry of Jewish refugees remained sacrosanct. Congressmen were not prepared to risk the White Anglo-Saxon Protestant and Roman Catholic backlash on that issue. More Jewish immigrants from Europe could be at the expense of Roman Catholics under the quota system. There was no question of American financial or military assistance for Britain to establish the Jewish state. Hardly any mention was made in the United States of the non-Jewish victims of Hitler.

The Foreign Office feared that a Jewish state in Palestine could end British predominance in the Middle East. The charges of inhumanity against the British policy on Jewish immigration seemed unfounded and hypocritical. They seemed a way of easing American consciences over the refusal to admit significant numbers of Jewish refugees to the United States, and a means of diverting the problem to an area over which the United States had no responsibility. Support for Zionism also conflicted with the spirit of the Atlantic Charter. In August 1942, Churchill pointed out to Roosevelt that its application to Asia and Africa could lead to claims by the Arab majority that they could expel the Jews from Palestine, and forbid further Jewish immigration.[36]

Early in 1945 Washington had to balance Zionist pressure and the claims of Ibn Saud. Bearing this in mind, James M. Landis, the American Director of Economic Operations in the Middle East, warned that the objective of a Jewish state had to be abandoned. Culbertson suggested trusteeship as a solution: Palestine, a land sacred to the three great monotheistic religions, should not be dominated by one. Local autonomy could be a solution.[37] The State Department envisaged British trusteeship for Palestine, the Zionists the Lowder-milk scheme to use the waters of the Jordan River for irrigation and hydroelectric power.[38] The Zionist Emergency Council urged on Roosevelt a Jewish commonwealth in 'an undiminished and undivided Palestine'.[39] On 14 February, on the Great Bitter Lake in Egypt, Ibn Saud told Roosevelt that the Arabs would rather die than yield their land to Jews.[40] Although his wife, Eleanor, remained a convinced Zionist and was prepared to risk a fight with the Arabs, Roosevelt was impressed. There were 15 to 20 million Arabs in and around Palestine and, in the long run, he thought these numbers would win.[41] The Democratic member for Brooklyn, Emmanuel Celler, upbraided Roosevelt for broken promises. On 18 March he warned that over 1 million Jews lived in Brooklyn: without their support New York City and state would have been lost to Roosevelt in the election. Indeed the nation might have been lost because the Jews held the balance in many metropolitan areas.[42] Ibn Saud was disturbed by this agitation. He wrote to Roosevelt on 23 March about Zionist preparations 'to create a form of Nazi-Fascism' in the midst of Arab countries loyal to the Allied cause. To bring Jewish immigrants into land 'already occupied and do away with the original inhabitants' was 'an act unparalleled in human history'. On 5 April 1945, Roosevelt assured Ibn Saud that he would make no move against the Arabs.[43] Roosevelt died on 12 April.

On 2 April 1945 the research and analysis branch of the Office of Strategic Services warned of the potential danger of Russia. It was in the American interest that the British, French and Dutch colonial empires be maintained: 'We have at present no interest in weakening or liquidating these empires or in championing schemes of inter-national trusteeship which may provoke unrest and result in colonial disintegration, and may at the same time alienate from us the Empire states whose help we need to balance the Soviet power.' On 19 May Joseph Grew argued that the result of the war would be merely to transfer the 'totalitarian dictatorship and power from Germany and Japan to Soviet Russia which will constitute in future as grave a danger to us as did the Axis'. American policy towards Russia should stiffen.[44] But Harry S. Truman became President, and after an initial stiffening, he followed the Roosevelt line of accommodation towards the Russians in the face of dire warnings from Churchill and Eden.[45]

Before Truman assumed office there had been tentative British hints that American help might be needed in Palestine. Early in April Sir Edward Grigg, Moyne's successor, condemned partition as a solution: it could endanger Britain's whole position in the Middle East. Instead he envisaged a bi-racial self-governing state. Western sympathy for Jewish suffering, 'combined with anti-Semitism in disguise', had led to an unrealistic conception of what Britain could do. American support was needed to guide Zionism away from militarism back to its original peaceful aims.[46] On 10 April, Eden advised the War Cabinet that Palestine policy had to be considered in relation to that of the whole of the Middle East where Britain had vital interests. British pre-eminence in the area was being challenged by the United States and Russia, both anxious to profit from British mistakes. An attempt to create a Jewish state in Palestine with unrestricted immigration would outrage the Arabs and imperil British interests. The Foreign Secretary could not recommend the partition scheme of the Palestine Committee. He warned of the danger of American irresponsibility, and the need to temper it with a direct interest in Palestine.[47] The Cabinet did not discuss the issue: it was preoccupied with the conclusion of the war. In considering alternative policies the Foreign Office concentrated on the United States, as discussion had suggested that British policy in Palestine might have to be decided in relation to opinion in that country. Michael Wright had sent an evaluation of this from the British embassy in Washington which Eden had endorsed. Wright pointed out that because there were 2,500,000 Jews in New York City, and most of the rest in towns of New England, Pennsylvania and Illinois, great areas of the United States had no immediate interest in Jewish questions. But in these few areas the Jewish vote was extremely important. The concentration of Jews in certain areas did lead to considerable anti-Jewish feeling. In the eastern United States Jews were barred from many universities and clubs. The lease of a house or apartment frequently contained a clause that subletting to Jews was forbidden. The public was not deeply moved over Palestine, but it was a source of trouble because politicians, with their eyes on the Jewish vote, could agitate about it at no cost to themselves.

Halifax emphasized the prominence of Jews in the White House and the administration, as well as the extent to which the Jewish vote in New York could be decisive in election years. There was, the ambassador pointed out, an unwritten bond between the Zionists and those disinterested in Palestine: 'the average citizen does not want them [the

Jewish refugees] in the United States and solves his conscience by advocating their admission to Palestine'. On this issue, the Zionists could carry with them both liberal humanitarians and many anti-Semites. He concluded: 'For the Americans to be able thus to criticize and influence without responsibility is the most favourable and agreeable situation for them, and, I must suppose, the exact converse for us.' Halifax proposed that the United States be invited to share Britain's responsibilities for the mandate of Palestine.[48] Churchill liked Halifax's suggestion. He recorded: 'I am not aware of the slightest advantage which has ever accrued to Great Britain from this painful and thankless task. Somebody else should have their turn now.' The United States could be invited to take over the mandate. The Foreign Office disagreed. The chiefs of staff were emphatic: Palestine was 'the bottleneck' of all land communications between Africa and Asia; a main centre of air routes between Britain and the eastern part of the Empire; it also included one of the key oil terminals. If Britain handed the mandate to the United States it would lose its predominant position in the Middle East with incalculable psychological effects on world opinion.[49] Churchill and Attlee went to meet the new President at Potsdam without any British solution to offer.

In 1944 Truman had told the Senate that his sympathy was with the Jewish people.[50] On 18 April Stettinius warned the new President of the danger of Zionist pressure: the Palestine issue should be handled with a view to American 'long-range interests'. The next day Wise saw Truman, and a statement was issued that the President was carrying out Roosevelt's policies for Palestine. Truman assured Cairo and Amman that no decision should be taken over Palestine without full consultation of both Arabs and Jews.[51] The Zionists, by organizing mass rallies, tried unsuccessfully to secure representation at the conference at San Francisco. The American Palestine Committee organized a petition from Congress. The Acting Secretary of State, Grew, pointed out to them that the proposed resolution referred only to the Nazi persecution of 'certain persons in Europe'. Grew advised Truman that this resolution for 'the creation of an independent Jewish State' could only inflame the Arabs at a most unfortunate time. Truman received a moderated petition signed by 54 Senators and 250 Representatives just before he left for Potsdam.[52]

The American administration also had details of Haganah's plans. Any solution condemning Jews to a permanent minority status in Palestine would be countered by military activity, resistance from the civilian population, including a general strike and the proclamation of death sentences against any Jews collaborating with the British administration. In the sections of Palestine it held, Haganah would establish a Jewish government. The Yishuv was 'a bridgehead in the conquest of the empty sixty percent of Palestinian land, where homes can be made for millions of distressed Jews in Europe'. Haganah would carry on illegal immigration, even if this led to clashes with Britain or any outside authority. If Britain attempted to stop or drastically curtail immigration the Irgun and the Stern gang would submit themselves to Haganah to form a united opposition. The Haganah leaders said they realized that the terrorists could be valuable political allies. Irgun membership was estimated by Haganah at 2,000, and that of the Stern gang, 200. It was widely believed that the Irgun received money, weapons and technical assistance from the Polish army forces in Palestine. Irgun's leader was Menachem Begin, a Polish soldier who came to Palestine in 1943 through Russia. It was also thought that the Stern gang was receiving aid from the French in the Levant.[53] Over the following three years Haganah implemented this policy. American intelligence also had reports that militancy within the Zionist movement was growing, both in the United States and abroad.[54]

At Potsdam Truman sent a minute to Churchill on 24 July: he referred to the passionate protests in the United States over the drastic restrictions imposed on Jewish immigration and hoped that Britain would find it possible to lift these. In the Foreign Office Harold Beeley minuted: 'The Zionists have been deplorably successful in selling the idea that even after the Allied victory immigration to Palestine represents for many Jews "their only hope of survival".'[55] Churchill did not reply: on 26 July he was defeated in the British general election. Labour was voted in. Clement Attlee became Prime Minister.

In December 1944 the Labour Party had adopted a resolution, framed by Hugh Dalton, endorsing a transfer of population in Palestine in favour of the Jews. During the election campaign Dalton had also made virtually the only statement on Palestine.[56] Some thought that Dalton would be Attlee's choice as Foreign Secretary. But the Palestine issue was not a factor in Attlee's choice of ministers. Ernest Bevin was picked as Foreign Secretary, unexpectedly, for reasons of personality conflicts.[57] Attlee regarded Russia as a power with imperialist ambitions 'whether ideological or territorial whether derived from Lenin or Peter the Great'.[58] He reassured Churchill that he believed in continuity in foreign policy, on 'the main lines which we have discussed together so often'.[59] Bevin, with his working-class background, temper and blunt turn of phrase soon 'became more devoted than any of his predecessors for a generation to the Career Diplomat and all the Old Boys in the F.O., so that "now all the old nags are going back to the stables" '.[60]

In Palestine Labour's victory raised Zionist expectations. The American Palestine Committee took immediate appropriate action. On 16 August Truman told a press conference of his Potsdam message to Churchill, but added the caveat that the matter would have to be worked out diplomatically between Britain and the Arabs: he did not want to send 500,000 American soldiers to Palestine.[61] In the State Department William Yale pointed out that among the 1,250,000

Jewish refugees in Europe there were many who would prefer to emigrate to the United States. He warned that the Arabs would consider mass Jewish immigration into Palestine an attempt to turn that country into a Zionist state. There would be disorder and troops would be needed. Yale advised that the United States should refrain from supporting a policy of large-scale immigration into Palestine during the interim period. Washington should not make any public statements on immigration before discussions with Britain.[62]

The officer administering the government of Palestine, J. V. W. Shaw, reported an explosive situation in the mandate. His analysis of the new Zionism confirmed that offered by Grigg in April. Shaw warned that the pressure of Zionism had been the main contributory factor to a sense of Arab nationalism. Jewish publicity and terrorism were persuading the Arabs that they would have to maintain their present position by force.[63] Against this background the Colonial Office developed a scheme drawn up by Sir Douglas G. Harris, the former treasurer in Palestine, of local autonomy for separate Arab and Jewish provinces.[64] On 30 August Bevin proposed a conference of British representatives in the Middle East to discuss general policy in the area. It decided that Britain should broaden the base of its influence in the Middle East, and develop an economic and social policy that would make for the prosperity and contentment of the area as a whole. But the Middle East was to remain largely a British sphere of influence: Britain 'should not make any concession that would assist American commercial penetration into a region which for generations has been an established British market'.[65] The Palestine Committee concentrated on Britain's strategic position. The attitude of the Arabs was of the first importance as the Middle East was a region of 'vital consequence' for Britain and the Empire. It formed the nodal point in the Empire communication system and was also the Empire's main reserve of oil. It also contained the Suez Canal and the principal naval bases in the eastern Mediterranean and at Alexandria. Britain was likely to have to depend on co-operation from independent Middle Eastern states. A policy unfavourable to the Arabs in Palestine could lead to widespread disturbances in Arab countries and endanger Britain's imperial interests.[66] On 4 October Bevin outlined a policy to the Cabinet based on these recommendations. Particular attention was paid to Britain's strategic position. It was reported that the chiefs of staff were considering the feasibility of basing forces needed for the protection of the Middle East on British territory rather than in Egypt. The Cabinet endorsed the new policy.[67]

The Palestine issue, however, was complicated by pressure from the United States. Truman, in June 1945, had sent Earl G. Harrison, the American representative on the Inter-Governmental Committee on Refugees, to investigate the condition of displaced persons in Europe. He recommended that the United States should, under existing immigration laws, allow reasonable numbers of Jewish refugees into the United States. Truman, realizing that Congress would not relax the immigration quotas, chose instead to assign the responsibility to Britain. The President overrode his State Department. There was an election in New York, and the Jewish vote seemed crucial. Truman wrote to Attlee on 31 August suggesting that the main solution lay in the quick evacuation of Jews to Palestine. Harrison had recommended that 100,000 be admitted.[68] Attlee was alarmed. He reminded Truman that Britain had to consider the Arabs as well. The Palestine problem also had to be considered in relation to India with its 90 million Muslims.[69] The State Department agreed: on 26 September it recommended that the United States publicly accept a British decision that it would be impossible to allow any large number of refugees into Palestine. Instead they should be settled in other countries, including the United States. Furthermore, if Roosevelt's promise to Ibn Saud were not kept there would be a serious threat to vital American interests in the Middle East. The War Department estimated that if Palestine were opened to Jewish immigration 400,000 men would be needed to maintain order, of which the United States would perhaps have to contribute over 300,000.[70] But Zionist agitation led by Rosenman, Silver, Wagner and Bernard Baruch mounted. In Congress Taft tried to link Britain's Palestine policy to the Anglo-American financial negotiations. Both Republicans and Democrats censured Britain for restricting immigration to Palestine. The New York election was only a few weeks away.[71]

In Cabinet Bevin mooted the idea of an Anglo-American commission to investigate the refugee problem. He explained on 11 October that agitation in the United States on the immigration issue was poisoning relations with that country. The Foreign Secretary could not accept that Jews could not live in Europe. The Cabinet agreed to Bevin's proposal. The Foreign Secretary forwarded it to Halifax with the observation that the United States had been thoroughly dishonest: 'to play on racial feeling for the purpose of winning an election is to make a farce of their insistence on free elections in other countries'.[72]

Truman, however, remained obsessed with the New York election of 6 November. Rosenman tried to persuade Truman not to give in to State Department pressure to publish Roosevelt's assurances to Ibn Saud in the letter of 5 April 1945. The new Secretary of State, James F. Byrnes, admitted to Halifax on 22 October that the Jews in the United States were not interested in the plight of the Jews in Europe. American Jews believed that they ought to have 'a country to call their own' and that was their main preoccupation. The New York election was the paramount consideration.[73] Bevin wanted to announce the Anglo-American commission in the House, and to point to its terms of reference that Palestine was not the only country for refugees. But Byrnes 'in shamefaced embarrassment' had to ask Bevin to postpone the statement till after polling day. The Secretary of State explained that the negative American attitude was a result of 'intense and growing agitation about the Palestine problem in the New York election campaign'.[74] Even after a Democrat was elected in New York with a resounding majority, the Zionists succeeded in delaying matters. London, worried about repercussions in India over the pilgrimage to Mecca, was disturbed. Halifax told Byrnes that American domestic difficulties were hardly comparable to the 'possibilities of outbreaks and dead bodies in Palestine'.[75] In Palestine Haganah was implementing its plan, and Bevin was increasingly upset by the murder of British Tommies with whom he felt a class affinity. He told Weizmann on 2 November that the Jewish Agency could no longer be regarded as an innocent party in relation to terrorist outrages.[76]

But Truman was threatened by another congressional resolution on Palestine organized by the American Palestine Committee. Wagner and Taft, aghast at the enormity of the Jewish tragedy – 5,700,000 had died at the hands of the Nazis – argued that Palestine was the only safe refuge for the remainder. They did not regard the United States as a suitable haven. Truman drafted a letter he did not send: 'I don't think that you or any of the other Senators, would be inclined to send a half dozen Divisions to Palestine to maintain a Jewish state.'[77] Despite Truman's requests for delay, in the middle of December the Senate and the House of Representatives endorsed a resolution mentioning Truman's request for the immediate entry of 100,000 refugees, and referring to a 'democratic commonwealth' in Palestine.[78]

On 9 November Bevin announced the appointment of an Anglo-American commission of inquiry to the House of Commons. He suggested that the commission should prepare a trusteeship agreement for Palestine, as well as a permanent solution for submission to the United Nations.[79]

By the end of 1945 the Arab–Zionist controversy had a new centre of focus. It had become subsumed into a conflict between British strategic interests in the whole of the Middle East and American domestic politics. Britain, after the end of the Second World War, wished to remain the paramount power in the Middle East. That area was vital for the Empire's strategic security and communications. At a time of the emergence of the Cold War Britain was increasingly worried about possible Russian advances into the area, and saw the Middle East as being essential to Western security. But to maintain this, Britain had to negotiate treaties with the new Arab states. This would hardly be possible if Britain were seen as the sponsor of a Zionist state in Palestine, to be achieved through Jewish immigration. In the United States, the State Department and the military appreciated Britain's predicament and advised Truman accordingly. But the new President, having reiterated Roosevelt's assurances to the Arabs, succumbed to Zionist pressure and threats of electoral punishment. To the British it seemed that winning the election in New York was more important to the President than dead bodies in Palestine. The American position appeared hypocritical: immigration quotas meant that the United States took hardly any Jewish refugees. Instead an alliance of Zionists, anti-Semites and Roman Catholics in the United States wanted Britain to be responsible for the refugees in Palestine. In Truman the Zionists found a President sensitive to his electoral position. American domestic politics became a principal component in the events leading to the outbreak of the Arab–Israeli Wars.

REFERENCES

1. ESCO Foundation, *Palestine. A Study of Jewish, Arab and British Policies*, Vol. I (New Haven 1947), pp. 252–3.
2. *Warren R. Austin Papers* (University of Vermont Library, Burlington), Box 23, Palestine Notebook 1936, ff. 47–56.
3. Llewelyn Woodward, *British Foreign Policy in the Second World War*, Vol. IV (London 1975), pp. 388–402.
4. *James F. Byrnes Papers* (Clemson University Library, North Carolina), Folder 95(1), Byrnes to Roosevelt, 17 Feb. 1944.
5. Woodward, op. cit., pp. 388–402.
6. *Foreign Relations of the United States* (hereafter cited as *FRUS*), 1943(4), pp. 786–7, Hull to Kirk, 26 May 1943.
7. Joseph B. Schechtmann, *The United States and the Jewish State Movement* (New York 1966), pp. 61–9.
8. Woodward, op. cit., pp. 351 7.
9. Michael Cohen, *Palestine: Retreat from the Mandate. The Making of British policy. 1936–45* (London 1978), pp. 162–3.
10. *RG 59* (National Archives, Washington), Decimal Files 1945–49, Box 6751, Alling to Dunn, 6 May 1945.
11. *FRUS* 1943(4), pp. 816–21, Memorandum by Merriam, 15 Oct. 1943; William D. Hasset, *Off the Record with F.D.R.* (New Brunswick, New Jersey 1958), p. 209, Diary, 6 Oct. 1943.
12. *Robert F. Wagner Papers* (Georgetown University Library, Washington), Palestine Files, Box 2, File 28, Wagner to Ben Hecht and Will Rogers Jr, 28 May 1944; Blank Invitation Form, 20 June 1944; see also Samuel Halperin, *The Political World of American Zionism* (Detroit 1961), pp. 179, 182–5, 275–81, 320, 374–5; Hertzel Fishman, *American Protestantism and a Jewish State* (Detroit 1975), pp. 71–3, 80–2; Esther Yolles Feldblum, *The American Catholic Press and the Jewish State 1917–1959* (New York 1977), pp. 58–9.
13. Doreen Bierbrier, 'The American Zionist Emergency Council: an analysis of a pressure group', *American Jewish Historical Quarterly*, LX (1970), 82–105; Stephen Wise, *Challenging Years* (New York 1949), pp. 216–32; 297–308; Schechtman, op. cit., p. 69.
14. *FRUS* 194(4), pp. 828–9, Halifax to Hull, 23 Dec. 1944.
15. Ibid., 1944(5), p. 562, Memorandum by Berle, 31 Jan. 1944.

16. *Marshall Library* (Lexington, Virginia), with WDCSA, McCarthy to Marshall, 5 Feb. 1944; *George C. Marshall Papers* (Marshall Library, Lexington, Virginia), Box 78, File 15, Marshall to Hull, 7 Feb. 1944 (not sent); Memorandum for Record by F. McCarthy, 7 Feb. 1944.
17. *Truman Papers* (Truman Library, Independence, Missouri), General File Jews, Truman to Dubinsky, 8 Feb. 1944.
18. *FRUS* 1944(5), pp. 574–7, Enclosure, McCloy to Marshall, 22 Feb. 1944; *Marshall Library*, WDCSA 381, Marshall to McCloy, 23 Feb. 1944.
19. *Samuel I. Rosenman Papers* (F. D. Roosevelt Library, Hyde Park, New York), Box 13, Rosenman to Wise, 3 Feb. 1944; Rosenman to Wise, 5 Feb. 1944; *F. D. Roosevelt Papers* (F. D. Roosevelt Library, Hyde Park, New York), McCormack to Roosevelt, 8 Feb. 1944; Enclosing Memorandum on the Jewish National Home; Department of Commerce, *Statistical Abstract of the United States 1944–45* (Washington 1945), p. 32; United States Office of Strategic Services, *Foreign Nationality Groups in the United States: A Handbook* (Washington 1943), p. 6.
20. *New York Times*, 10 March 1944; *F. D. Roosevelt Papers*, OF 700, Roosevelt to J. Melville Broughton, 17 March 1944.
21. *FRUS* 1944(5), pp. 600–3, Memorandum by Kohler, 11 April 1944; pp. 603–5, Memorandum by Kohler, 19 April 1944.
22. *F. D. Roosevelt Papers*, OF 700, Nathan Hilfer to Senator Theodore Francis Green, 7 April 1944.
23. *FRUS* 1944(5), p. 605, n. 99; p. 606, Hull to Roosevelt, 26 July 1944.
24. Ibid., pp. 614–15, Memorandum by Murray, 30 Sept. 1944.
25. *F. D. Roosevelt Papers*, OF 700, Wise to Roosevelt, 16 Sept. 1944; Silver to Roosevelt, 26 Sept. 1944; Roosevelt to Wise, 9 Oct. 1944; Wagner to Roosevelt, 29 Sept. 1944; Memorandum for Watson, 13 Oct. 1944; *FRUS* 1944(5), pp. 615–16, Roosevelt to Wagner, 15 Oct. 1944.
26. *W. S. Culbertson Papers* (Library of Congress, Washington), Box 99, *Ventures in Time and Space*, Ch. 27, f. 24; *RG 59*, Decimal Files 1945–49, Box 6750, Extract from Report of Culbertson Mission, 15 Nov. 1944; *FRUS* 1944(5), p. 39, n. 6.
27. Woodward, op. cit., pp. 368–9; Cohen, *Palestine*, pp. 173–4; Trefor E. Evans (Ed.), *The Killearn Diaries 1934–46* (London 1972), p. 281, 21 Feb. 1944.
28. Woodward, op. cit., pp. 369–72; Cohen, *Palestine*, pp. 175–9.
29. *United Kingdom Parliamentary Debates House of Commons*, 404, col. 2242, 17 Nov. 1944; *Cab 66*, 65, ff. 272–3, WP (45) 306, Memorandum by Stanley, 16 May 1945.
30. *Stettinius Papers* (University of Virginia Library, Charlottesville), Box 229, Palestine Resolution.
31. Ibid., Box 372, NEA Weekly Political Review, 15 Nov. 1944; *FRUS* 1944(5), pp. 624–6, Murray to Stettinius, 27 Oct. 1944; Annex, Memorandum by Murray, 25 Oct. 1944.
32. *FRUS* 1944(5), pp. 634–5, Murray to Stettinius, 8 Nov. 1944.
33. Ibid., p. 637, Stettinius to Roosevelt, 15 Nov. 1944; p. 640, Memorandum by Stettinius, 23 Nov. 1944; p. 641, Murray to Stettinius, 24 Nov. 1944; p. 638, Tuck to Hull, 21 Nov. 1944; pp. 638–9, Tuck to Hull, 21 Nov. 1944; *F. D. Roosevelt Papers*, OF 700, Stettinius to Roosevelt, 17 Nov. 1944; Wise to Stettinius, 16 Nov. 1944; Roosevelt to Stettinius,

20 Nov. 1944; *Stettinius Papers*, Box 229, Palestine Resolution; Elliott Roosevelt (Ed.), *FDR: His Personal Letters 1928–1945*, Vol. II (New York 1950), pp. 1559–60, Roosevelt to Wagner, 3 Dec. 1944.

34.   *Stettinius Papers*, Box 245, Record, Section 1 ff. 17–20; Record, Section 2, f. 1; Box 229, Palestine Resolution.

35.   Naomi W. Cohen, *American Jews and the Zionist Idea* (New York 1975), pp. 58–9; Philip J. Barum, *The Department of State in the Middle East 1919–1945* (Philadelphia 1978), p. 294.

36.   Francis L. Loewenheim et al. (Eds), *Roosevelt and Churchill. Their Secret Wartime Correspondence* (New York 1975), p. 234, No. 128, Churchill to Roosevelt, 9 Aug. 1942; *FRUS* 1942(4), pp. 538–40, Murray to Hull, 2 July 1942 and Enclosures.

37.   Elliott Roosevelt, op. cit., Vol. II, pp. 1564–5, Roosevelt to Landis, 11 Jan. 1945; *FRUS* 1945(8), pp. 680–2, Landis to Roosevelt, 17 Jan. 1945; *W. S. Culbertson Papers*, Box 99, *Ventures in Time and Space*, Ch. 27, f. 49, Comments on the Arab–Jewish Question in Palestine, 22 Jan. 1945.

38.   *FRUS* 1945(8), pp. 683–7, Memorandum prepared in the Department of State, 30 Jan. 1945; Walter Clay Lowdermilk, *Palestine Land of Promise* (New York 1944), esp. pp. 9–10, 80, 168–79.

39.   *F. D. Roosevelt Papers*, OF 700, Memorandum of the American Zionist Emergency Council, 19 Jan. 1945.

40.   *FRUS* 1945(8), pp. 2–3, Memorandum of Conversation between Ibn Saud and Roosevelt, 14 Feb. 1945; William A. Eddy, *FDR meets Ibn Saud* (New York 1954).

41.   *RG 59*, Decimal Files 1945–49, Box 6750, Hoskins to Alling, 5 March 1945.

42.   Schechtmann, op. cit., pp. 114–15.

43.   *RG 59*, Decimal Files 1945–49, Box 6750, Ibn Saud to Roosevelt, undated; Roosevelt to Ibn Saud, 5 April 1945.

44.   *Joint Chiefs of Staff Leahy Records* (National Archives, Washington), Folder 88, Research and Analysis Branch of OSS: Problems and Objectives of United States Policy, 2 April 1945; *RG 59*, Records of Charles E. Bohlen 1942–52, Box 1, Memorandum by Grew, 7 April 1947; Private Memorandum by Grew, 19 May 1945.

45.   Ritchie Ovendale, 'Britain, the U.S.A. and the European Cold War 1945–1948', *History*, **67** (1982), 219–29.

46.   *Cab 66*, 64, ff. 58–68, WP (45) 214, note by Grigg, 4 April 1945.

47.   Ibid., ff. 120–2, WP (45) 229, Memorandum by Eden on Palestine, 10 April 1945.

48.   *FO 954*, 19A, ff. 76–8, Michael Wright to G. E. Millard, 17 March 1945; Minute by Eden, 26 March 1945; *FO 371*, 45378, E 4849/15/31G, Halifax to Eden, 1 July 1945.

49.   *FO 371*, 45378, E 4939/15/31G, Churchill to Stanley and Chiefs of Staff Committee, 6 July 1945; E 5141/15/31G, COS (45) 175th Meeting, 12 July; JP (45) 167 (Final), 10 July 1945.

50.   Reuben Fink, *America and Palestine* (New York 1945), p. 153.

51.   *FRUS* 1945(8), pp. 704–5, Stettinius to Truman, 8 April 1945; pp. 706–7, Grew to Truman, 15 May 1945; p. 707, Truman to Abdullah, 17 May 1945; p. 708, Grew to Truman, 2 June 1945; pp. 708–9, Truman to Nokrashy, 4 June 1945; *RG 59*, Decimal Files 1945–49, Box 6751,

Memorandum for Truman by Grew, 1 May 1945; Note to Grew, 2 May 1945; Grew to Stettinius, 4 June 1945.

52. *Robert F. Wagner Papers*, Palestine Files, Box 2, File 31, Wagner and Taft to Senators, 18 May 1945; Green to Wagner, 23 May 1945; Grew to Green, undated; Senators and Representatives to Truman, 2 July 1945; *RG 59*, Decimal Series 1945–49, Box 6750, Grew to Truman, 26 May 1945.

53. G-7333 (National Archives, Suitland), Palestine – Jewish terrorist gangs, 22 March 1945; G-7090, Polish support of Irgun activities, 13 Feb. 1945; G-6716, 12 Dec. 1944; *RG 84* (National Archives, Suitland), Entry 56A336, Box 254, 800 Palestine, State Department to London Embassy, 17 July 1945; Enclosing OSS Field Memorandum 253 (FR-446), 8 June 1945.

54. *RG 84*, Entry 59A543 part 5, Box 1057, 800 Palestine, State Department to London Embassy, No. 5686, Enclosing OSS Report No. B-378, 14 June 1945.

55. *FO 371*, 45378, E5474/15/31C, Truman to Churchill, 24 July 1945; Minute by Beeley, 27 July 1945.

56. *RG 59*, Decimal Files 1945–49, Box 6751, Hare to Byrnes, 1 Aug. 1945.

57. *Attlee Papers* (Bodleian, Oxford), 2, Plans for New Government 1945; List A; Next Draft; *Attlee Papers* (Churchill College, Cambridge), 1/17, Labour in Power; *Dalton Diaries* (British Library of Political and Economic Science, London), 33, ff. 4–4v, 27–8 July 1945; *Oliver Harvey Diaries* (British Library, London), 8, 28 July 1945.

58. *Attlee Papers* (Churchill College, Cambridge), 1/17, Labour in Power.

59. Ibid., 1/24, Notes on Post-war Problems.

60. *Dalton Diaries*, 34, 25 Feb. 1946.

61. *FRUS* 1945(8), p. 722, Byrnes to Pinkerton, 18 Aug. 1945.

62. *RG 59*, Decimal Series 1945–49, Box 6751, Henderson to Byrnes, 30 Aug. 1945.

63. *Cab 129*, 2, ff. 47–9, CP(45) 165, Shaw to Hall, 24 Aug. 1945 (extracts).

64. *FO 371*, 45379, E 656/15/31G, Memorandum on Future Policy for Palestine, Aug.–Sept. 1945.

65. *Cab 129*, 2, f. 91, CP(45) 174, Memorandum by Bevin on Middle East Policy, 17 Sept. 1945.

66. Ibid., f. 20, CP(45) 156, Great Britain's Position in the Middle East, 8 Sept. 1945.

67. *Cab 128*, 1, f. 81, Cab 28(45)6, 4 Oct. 1945.

68. *FRUS* 1945 (8), pp. 738–9, Truman to Attlee, 31 Aug. 1945; 'Report of Earl G. Harrison', Department of State *Bulletin*, 30 Sept. 1945, p. 456.

69. *FRUS* 1945 (8), pp. 740–1, Attlee to Truman, 16 Sept. 1945.

70. Ibid., pp. 745–8, Merriam to Henderson, 26 Sept. 1945; pp. 751–3, Henderson to Acheson, 1 Oct. 1945; pp. 753–5, Acheson to Truman, 2 Oct. 1945; p. 762, Henderson to Byrnes, 9 Oct. 1945.

71. *Rosenman Files* (F. D. Roosevelt Library, Hyde Park), Rosenman to Truman, 1 Sept. 1945; *Robert F. Wagner Papers*, Palestine Files, Box 2, File 31, Silver to Wagner, 27 Aug. 1945; 6 Sept. 1945; *Baruch Papers* (Princeton University Library), Vol. LXII, Silver to Baruch, 21 Sept. 1945; *FO 371*, 45400, E 7449/265/31, Halifax to Bevin, 4 Oct. 1945.

72. *FO 371*, 45381, E 7757/15/31 G, Bevin to Halifax, 12 Oct. 1945.

73. *Rosenman Files*, Memorandum by Rosenman, 18 Oct. 1945; *RG 59*, Office of Near Eastern Affairs, Box 2, Minutes of Conversation between Byrnes and Halifax, 22 Oct. 1945.
74. *FRUS* 1945(8), pp. 794–5, British Embassy to Department of State, 26 Oct. 1945; pp. 795–9, Halifax to Byrnes and Enclosure, 26 Oct. 1945; *FO 371*, 45382, E 8160/15/31 G, Balfour to Bevin, 27 Oct. 1945.
75. *FO 371*, 45383, E 8539/15/G, Halifax to Bevin, 7 Nov. 1945.
76. *FRUS* 1945 (8), pp. 812–13, British Embassy to Department of State, 6 Nov. 1945; *FO 371*, 45383, E 8437/15/31a, Minute by Bevin, 2 Nov. 1945.
77. *Robert F. Wagner Papers*, Palestine Files, Box 2, File 32, Wagner and Taft to various Senators, 16 Nov. 1945; *Truman Papers*, Box 184, PSF, Truman to Joseph H. Bull, 24 Nov. 1945; Minute by Truman, undated.
78. *Robert F. Wagner Papers*, Truman to Wagner, 10 Nov. 1945; *FRUS* 1945 (8), pp. 841–2, State Department Memorandum, 17 Dec. 1945.
79. *United Kingdom Parliamentary Debates House of Commons*, 415, cols. 1930–2, 13 Nov. 1945.

Chapter 6

THE ARAB AND ZIONIST CASES IN BRITISH AND AMERICAN EYES

The Anglo-American commission met against a background of Arab agitation over Haganah's policy of promoting illegal Jewish immigration into Palestine, Zionist protests over Britain's establishing Transjordan as an independent state with Abdullah as king,[1] and fears that there could be war with Russia over Iran. Indeed, in March 1946, Attlee urged the Defence Committee to consider abandoning the Mediterranean route, withdrawing from the Middle East, and concentrating instead on a line of defence across Africa from Lagos to Kenya. This was supported by Captain B. H. Liddell Hart who preferred Africa to the Middle East.[2] But these ideas were not pursued as the United States finally decided to stand against Russian expansion, starting in Iran in March 1946.[3]

Of the six American members of the commission, two, James G. McDonald and Bartley Crum, were known to be Zionists. The State Department felt unable to give Crum security clearance, but Truman was persuaded by David Niles to allow Crum to serve.[4] The Zionists, however, saw the co-chairman Judge Joseph C. Hutcheson, as unsympathetic to their aspirations,[5] and another, William Phillips, soon found Zionism intransigent.[6] The British delegation was led by Sir John Singleton who had a horror of terrorism after experiences in Ireland, and was also conscious of the need for Anglo-American co-operation in the face of the Russian threat. The only member with overriding Zionist sympathies was Richard Crossman who had been married to a Jewess, and later admitted that his loyalty to Zionism was greater than that to his king.[7] The commission first sat in Washington, and there Crossman established a rapport with the Zionist, David Horowitz. The Arabs argued their case in London: they did not object to a Jewish national home, but a Jewish state would bring Jewish political domination. Bevin implied to the commission that he would try to follow its advice provided the report were unanimous. The Foreign Secretary apparently thought he had Crossman's assurance that this would not happen unless British interests were taken into account. Zionist propaganda in the refugee camps in Europe meant that the commission was told that refugees were not prepared to settle anywhere other than Palestine. Against this, in the Middle East, the Arabs protested that there was no reason why they, the one race with no anti-Semitic tradition, should have to bear the sins of Christian Europe. The commission held its final deliberations at Lausanne in Switzerland. Anglo-American unity had to be sustained in the face of the perceived Russian menace, and it was thought that a unanimous report was essential. Crossman and Crum argued for partition, but were persuaded to subscribe to a unanimous document recommending a binational state and the immediate admission of 100,000 Jewish refugees.[8]

The American members of the commission were appraised of the report by the Bureau of Intelligence and Research that Palestine was on the imperial lifeline and could become the headquarters of the British armed forces in the Near East, and also by that of the joint chiefs of staff that the importance for Britain of the Middle East was comparable to the significance for the United States of the Caribbean and the Panama Canal zone.[9] Truman also knew through conversations between Crum and Niles of the direction in which the commission was moving.[10] At a time of attempts to renegotiate the Anglo-Egyptian treaty Britain wanted a few days to consider the commission's report, and it was agreed that it would be released simultaneously in Washington and London.[11]

A special committee, chaired by Sir Norman Brook, considered the commission's report in London. It concluded that adoption of the report woud have 'disastrous effects' on Britain's position in the Middle East and unfortunate repercussions in India. Furthermore, it would not silence Zionist clamour in the United States. The financial burden would be enormous, and it was intolerable that the British taxpayer should have to pay. On 29 April the Cabinet, against the background of the murder of six British soldiers by Zionist terrorists in Palestine, agreed that Bevin should ask the Americans how far they were prepared to help with money and troops.[12] The Zionist lobby, however, once again exerted decisive influence on Truman. Crum suggested to the Zionist Emergency Council that Truman merely endorse the recommendations acceptable to the Zionists. Crum took a possible presidential statement to the White House. Wagner released a press statement that the long-range recommendations were at variance with the overwhelming sentiment in the United States for a Jewish commonwealth in Palestine.[13]

On 30 April, without first consulting London, Truman endorsed the recommendation that 100,000 certificates be issued and two other aspects favourable to Zionism. The clauses conciliatory to the Arabs were dismissed as long-range considerations. The British public was outraged: British soldiers had just been murdered by Zionist terrorists. Attlee himself drafted the key section of his speech to the

House of Commons on 1 May. The Prime Minister said that a large number of Jewish immigrants could not be absorbed into Palestine in a short time unless the illegal organizations were disbanded and disarmed. It raised the question of active American participation.[14] On 24 May the chiefs of staff insisted that Britain had to be able to place in Palestine any forces it considered necessary. The Viceroy warned of the intensity of Indian feeling.[15] Bevin, at the Labour Party conference at Bournemouth, made a speech in which, following Foreign Office policy, he drew a distinction between 'Jew' and 'Zionist'.[16] The Foreign Secretary then referred – according to the information he had, quite accurately – to the Jews in the United States wanting the refugees to go to Palestine as they did not want them in New York. The Zionist organizations considered trying to defeat, or at least delay, the American loan to Britain. But Niles stopped this, and the loan was passed by Congress.[17] Niles, however, advanced a pro-Zionist policy to Truman. The President should not be deterred by worries about Ibn Saud and Arab threats of violence.[18] At this time the Zionist position was strengthened by the arrival of the new British ambassador, Lord Inverchapel (Sir Archibald Clark Kerr), who had strong Zionist sympathies, and the merging of the American Palestine Committee and the Christian Council on Palestine to form the American Christian Palestine Commitee under Wagner.[19] Wagner and Taft claimed that Bevin's distinction between Jews and Zionists was without foundation: 89.95 per cent of United States Jews who had an opinion were united behind the Zionist programme.[20]

The State Department, however, agreed with Bevin: the United States and other countries should take more Jewish refugees. J. C. Satterthwaite suggested 200,000 be admitted to the United States. Even Eleanor Roosevelt, a self-confessed Zionist, suggested in her syndicated column that the United States should relax its immigration laws: Bevin's speech 'had point'.[21] The chiefs of staff pointing to Britain's role in the Middle East in the defence of the West, and the importance of oil, warned that Russia could replace British and American influence throughout the area.[22] Indeed, conversations between British and American officials at the end of June led to the War Department agreeing to provide the necessary transportation to move 100,000 Jews from Europe to Palestine.[23]

The British position hardened, however, at the end of June: Zionist terrorists kidnapped five British officers in a series of attacks. The probability of Arab violence forced the Cabinet to take a strong stand. It decided to suppress the illegal organizations: this necessitated raiding the offices of the Jewish Agency as there was evidence of its connections with Haganah. Washington was informed just before the raids.[24] The Cabinet considered the worsening situation on 11 July. The Colonial Secretary, George Glenville Hall, advocated a new long-term policy with provincial autonomy as a convenient stepping-stone to either federation or partition. From Paris, Bevin objected: the Foreign Secretary suggested that the major part of the Arab province should be assimilated into Transjordan and the Lebanon, and the Jewish province, possibly enlarged, should form an independent Jewish state. Largely on strategic grounds the Cabinet favoured Hall's scheme.[25]

Hall's plan was the brainchild of Sir Douglas Harris in the Colonial Office. It was similar to one William Yale had drawn up in the State Department for a trusteeship of Palestine.[26] The Anglo-American Cabinet Committee that met in London in July 1946 concentrated on these schemes of provincial autonomy. Before the American delegates left, Truman indicated that he would support the idea that Palestine should be neither a Jewish nor an Arab state, that future announcements would emphasize the larger interests of the United States in the Middle East and would ask Congress to admit 50,000 non-quota Jewish refugees. As a result of Nazism in Europe the United States had admitted 275,000 refugees, including 180,000 Jews. Between May 1945 and September 1946, however, only 5,718 Jewish refugees were allowed entry. Britain had received over 300,000 refugees, including 70,000 Jews.[27] The British chiefs of staff preferred provincial autonomy to the binational scheme, but insisted that Britain should be able to control Palestine.[28] This proviso influenced the British delegates. The British position was also made more resolute by the blowing up of the King David Hotel in Jerusalem, a wing of which was used as British army headquarters: ninety-one were killed. This was perpetrated by Begin's Irgun working in alliance with Haganah. Begin has claimed that the British were warned, but no satisfactory evidence has been produced.[29] Truman initially endorsed three recommendations of what came to be known as the Morrison–Grady plan: it should definitely be settled that Palestine should be neither an Arab nor a Jewish state; the immigration of the 100,000 and thereafter an opportunity for future immigration; that other measures should be introduced to deal with the problem of displaced Jews.[30]

On 26 July, however, the American press published an account of the Morrison–Grady plan based on leaks, probably from Crum, and the Zionist lobby went to work. McDonald and leaders of the American Christian Palestine Committee, including Wagner, saw Truman and insisted on the need for a Jewish state.[31] Celler and eight other New York members of the House of Representatives saw Truman on 30 July. Over the next few days the Zionists warned explicitly that 90 per cent of the 4 million American Jews were pro-Zionist and were influential in elections in large urban centres including Boston, New York, Philadelphia, Chicago, Cincinatti, Cleveland, Los Angeles, Hartford, New Haven and elsewhere.[32] Truman informed Attlee on 31 July that he could no longer agree that the Morrison–Grady plan should be thought a joint Anglo-American venture. Loy W. Henderson of the State Department admitted to Inverchapel that this 'deplorable display of weakness was solely attributable to domestic politics: the executive could not afford the risk of antagonizing the powerful Zionist lobby in an election year'.[33]

Britain was faced with a rapidly deteriorating situation in Palestine, and fading morale. After the King David Hotel explosion the British army commander, Lieutenant-General Sir Evelyn Barker, had spoken of 'punishing the Jews in a way the race dislikes – by striking at their pockets'. Zionist propaganda took over. Herbert Morrison's disavowal in Parliament of Barker's subsequent non-fraternization order, according to the *Washington Post*, would not repair the damage done to the British administration: this colonial–militarist policy smacked of a Goering model.[34] From the floor of the House Churchill suggested that Britain abandon the mandate: the Zionists' claims went beyond anything agreed upon by Britain.[35] But, towards the end of August, the military had the situation in Palestine under control, and the Arab states accepted an invitation to consultations in London. Weizmann and other Zionist delegates went as well.

The Arabs showed inflexible opposition to the establishment of a Jewish national state in Palestine: that would be a bridgehead for Jewish economic and political penetration into the whole Arab world. The Arabs feared that the Zionists would fill their state with immigrants from Europe, creating conditions which would warrant a demand for more *lebensraum*. The Arabs wanted a unitary state in Palestine with a permanent Arab majority. The conference was adjourned on 2 October for several months to give Britain time to study the Arab proposals.[36] On 1 October Bevin and Hall saw Weizmann and other Zionist delegates. Weizmann was prepared for a transitional period of several years before partition. Bevin was blunt: the British government had not 'taken the initiative in blowing people up'. He had never known such strong latent anti-Semitism in Britain. Relatives of British soldiers in Palestine felt that they had been badly treated by the Jews. Britain could not allow its young soldiers in Palestine to be slaughtered. It also had to ensure that the rights and position of other inhabitants of Palestine were not prejudiced: 'If a person's land and livelihood had to go in order to make room for another, his rights and position were certainly prejudiced.' Rather than force partition on the Arabs at the point of British bayonets he would hand the problem to the United Nations. Bevin could not accept that Palestine was the only home for the Jewish people: he hoped the Jews would be a great force in the reconstruction of Europe. There were hopes that agreement could be reached about the release of detainees in Palestine, and that the Jewish delegates could be brought into conference even before the return of the Arabs.[37]

This prospect was destroyed by Zionist agitation in the United States. Wise and others urged Truman to make an immediate statement in favour of partition. The State Department advised against this, as did the joint chiefs of staff: partition might alienate the Arabs from the West.[38] But Niles working with Eliahu Epstein, the official for the Jewish Agency for Palestine, urged Crum to send a letter to Robert E. Hannegan, the chairman of the Democratic National Committee, emphasizing the positive political implications of a presidential statement favourable to the Jews.[39] Attlee asked Truman to delay making this statement. Bevin pointed out that Truman's claim that the work had come to an end was incorrect: the Zionists had agreed to discuss joining the conference on Palestine.[40]

On 4 October Truman said that he believed a solution along the lines of partition originally proposed by the Jewish Agency on 5 August would 'command the support of public opinion in the United States'. There should be immediate and substantial immigration to Palestine in which the United States would assist.[41] Truman refused Attlee time for consultation. Acheson explained to Inverchapel that the President felt threatened by immediate dangers such as the Jewish Day of Atonement on 5 October, and a speech by his likely opponent in the presidential election, Thomas E. Dewey, envisaged for 6 October, and designed to catch the Jewish vote in five major eastern states that tended to dominate the presidential elections: 'For this reason Mr. Truman dare not keep quiet.'[42]

Faced with the situation where the security interests of the West could be sacrificed on the altar of American domestic politics, the British government started investigating seriously the possibility of taking the Palestine question to the United Nations. Both the Colonial and the Foreign Offices considered this option. Inverchapel argued it from Washington. On 5 October Arthur Creech Jones, a known Zionist sympathizer, became Colonial Secretary, and his office took the initiative in advancing schemes of partition, but this was resisted by the Foreign Office and some of his own officials including Sir Douglas Harris and Sir George Gater.[43]

Truman faced the anger of Ibn Saud: the President would surely agree that 'no people on earth would willingly admit into their country a foreign group desiring to become a majority and to establish its rule over that country'. The United States would not admit 100,000 Jewish refugees as it was contrary to its laws 'established for its protection and the safeguarding of its interests'.[44] Truman's Day of Atonement speech did not win the Democrats the November congressional elections: for the first time since 1928 the Republicans secured a majority in both Houses.[45] Privately Truman wrote: 'the Jews themselves are making it almost impossible to do anything for them. They seem to have the same attitude towards the "under dog" when they are on top as they have been treated as "under dogs" themselves. I suppose that is human frailty.'[46] At this time the embassy in Washington reported to London that although Zionist pressure would continue, with no elections for two years in the United States, it was doubtful whether it would be effective.[47]

As attempts to renegotiate the Anglo-Egyptian treaty reached impasse the Cabinet, in December 1946, decided to move a further division from Egypt to Palestine. The importance of Palestine as a British military base in the Middle East increased.[48] Against this background Bevin visited the United States at the end of the year. He was met by Zionist demonstrators and compared to Hitler. On the Palestine issue Bevin did not receive much encouragement from Byrnes or Truman, though the President did agree that the United States would have to take more Jewish refugees. There were hints, however, that the United States was prepared to take over Britain's responsibilities in Greece and Turkey, and to commit itself to Europe. Hostile domestic reaction in the United States to a continuing British presence in Palestine could jeopardize that great advance. Bevin became convinced that Britain should consider abandoning the mandate.[49] Towards the end of December Bevin was against any continuing British military commitment in Palestine, and felt that before surrendering the mandate to the United Nations it should be offered to the United States.[50] At this time opinion in Britain was antagonized by unusual terrorist activities in the mandate. A sixteen-year-old convicted Zionist terrorist, too young to hang, was sentenced to eighteen years imprisonment and given eighteen cuts with a cane. This sudden indulgence in 'the English vice' by public school men[51] outraged Begin. His Irgun kidnapped and flogged four British officers, giving them eighteen strokes each with rawhide whips or a rope's end.[52] The Palestine administration stopped using judicial corporal punishment. British morale was further eroded at a time when withdrawal from Palestine was being considered. From the floor of the House, Churchill deplored this giving way to terrorism.

At the beginning of January 1947 the Cabinet was advised of the vital importance for Britain and the Empire of the oil resources of the Middle East. The chiefs of staff also continued to insist that Palestine was the only area able to accommodate Britain's Middle East reserve. Imperial communications also necessitated air bases there.[53] The Foreign Office emphasized the danger of the Russian threat.[54] Influenced by the military arguments that the retention of Britain's position in the Middle East was cardinal for the future defence of the Commonwealth, Bevin suggested to the Cabinet on 15 January that the Morrison–Grady proposals could be amended to point towards a unitary state. The Foreign Secretary did not examine the alternative, withdrawal, because of the insistence of the chiefs of staff that Britain's strategic interests necessitated the stationing of troops in Palestine. Creech Jones argued the Zionist case, and was supported by Dalton and Aneurin Bevan. Creech Jones then drew up a memorandum suggesting that Britain recommend a plan of partition to the United

Nations, and indicate the difficulties inherent in alternative schemes. The Cabinet discussed this on 22 January, and seemed convinced that if there were no agreed settlement the matter would have to go to the United Nations.[55]

Washington indicated to London that, because of domestic considerations, partition would be the easiest solution for the United States to back. But the State Department advised that the United States could not advocate partition: that would place it in the position of favouring the creation of a state against the wishes of the indigenous inhabitants.[56] London took the unusual step of keeping Washington fully informed of its discussions with the Arabs and the Zionists. Creech Jones arranged with Ben-Gurion that responsible members of the Jewish Agency would be in London for informal discussions. British officials spoke to the Arab delegates at the reconvened Palestine conference. The protagonists were intransigent. The Palestinian Arabs, led by Jamal Husseini, spoke of inflexible opposition to partition: the Arabs wanted self-determination. It was pointed out by an Iraqi delegate that the Arab peoples were the only ones who seemed to be called upon to pay for what Hitler had done to the Jews. Faris Bey Khouri of Syria argued that the real obstacle lay in the Jews looking upon non-Jews as subordinates 'whom they would use for their own ends and for this they considered they had biblical warrant'; the Jews had to be persuaded to abandon the idea of a state based on religious and racial principles. The British delegates were asked by C. Bey Chamoun of the Lebanon to substitute the words 'Great Britain' for Palestine and to say what the reaction would be in Britain 'if a third Power were to impose upon her an alien element whose presence was of a nature to disrupt her national life and her political and territorial unity'.[57] Ben-Gurion ceded that the Arabs had a right to stay in Palestine, but insisted that the future of the Arab peoples and culture did not depend on that country: 'For the Jews that little country was the only one in which they could ensure the continuance of their race.' Palestine was needed for the unborn generations of the Jewish people: the Zionists wanted to create there 'something worthy of the generations of Jewish martyrs'. Ben-Gurion ceded that 'state' had not been used in the mandate, but argued that 'national home' meant more than that a number of Jews would be allowed to live in Palestine. Bevin replied that it was a 'dreadful thing that Jews should be killing the British soldiers who had fought their battles for them against Germany'.[58]

These meetings weaned Creech Jones away from his Zionist sympathies. Ben-Gurion had spoken of 1,200,000 Jewish immigrants. For Britain that was unacceptable. The Colonial and Foreign Secretaries submitted a joint solution to the chiefs of staff and the Cabinet. It envisaged self-government in Palestine leading to independence after a transitional period of five years under trusteeship. The plan provided for 100,000 Jewish immigrants over the following two years: immigration after that would be by the agreement of the two communities, and failing that through United Nations arbitration. The chiefs of staff were worried about the loss of British military rights in Palestine. Bevin warned the Cabinet on 7 February that, if the parties would not acquiesce to this plan, Britain would have to submit the Palestine problem to the United Nations without making any recommendations.[59]

In the United States, Henderson commented that the 'plan should not be so objectionable to the Arabs as to the American Jews'. Ben-Gurion argued that Britain envisaged a state composed of Palestinian nationals of Arab and Jewish race. That was unacceptable: 'They were first and foremost Jews and they wanted a Jewish state in Palestine in which the Jews would be a majority.' Bevin responded: 'under the Jews the Arabs would have no rights but would remain in a permanent minority in a land they had held for 2,000 years'. The Arab delegates also rejected the new proposals: they could lead to partition and provided for further Jewish immigration.[60]

On 14 February the Cabinet decided to submit the problem to the United Nations without any recommendation for a solution. Attlee insisted that during the interim period there should be no concessions on Jewish immigration. The United States under its new Secretary of State, George C. Marshall, assisted by Robert A. Lovett, remained without a definite policy for Palestine. Bevin announced that the Palestine issue would be referred to the United Nations. He told the House of Commons on 25 February: 'In international affairs I cannot settle things if my problem is made the subject of local elections.' This attack on Truman was cheered in the House only a few days after the United States had decided to take over Britain's responsibilities in Greece.[61] With the emergence of the Cold War Britain had succeeded in isolating the Palestine question from the overall development of the Anglo-American special relationship. The Zionists realized this, and tried, unsuccessfully, to force Washington to link the Palestine question with negotiations over Greece and Turkey. Wagner suggested to Senator Arthur Vandenberg, a fellow member of the American Christian Palestine Committee, that as the United States was relieving Britain of a financial burden in Greece, Britain should relieve the United States of the burden of supporting 250,000 displaced Jews in Germany, and admit them to Palestine. Wagner hinted that British military personnel employed in Palestine could be used in Greece.[62]

At a time when opinion was roused in Britain over sensational kidnappings in Palestine in retaliation for death sentences passed on Zionists, and the death of twenty British soldiers in an attack on the Jerusalem officers' club,[63] the British government became increasingly concerned about the Haganah's policy of bringing pressure to bear through the traffic in illegal immigrants, and raised the issue with

Washington, as most of the ships concerned originated in the United States and were crewed by American citizens. This operation was financed largely by tax-free contributions from American sympathizers. Attlee complained directly about a report that the Mayor of New York had initiated a Zionist drive to raise nearly £2m. for the purchase of 'men, guns and money'. The Prime Minister protested: 'the guns which are being subscribed for in America can only be required to shoot at British soldiers in Palestine, and it is a matter for the greatest regret that they should be supplied from the United States'. Washington, however, felt that it could not stop the publication of advertisements, and that the tax-exemption issue raised complicated legal issues. No legal authority could be found to stop the sale of ships for illegal immigration, or to prevent their departure. Every possibility was being investigated to halt the purchase of surplus American army material by the Zionist terrorists.[64]

The United States blocked the formation of an *ad hoc* United Nations committee of inquiry on Palestine. A special session, however, on 15 May established a fact-finding committee. Russia insisted that the committee's membership be increased from seven to eleven, and that the solution of partition be considered. Beeley consequently thought that Russia hoped to be associated with a joint trusteeship over Palestine. The United Nations Special Committee on Palestine (UNSCOP) consisted of eleven neutral states and had broad powers of investigation.[65] Throughout this period the State Department and the White House were subjected to a barrage from the Zionists. Truman wrote to Niles on 13 May that the Palestine problem could have been settled but for American politics: 'terror and Silver are the contributing cause of *some*, if not all of our troubles'.[66]

UNSCOP went to Geneva to deliberate in August. The partition bloc crumbled, and it appeared that the majority favoured a ten-year period of probably British trusteeship. Crossman rushed to Geneva, and seemingly managed to change this. UNSCOP's report was finally signed on 31 August. The majority plan suggested partition into an Arab state, a Jewish state and the city of Jerusalem under international trusteeship. Britain would administer the mandate during the interim period and admit 150,000 refugees into the Jewish state. The minority plan proposed an independent federal state.[67]

The period of the UNSCOP inquiry saw the final wearing down of British morale in Palestine. Even Creech Jones was conscious that there were limits to the forbearance of the troops and the civilian administration. It was also expensive: the estimated military expenditure for the army and air force alone was £23.5m.[68] Zionist activities in the United States did not help. The Foreign Office protested to Lewis Douglas, the American ambassador in London, about the probability of funds openly collected in the United States being passed on to the Irgun. In particular it objected to Ben Hecht's encouragement of the

101

terrorists by advertisements. The profits from Hecht's Zionist musical, *A Flag is Born*, went to the Irgun, tax free, as contributions to charity.[69] Eleanor Roosevelt, perhaps conscious of her latent anti-Jewish prejudice, was active in the fund-raising campaign.[70] Britain repeatedly asked the United States to deny illegal immigrant ships bunkering facilities, but a decision at 'a high level' ruled that this could not be done. But Washington did take action over the issuing of improper identification documents for illegal immigrants by officials of the International Red Cross.[71] Bevin protested directly to Marshall who took limited action to stem the flood of illegal immigrants.[72]

Two incidents convinced Britain that it had to withdraw from Palestine. The one was the arrival in Palestine of the *President Warfield*, renamed *Exodus*, with 4,493 illegal immigrants. These were returned to their French port of embarkation. But the French declined to force the refugees to land. The fate of these immigrants was determined by Begin's Irgun: in retaliation for the execution of Zionist terrorists the Irgun hanged two British sergeants and booby-trapped their bodies. These were found on 31 July. From Jerusalem the American consul reported on the 'utter horror' at this act of the Irgun. The cold-blooded letter from the terrorist organization explaining that this was an act of war, the innocence of the victims, the atrocious nature of the murder and the bloody booby-trapping of the bodies led the consul to dilate on the 'mentality lurking behind outrages of this type'. He argued that the terrorist thinking was based on the premise, proclaimed by both the Irgun and the Stern gang, that all of Palestine and Transjordan belonged to the Jewish people: the British were merely there to bring about the unchallenged Jewish occupation and government of those two states. The consul concluded: 'During the time of the Nazis it was a commonplace to hear the opinion that Hitler and his followers were deluded to the point where their sanity was questionable. If such generalizations are permissible, it may be well to question whether the Zionists, in their present emotional state, can be dealt with as rational human beings.'[73] There were widespread outbreaks of anti-Semitism in Britain, and synagogues were daubed with swastikas. The British public blamed the Americans for giving the terrorists money: the *Daily Mail*, on 1 August, appealed to the feelings of 'American women whose dollars helped to buy the rope'. The press and some Members of Parliament demanded an early evacuation of British troops from Palestine: Britain could no longer support the moral and financial drain. An American official warned that British patience had been exhausted by the 'deliberate murder of two innocent men'. With opinion like this in Britain, any landing of refugees from the *President Warfield* was out of the question. Bevin explained to Inverchapel that Britain had no alternative other than to send them back to Germany. They were shipped back to Hamburg, giving the Zionists their most notable propaganda success of the time.[74]

On 20 September Bevin told the Cabinet that, failing a satisfactory settlement, Britain should announce its intention to surrender the mandate of Palestine, and plan for an early withdrawal of British forces and administration. Attlee saw a parallel between the situation in Palestine and the British withdrawal from India. He did not think it reasonable to ask the British administration to continue. The Cabinet accepted this policy of withdrawal.[75] The military, though it did not like withdrawal, had to accept it as well. The service directors of intelligence had estimated that the abandonment of the Palestine mandate would lead to the total collapse of Britain's position in the Middle East. The joint planning staff was worried that the Arabs, unless they were convinced that British withdrawal was dictated by a refusal to implement a solution unjust to them, would be alienated. This could leave Britain with no footing in the Middle East, apart from Cyprus, and Britain could lose the oilfields. Russia would be able to infiltrate and eventually dominate the area.[76] Informal political and strategic talks on the Middle East with American officials between 16 October and 7 November, however, reassured Britain to a limited extent. Bevin opposed any combined Anglo-American policy for the Middle East, as the area was primarily of strategic and economic interest to Britain. Both Truman and the British Cabinet endorsed the recommendations of the officials, though there was no formal agreement. The American participants recommended that their government strengthen the British strategic, political and economic position throughout the Middle East. This would include American diplomatic support for Britain, and also at the United Nations, over the retention of facilities in Egypt, Cyrenaica and Iraq. The United States also favoured the retention of Britain's strategic position in the Sudan, Gibraltar, Aden and Cyprus.[77]

It was at this time that the United States was forced into enunciating a specific policy on Palestine. The research and intelligence organization of the State Department regarded the UNSCOP majority plan as objectionable: it established two theocratic states in which majorities would apparently have special privileges. A single secular state was more in accord with American thinking. William A. Eddy, the special assistant to the Secretary of State, bluntly said that what was important was whether there should be 'a theocratic racial Zionist state' and secondly, whether there should be 'area self-determination, and an end to outside pressure and artificial economy'. He warned that acceptance of the majority report would damage American interests and leadership: it was contrary to America's 'example of non-clerical political democracy, without prejudice to race or creed'. It was 'an endorsement of a theocratic sovereign state characteristic of the Dark

Ages'. The Arab League would immediately align itself with Russia for survival.[78] Niles, however, secured the appointment of John Hilldring to the American delegation to the UN, and he sustained the Zionist viewpoint.[79] Marshall warned that delegation on 15 September that if the majority report were adopted there would be a *rapprochement* between the Arabs and Russia. But the American decision to support partition was taken in New York, without reference to the State Department and indeed to the consternation of its officials who feared Russian participation. Marshall went along with this.[80] On their own initiative the military opposed the move. The joint chiefs of staff warned on 6 October of the strategic consequences of partition: it would curtail American influence in the Middle East to that which could be maintained by military force. If the people of that area turned to Russia this would have an impact on American strategic and security interests similar to military conquest of the area by Russia. Partition would gravely prejudice American access to the oil of Iran, Iraq and Saudi Arabia. If it lost these resources America might have to fight an oil-starved war. Russia would be in a better position to fight such a war. There was a danger of Russian participation in any United Nations agreement which could establish for Russia a strategic interest in the Middle East incompatible with that of the United States.[81]

On 26 September Creech Jones told the *ad hoc* Palestine Committee of the United Nations that if the General Assembly recommended a policy not acceptable to the Arabs and Jews, Britain would not be able to implement it.[82] Russia, on 13 October, 'mystified' Britain and the United States by announcing its support for the partition of Palestine. Russian delegates to the United Nations hinted privately that Moscow wanted to create chaos in the Middle East, destroy American influence there, hasten the withdrawal of British troops and establish a Russian bridgehead instead, and, finally, to set a precedent for similar action in Kurdistan, Azerbaijan and even Macedonia.[83] Bevin drew up a timetable for Britain's withdrawal. The Foreign Secretary insisted that, in line with its treaty obligations, Britain was obliged to supply military equipment to various Arab armies. Britain would also continue to finance and loan British officers to the Arab Legion in Transjordan, and the British military missions which were a vital link with the armies of Egypt, Iraq and Saudi Arabia would continue. The position would have to be reviewed if the Arab armies became involved in the fighting in Palestine.[84]

Washington realized that it would be impossible to persuade Britain to stay in Palestine, and so the State Department considered the likelihood of having to use American forces there. However, it remained determined not to yield to demands of the Jewish Agency and the American Zionist Emergency Council for the inclusion of the Negeb in the Zionist section.[85] Then Weizmann saw Truman on 19 November about this. Hilldring supported Weizmann. Under White

House instructions Hilldring was given a free hand: Truman and Weizmann had their way on the question of the Negeb.[86] The British chiefs of staff became worried that a communist regime could be set up in Palestine after the British withdrawal on 15 May 1948,[87] but Bevin insisted on a British attitude of neutrality in the United Nations. On 24 November Bevin dined with Marshall and told him that Britain would abstain in the United Nations vote. It was deplorable that Britain was once again being held up to 'ignominious abuse'. Bevin had thorough legal advice that the Balfour Declaration did not commit the British government to developing a Jewish state. 'This great issue' had been handled by the United States more with 'the electoral situation in New York City in mind than the large issues of foreign policy which were involved'. Anti-Semitism was growing in Britain and feelings were running high in the House of Commons. The callous murder of the two British sergeants was responsible. Before that, Bevin had felt that the situation in Palestine could be held. Britain could not be committed to a position which might involve military action against the Arabs.[88]

On 29 November the General Assembly voted for partition. Prior to the vote, and particularly during the immediately preceding three days, the American Zionists exerted unprecedented pressure on the administration, and both delegations to the United Nations and their governments, to secure the necessary majority. Some correspondence suggests that Truman himself might have intervened at the last minute to ensure success for partition.[89] The State Department acknowledged that the votes of Haiti and the Philippines, at least, had been secured by the unauthorized intervention of American citizens.[90]

While the situation in Palestine deteriorated and, as Bevin told Marshall on 17 December, the Arab reaction was worse than expected, the Zionists in the United States celebrated. The Roman Catholic, Wagner, was singled out for particular praise. Silver acknowledged how magnificently he had championed the Zionist cause throughout the years and at this hour 'of joyous consummation' offered his people's gratitude.[91] The American Zionists had successfully sidestepped attempts to secure the entry of Jewish refugees into the United States by the bill introduced into the House of Representatives in the middle of 1947. This would have allowed 400,000 displaced persons into the United States and coped with the whole Jewish refugee problem in Europe. The Zionists contributed only eleven of the 693 pages of testimony.[92]

As the Cold War was joined in Europe, the Zionists and Arabs argued the relative merits of their claims on Palestine. In the end what they said counted for little. The Arabs were, perhaps, unfortunate in that they did not have an effective propaganda machine, or even easy access to the mass media of the West. The Zionists, however, were able to mount a campaign based on sympathy for the victims of the holocaust. Zionist propaganda was able to turn the King David Hotel incident from a terrorist atrocity into an instance of British anti-Semitism. Most successful of all was the publicity surrounding the *Exodus*. This, combined with terrorist activities in the mandate, especially the hanging of the two sergeants, eroded British morale. Britain, conscious of the dangers of Russian penetration in the Middle East, the vital strategic importance of the area and the significance of oil, was faced with a public opinion that would not tolerate a continued British presence in Palestine. To safeguard its interests the British government tried to leave in a way least likely to offend the Arabs. British policy was governed by a determination to maintain British paramountcy in the Middle East, and to prevent an increase of American influence in an area of traditional British concern. By the end of 1947 Russia hoped to establish a bridgehead in the area either through the United Nations or in the chaos following the end of the Palestine mandate. There was no one American view. The State Department and the military offered a diagnosis identical to that of Britain. The State Department was particularly conscious that support for partition would place the United States in the position of favouring the creation of a state against the wishes of its indigenous inhabitants. That would be un-American. But it was Truman who controlled policy. His private correspondence suggests that the President had no particular sympathy for the Jews. But he wanted to be re-elected. In his diagnosis the Jews in the United States could do that. After the First World War the Middle East was divided by the Great Powers in their own imperial interests. In the years immediately following the conclusion of the Second World War the politics of the powers with their concern for prestige, oil, strategic interests and communications to a large extent controlled developments in the area. But, in the end, the crucial factor was the United States, and its domestic politics determined the fate of the Middle East.

REFERENCES

1. *Robert F. Wagner Papers*, Palestine Files, Box 3, File 41, Memorandum by Handler, 27 March 1946.
2. *Dalton Diaries*, 34, f. 12, 22 March 1946; *Attlee Papers* (Bodleian, Oxford), 5, Liddell Hart to Attlee, 10 May 1946; Memorandum on Africa or the Middle East by Liddell Hart, 20 March 1946.
3. Ritchie Ovendale, 'Britain, the U.S.A. and the European Cold War, 1945–48', *History*, **67** (1982), 217–36 at 229–31.
4. *Truman Library*, Oral History Interview with Loy W. Henderson, ff. 108–10.
5. *Robert F. Wagner Papers*, Palestine Files, Box 3, File 14, Memorandum by Milton Handler, 27 March 1946.
6. William Phillips, *Ventures in Diplomacy* (Boston 1952), pp. 343–96.
7. Richard Crossman, *Palestine Mission* (New York 1947), pp. 15–17.

8.   Bartley C. Crum, *Behind the Silken Curtain* (New York 1947), pp.
      12–30, 85–6, 147–8, 195, 262–83; Crossman, op. cit., pp. 40–1, 165–87;
      David Horowitz, *State in the Making* (New York 1953), pp. 35–50, 91–2;
      Phillips, op. cit., pp. 425–6; James G. McDonald, *My Mission in Israel
      1948–1951* (New York 1951), p. 24; for the minutes of the public
      hearings before the Anglo-American commission see *PRO 30* (Public
      Record Office, London), 78.
      RG 59, OSS Bureau of Intelligence and Research, R + A 3652 D
      Intelligence, Current United States Policy towards Palestine, Feb. 1946;
      Joint Chiefs of Staff Leahy Records (National Archives, Washington),
      Folder 110, State Department, 1946, Leahy to Byrnes, Top Secret, 13
      March 1946; *RG 59*, Decimal Files 1945–49, Box 6754, 867N.01/3-746,
      William F. Finan to Leslie Rood, 7 March 1946.
10.   *Truman Papers*, Box 771, OF 204, Truman to Niles, 18 April 1946; Niles
      to Connelly, April 1946.
11.   *RG 84*, Entry 59A 543 part 5, Box 1057, 800 Palestine 4/25, Department
      of State to London Embassy, 25 April 1946.
12.   *Cab 129*, 9, ff. 127–9, CP(46)173, Report of Committee of Officials on
      Palestine, 27 April 1946; *Cab 128*, 5, f. 174, Cab 38(46)1, Secret, 29 April
      1946; see Ritchie Ovendale, 'The Palestine policy of the British Labour
      Government, 1945–1946', *International Affairs*. 55 (1979), 409–31 at
      416–20.
13.   Joseph B. Schechtmann, *The United States and the Jewish State Move-
      ment* (New York 1966), p. 156; *Robert F. Wagner Papers*, Palestine Files,
      Box 3, File 42, Press Statement for Release after 30 April 1946.
14.   *Prem 8*, 627 Part 2, House of Commons, 1 May 1946 (drafted in Attlee's
      hand).
15.   *FO 371*, 52527, E506A/4/31G, Chiefs of Staff Conclusions, 24 May 1946;
      52531, E5816/3/31, Wavell to Pethick-Lawrence, 11 June 1946.
16.   *FO 371*, 52503, E 178/4/31, Minute by Beeley, 14 Dec. 1945.
17.   John Snetsinger, *Truman, the Jewish Vote, and the Creation of Israel*
      (Stanford 1974), pp. 38, 155.
18.   *Truman Papers*, Box 184, PSF, Truman to Niles, 7 May 1946; Box 771,
      OF 204-Misc, Niles to Truman, 27 May 1946.
19.   Dean Acheson, *Present at the Creation* (New York 1969), p. 178; *Robert
      F. Wagner Papers*, Palestine Files, Box 3, File 41, Howard M. Le Sourd
      to Wagner, 16 March 1946; File 42, Press Announcement, 23 May 1946.
20.   *Robert F. Wagner Papers*, File 30, Joint Statement by Wagner and Taft
      on Roper Survey.
21.   *RG 59*, Decimal Files 1945–49, Box 6755, 867N.01/6-1146, Howard to
      Merriam and Jones, 11 June 1946; undated Minutes by Officials; Joseph
      P. Lash, *Eleanor: The Years Alone* (New York 1972), p. 117.
22.   *Truman Papers*, Box 184, PSF, McFarland to State–War–Navy Co-
      ordinating Committee, 21 June 1946.
23.   *RG 59*, Decimal Files 1945–49, Box 6756, 867 N 01/7-846, J. H. Hilldring
      to Robert P. Paterson, 8 July 1946.
24.   *Cab 128*, 5, f. 25, Cab 60(46)3, 20 June 1946; *FRUS* 1946(7), 867N.01/6-
      2946; Telegram, Attlee to Truman, undated.
25.   *Cab 129*, 11, f. 27, CP (46) 258, 8 July 1946; ff. 38–50, CP (46) 259, 8 July
      1946; *Cab 128*, 6, ff. 19–21, Cab 4 (46) 4, 11 July 1946.
26.   *FO 371*, 52551, E7713/4/31, Minute by Beeley, 9 Aug. 1946; *RG 59*,

Office of Near Eastern Affairs, Box 1, Merriam to Henderson, undated, DA 65, Draft Terms of Trusteeship for Palestine.
27. *Foreign Relations of the United States* (hereafter cited as *FRUS*), 1946 (7), pp. 644–5, Memorandum to be considered by London Conference; *RG 59*, Office of Near Eastern Affairs Palestine, Box 1, Summary of Cabinet Committee Plan for Palestine, July 1946; Zorach Warhaftig, *Uprooted Jewish Refugees and Displaced Persons after Liberation* (New York 1946), p. 72.
28. *Prem 8*, 627, Pt. 3, Ismay to Attlee, 15 July 1946.
29. *The Observer*, 13 Nov. 1977.
30. *RG 59*, Office of Near Eastern Affairs Palestine, Box 1, Proposed Policy for Palestine, undated.
31. *Robert F. Wagner Papers*, Palestine Files, Box 3, File 43, McDonald to Wagner, 29 July 1946; McDonald to Truman, 29 July 1946; *Truman Papers*, Box 775, OF 204 C, Memorandum by Connelly, 30 July 1946.
32. *Robert F. Wagner Papers*, Palestine Files, Box 3, File 1, Memorandum No. 2, The Palestine Question Zionism, 7 Aug. 1946.
33. *Prem 8*, 627 Pt. 3, British Delegation Paris to Attlee, 31 July 1946.
34. Christopher Sykes, *Crossroads to Israel* (London 1965), pp. 358–9; *FO 371*, 52548, E7474/4/31, Inverchapel to Bevin, 3 Aug. 1946.
35. *United Kingdom Parliamentary Debates House of Commons*, 426, col. 1257, 1 Aug. 1946.
36. *Cab 129*, 13, ff. 26–7, CP (46) 358, 5 Oct. 1946.
37. *FRUS* 1946 (7), pp. 700–1, Attlee to British Embassy Washington, 2 Oct. 1946; *FO 371*, 52560, E10030/4/31, Minutes of Meeting at Foreign Office, 1 Oct. 1946; *Prem 8*, 627, Part 5, Note by G. H. Gater of Interview between Bevin and Weizmann on 29 Sept. 1946; *Cab 129*, 13, ff. 26–7, CP (46) 358, 5 Oct. 1946.
38. *FRUS* 1946 (7), pp. 693–5, Clayton to Truman, 12 Sept. 1946; Annex, Draft Statement by President.
39. *Truman Papers*, Box 184, PSF, Hannegan to Truman, 1 Oct. 1946; Crum to Hannegan, 10 Oct. 1946; *Weizmann Archives* (Truman Library, Independence), Box 1, Epstein to Nahum Goldmann, 9 Oct. 1946.
40. *FO 371*, 52560, E9966/4/31, Bevin to Attlee, 4 Oct. 1946.
41. *FRUS* 1946 (7), pp. 701–3, Truman to Attlee, 3 Oct. 1946.
42. *FO 371*, 52560, E9987/4/31, Inverchapel to Attlee, 4 Oct. 1946.
43. *CO 537* (Public Record Office, London), 1783, Palestine Conference 1946, 28 Oct. 1946; 19 Nov. 1946; Meeting between Colonial Office and Creech Jones, 27 Nov. 1946.
44. *FRUS* 1946 (7), pp. 717–20, Ibn Saud to Truman, transmitted 2 Nov. 1946.
45. Eric F. Goldman, *The Crucial Decade and After: America 1945–1960* (New York 1972), pp. 17–90.
46. *Truman Papers*, PSF, Palestine–Jewish Immigration Files, Truman to Pauley, 22 Oct. 1946.
47. *CO 537*, 1737, Balfour to Creech Jones, 22 Nov. 1946; Enclosing Memorandum by Branley over State of Jewish Affairs.
48. *Cab 128*, 6, f. 157, Cab 96 (46) 3, 14 Nov. 1946; f. 193, Cab 105 (46) 4, 12 Dec. 1946.
49. *FO 371*, 61762, E 221/46/9, Conversation between Truman and Bevin (extract), 8 Dec. 1946.

50. Ibid., 61761, E 74/1/46, Minute by Beeley to read as Bevin to Attlee, undated.
51. See Ian Gibson, *The English Vice* (London 1978) for an account of the role of corporal punishment in the administration of the Empire.
52. *FO 371*, 61761, E 53/46/31, Cunningham to Creech Jones, 30 Dec. 1946.
53. *Cab 129*, 16, f. 49, CP (47) 11, Memorandum on Middle East Oil, 3 Jan. 1947; *FO 371*, 61763, E 463/46/G, COS(47)4, JP(47)1, 6 Jan. 1947; *Prem 8*, 627 Part 6, COS 161/7, Top Secret, 6 Feb. 1947.
54. *FO 371*, 61874, E 2932/951/31, Minute by McGarran, 6 Jan. 1947.
55. *Cab 128*, 11, ff. 7–9, Cab 6(47)3, Confidential Annex, 15 Jan. 1947; ff. 20–2, Cab 11(47)2, Confidential Annex, 22 Jan. 1947; Ritchie Ovendale, 'The Palestine policy of the British Labour Government 1947: the decision to withdraw', *International Affairs* 56 (1980), 73–93 at 76–86.
56. *FO 371*, 61764, E 743/46/G, Inverchapel to Bevin, 21 Jan. 1947; *RG 59*, Office of Near Eastern Affairs Palestine, Box 1, Merriam to G. Lewis Jones, 10 Jan. 1947.
57. *Cab 133*, 85, f. 3, Meeting 8, 27 Jan. 1947; f. 17, Meeting 9, 30 Jan. 1947; f. 10, Meeting 10, 4 Feb. 1947.
58. Ibid., f. 5, Jewish Delegation Meeting, 29 Jan. 1947; f. 16, Jewish Delegation Meeting 2, 3 Feb. 1947; ff. 12–13, Jewish Delegation Meeting 3, 6 Feb. 1947.
59. *Cab 129*, 16, ff. 322–6, Joint Memorandum by Bevin and Creech Jones on Palestine, 6 Feb. 1947; *Prem 8*, 627 Pt. 6, CO 161/7, 6 Feb. 1947; *Cab 128*, 9, ff. 76–7, Cab 18 (47) 2, 7 Feb. 1947.
60. *FRUS* 1947(5), pp. 1038–9, Henderson to Acheson, 10 Feb. 1947; *Cab 133*, 85, ff. 1–14, Jewish Delegation Meeting 4, 10 Feb. 1947; f. 8, Jewish Delegation Meeting 5, 13 Feb. 1947.
61. *Cab 128*, 9, ff. 92–4, Cab 22(47)2, 14 Feb. 1947; *FRUS* 1947(5), pp. 1054–5, Marshall to Bevin, 21 Feb. 1947; *United Kingdom Parliamentary Debates House of Commons*, 433, col. 985, 18 Feb. 1947; col. 1901, 25 Feb. 1947.
62. *Robert F. Wagner Papers*, Box 3, File 47, Confidential Memorandum, 13 March 1947; Wagner to Vandenberg, 19 March 1947.
63. Nicholas Bethell, *The Palestine Triangle. The Struggle between the British, the Jews and the Arabs 1935–1948* (London 1979), pp. 297–304.
64. *RG 84*, Entry 59A543 Part 5, Box 1076, 800 Palestine 3/20, Memorandum of Conversation between Inverchapel, Acheson and Henderson, 20 March 1947; 800 Palestine 4/16, G. Lewis Jones to Marshall, No. 527, 16 April 1947; 800 Palestine 4/26, Sargent to Douglas, Enclosing Attlee to Stassen (draft), 26 April 1947; *RG 59*, Office of Near Eastern Affairs Palestine, Box 1, Acheson to Douglas, 1 May 1947 (draft).
65. *FO 371*, 61777, P. Garran to Sargent, 23 May 1947; for an analysis of the UNSCOP hearings see Jacob Robinson, *Palestine and the United Nations* (Washington 1947), pp. 140–251.
66. *Truman Papers*, Box 184, PSF, Truman to Niles, 13 May 1947.
67. *FO 371*, 61784, E 7453/46/G, Minute by Beeley, 15 Aug. 1947; 61785, E 7568/46/G, Beeley to MacGillivray, 13 Aug. 1947; Horowitz, op. cit., pp. 202–9; *FO 371*, 61786, E 7855/46/31, Minute by Beeley, 29 Aug. 1947.
68. *FO 371*, 61931, W. A. C. Mathieson to C. W. Baxter, 19 June 1947;

61941, British Middle East Office to Foreign Office, 7 July 1947.

69. *RG 84*, Entry 59A543 part 5, Box 1076, 800 Palestine 5/29, Sargent to Douglas, 29 May 1947; David Hirst, *The Gun and the Olive Branch* (London 1977), p. 119.

70. Joseph P. Lash, *Eleanor and Franklin* (New York 1971), p. 214; Hirst, op. cit., p. 119.

71. *RG 59*, Office of Near Eastern Affairs Palestine, Box 1, Memorandum of Meeting of British and American Officials, 27 June 1947; Satterthwaite to Henderson, 2 July 1947.

72. S. Villard to Douglas, 11 Aug. 1947, Enclosing E 50001/48/G, Bevin to Marshall, 27 June 1947.

73. *RG 59*, Decimal Files 1945–49, Box 6760, Robert B. Macatee to Merriam, 4 Aug. 1947; Enclosing Memorandum, 3 Aug. 1947.

74. *RG 84*, Entry 59A543 part 5, Box 1076, 800 Palestine 8/14, Jones to Marshall, 14 Aug. 1947; 800 Palestine 8/15, Jones to Marshall, 15 Aug. 1947; *RG 59*, Decimal Files 1945–9, Box 6760, Clark to Marshall, 6 Aug. 1947; *CO 537*, 2313, Bevin to Inverchapel, 16 Aug. 1947; *RG 59*, Decimal Files 1945–9, Box 6760, R. S. Huestis to Marshall, 13 Sept. 1947; David Leitch, 'Explosion at the King David Hotel', in Michael Sissons and Philip French (Eds), *Age of Austerity 1945–1951* (London 1964), pp. 58–85 at pp. 73–9.

75. *Cab 128*, 10, ff. 148–50, Cab 76(47)6, 20 Sept. 1947.

76. *FO 371*, 61789, E 8913/46/G, Hayter to Warner, 20 Sept. 1947; E 8913/46/G, JP(47)131 (Final), Report by the Joint Planning Staff, 19 Sept. 1947.

77. *FO 371*, 61114, AN 3997/45/C, Record of Informal Political and Strategic Talks in Washington on the Middle East held from 16 Oct. to 7 Nov. 1947; AN 4080/3997/45/G, Bevin to Inverchapel, 13 Dec. 1947.

78. *RG 59*, Decimal Files 1945–49, Box 2182, 501 BB Palestine/9-1447, Appendix Cleland to Eddy, 12 Sept. 1947; 501.BB Palestine/9-1347, Comment by Eddy on the UNSCOP Report.

79. *Truman Papers*, Box 184, PSF, Niles to Truman, 29 July 1947; Truman to Under-Secretary, 6 Aug. 1947.

80. *FRUS* 1947 (5), pp. 1147–51, Meeting of United States Delegation to United Nations, 15 Sept. 1947; p. 1151, Statement by Marshall, 17 Sept. 1947; pp. 1152–3, Henderson to Lovett, 18 Sept. 1947; *Marshall Library*, Xerox, Hamilton to Forrestal, 20 Sept. 1947; *RG 59*, Decimal Files 1945–49, Box 2182, 501.BB Palestine/10-2847, Merriam to Henderson, 28 Oct. 1947; 501.BB Palestine/10-347, Henderson to Lovett, 6 Oct. 1947.

81. *Joint Chiefs of Staff Leahy Records* (National Archives, Washington), Folder 56, JCS 1684/5, Strategic and Military Implications of Partition, Approved 10 Oct. 1947.

82. *FRUS* 1947 (5), p. 164, note 2.

83. *Joint Chiefs of Staff Leahy Records*, Folder 118, US/A/AC 14/113, Wadsworth to Johnson, 22 Oct. 1947.

84. *FO 371*, 61793, E 10281/46/G, Memorandum by Bevin, undated,? 22 Oct. 1947.

85. *FRUS* 1947(5), pp. 1269–70, Lovett to Austin, 19 Nov. 1947.

86. *Truman Papers*, Box 773, OF 204–Misc., Memorandum for Truman, 22

Nov. 1947; Connelly to Truman, 22 Nov. 1947.
87. *FO 371*, 61794, E 10832/46/G, COS(47) 141, 14 Nov. 1947.
88. Ibid., 61796, E 11310/46/G, Note of Discussion between Bevin and Marshall, 25 Nov. 1947; see 61783, E 6586/43/31 for legal arguments.
89. *Truman Papers*, Box 773, OF 204-Misc., Celler to Truman, 26 Nov. 1947; Celler to Truman, 3 Dec. 1947; Celler to Matthew Connelly, 3 Dec. 1947.
90. *RG 59*, Office of Near Eastern Affairs Palestine, Box 1, Merriam to Henderson, 11 Dec. 1947.
91. *Robert F. Wagner Papers*, Palestine Files, Box 3, File 47, Silver to Wagner, 1 Dec. 1947.
92. *Senate Library*, Vol. 1174 (4), 80th Congress, HR 2910, 4–27 June 1947; 2–18 July 1947.

Chapter 7

THE RECOGNITION OF ISRAEL AND WAR

The United Nations vote in favour of the partition of Palestine confirmed Arab fears, and seemed to presage the establishment of an alien and hostile Zionist state in their midst. As the West prepared to stand against Russian advances in Europe, the Arabs began to fight. Britain had decided to withdraw from Palestine: Zionist terrorism had eroded British morale and the government felt that the public would not allow the troops to stay. Bevin blamed Truman and the President's concern for his domestic position. But at a time when oil was needed for Marshall aid for Europe, election politics in the United States had to be balanced against other factors. And, for the first few months of 1948, it was the United States that had the power to determine what happened in Palestine. The Zionists made their position clear: on 23 March 1948 the Jewish Agency warned that the Jewish people in Palestine and the rest of the world would oppose any initiative designed to prevent or postpone the Jewish state.[1]

In the United States the Zionists mounted mass public rallies, lobbied Truman, Marshall and congressmen and ran advertisements in the press.[2] They were in a strong position: New York with its forty-seven electoral votes was seen as the key state in the forthcoming presidential election. There, in February, Henry Wallace, whom Truman had dismissed for anti-containment speeches, supported a candidate in a district where the Jewish votes counted for 55 per cent. They ran their campaign on a militantly pro-Zionist platform and won a resounding victory. Beeley commented to G. Lewis Jones of the American embassy in London that there was no need for Russia to change its attitude to Palestine: Russia's policy had successfully embroiled the United States with the Arabs and 'helped to win the Bronx for Wallace'.[3] Truman's electoral adviser was the young and elegant Clark McAdams Clifford. Initially, Clifford did not advocate the wooing of the Jewish vote through an appropriate Palestine policy. But, after the defeat in New York, Clifford changed the strategy.[4]

George Kennan and the policy planning staff warned that pressures for the United States to shoulder a major responsibility for the maintenance, and even the expansion, of a Jewish state in Palestine, operated against major security interests in that area: it could mean the presence of communist troops and that the United States had been guided 'not by national interest but by other considerations'. The joint chiefs of staff argued that partition would lead to Arab hatred, the loss of oil, Russian penetration in the area in the guise of enforcing the United Nations plan, and a call for American troops for Palestine.[5] In the view of the State Department and the policy planning staff the presence of Russian forces in Palestine enforcing partition would constitute an outflanking of the American position in Greece, Turkey and Iran, and be a potential threat to the stability of the entire eastern Mediterranean. The United States should investigate the possibility of a federal state or trusteeship for Palestine.[6] On 16 January 1948 the Secretary of Defense, James S. Forrestal, told the Cabinet that without access to Middle Eastern oil the Marshall Plan could not succeed, the United States could not fight a war or even maintain the peace-time tempo of its economy. He drew up a paper in which he argued that it would be 'stupid' to endanger permanently relations with the Muslim world or 'stumble into war' on the Palestine issue.[7] Then, on 29 January, Kennan warned that British relations with the Arabs, and the remaining British strategic positions in the Middle East were among the few 'real assets' the United States still had in the area.[8]

Washington began to move away from partition. On 19 February Truman told Marshall to pursue the right course and to 'disregard all political factors'.[9] Warren Austin, the American representative at the United Nations, said on 24 February that the Security Council's action was 'directed to keeping the peace and not to enforcing partition'.[10] Senior Democratic leaders told Truman that only positive action by the administration for partition could keep New York state in the Democratic camp in the forthcoming November elections.[11] On 28 February the Central Intelligence Agency reported that partition could not be implemented and that its failure was already evident.[12] American policy moved towards supporting trusteeship. Truman endorsed this change, but was not specifically informed when Austin was to announce it. The President was preoccupied with the Russian coup in Czechoslovakia.[13] Clifford, at this time, advocated partition and a policy that coincided closely with the demands of the Jewish Agency.[14] On 18 March, at Zionist instigation and through the intervention of the President's old business associate, Edward Jacobson, Truman finally saw Weizmann. Weizmann impressed on the President the need for the future Jewish state of the Negeb area.[15] The next day Austin urged the Security Council to suspend its efforts to implement partition, and to establish instead a United Nations temporary trusteeship without prejudice as to the character of the eventual settlement.[16]

Britain, however, would not shift. The Cabinet, on 22 March, rejected American suggestions that order should be maintained in

Palestine by joint forces from Britain, France and the United States. Instead it instructed the chiefs of staff to investigate accelerating the British withdrawal.[17] Two days later Bevin instructed Sir Alexander Cadogan to maintain Britain's line of abstention in the United Nations.[18] That same day the Office of Near Eastern and African Affairs offered an alarming assessment to Marshall: support for temporary trusteeship could lead to American troops in Palestine, and the shedding of American blood. Without full Anglo-American co-operation no Palestine policy could be successful. That would be difficult unless Britain were assured that the administration refused to be influenced by Zionist pressure; informal undertakings would be needed that Zionism and Palestine would not be an issue in the forthcoming presidential elections. There would also need to be a campaign to free many American Jews from the domination of Zionist extremists.[19] But London told Marshall that there was overwhelming popular demand in Britain to get the boys back home from Palestine: the long experience of being shot at by both sides and being vilified by Zionists and by some countries had 'so calloused that British conscience that it is insensate on this particular subject'.[20] Then, under pressure from Niles and other Zionists, Truman, on 25 March, told a press conference that he remained in favour of partition at some future date. Beeley minuted that the President had 'destroyed the possibility of Arab cooperation in discussions on the basis of trusteeship'.[21]

American overtures for British co-operation on the implementation of trusteeship were turned away. Bevin told Lewis Douglas, the American ambassador, on 15 April that any British statesman suggesting further British responsibility for Palestine would not survive a moment.[22] Threats that this British attitude could have repercussions on Anglo-American co-operation throughout the world left Bevin unmoved. The Foreign Secretary told Douglas that troops might not be necessary if a firm decision were reached for the creation of a unitary state in Palestine. The problem would then be the breaking up of illegal organizations like the Stern gang and the Irgun, a possible task for organizations such as the American Federal Bureau of Investigation. Bevin felt that the fundamental difficulty over Palestine was that the Jews refused to admit that the Arabs were their equals: if the Jews could be brought to see that the principle of one man one vote applied in Palestine to Arabs and Jews alike as much as everywhere else the difficulties would be solved. Bevin wondered, as the Jews would be reluctant to fight Americans, whether the United States could not send troops into Palestine.[23]

Austin, on 20 April, speaking in the United Nations called for a truce in Palestine and the establishment of a trusteeship.[24] The British military authorities in the Haifa area started withdrawing their forces on 21 April. The Zionists and the Arabs clashed. The Zionists won, and the Arabs started fleeing. Arab states complained that this British withdrawal was contrary to the understanding under which they agreed to refrain from intervention in Palestine until 15 May. They accused Britain of giving the Zionists an advantage.[25] Nahum Goldman of the Jewish Agency was elated by the Zionist successes: the Haganah units had expert training. He did not see why the Zionists should accept an unfavourable truce when they were winning. The Zionists had 30,000 trained men in Palestine and that was likely to increase soon to 40,000. Shortly after 15 May there would be an additional 20,000 from outside Palestine. They faced only about 18,000 Arab troops.[26] On 21 April Bevin told Douglas that Britain would not like any part in arranging or supervising a truce. In any case Douglas did not expect a truce: the Zionists with trained men and munitions were in a position to win with their goal in sight. Bevin thought that the Zionists might win initially, but that the fighting would be wider than anticipated. Britain had close bonds not only with the Arabs but with the Muslims generally. The whole Muslim world might be inflamed. This could go on for two or three years, but the real bloodshed might not come for some time.[27]

Britain remained uncooperative. Dean Rusk threatened that this could lead to Russia using Palestine as a point of entry into the Middle East, and the United States would then have to reconsider the value of its commitments to Greece, Turkey and Iran.[28] Douglas saw Attlee and Bevin in the House of Commons on 28 April. The ambassador was worried about the threatened invasion of Palestine by Abdullah's troops. Bevin retorted that Abdullah had little option. Transjordan's entry to the United Nations had been blocked by Russia so the charter could hardly apply to him. Were the Jews to be allowed to be the aggressors on Abdullah's co-religionists and fellow Arabs in the state of Palestine while he had to stand by idly doing nothing? The Foreign Secretary had the impression that American policy was to allow no Arab country to help their fellow Arabs anywhere, while the United States assisted the Zionists to crush the Arabs within Palestine and to allow the slaughter to continue, and then to ask the British government to restrain Abdullah. The Jews appeared to be aggressive and arrogant, and to disregard United Nations' appeals. Bevin and Attlee insisted that any 'little acts' the Arabs had committed had been exaggerated: 'After all, Palestine was an Arab country.'

The Prime Minister asked whether it was aggression for the Arabs to come into Palestine from their own countries, and non-aggression for Jews to come in by sea to the tune of thousands? He rejected Douglas's protest that the Jews were unarmed: that was Hitler's method. Hitler put people in as tourists, but they were soon armed once they got in.[29]

On 28 April Truman, influenced by Niles and political considerations, appointed Hilldring as special assistant to the Secretary of State for Palestine affairs. A few days previously Hilldring had supported partition at a Zionist rally and told reporters that no man could say that the Jews should not be allowed to defend themselves or helped to defend themselves. The pro-Zionist press welcomed the appointment. Forrestal was disturbed. Henderson learnt of it from a wireless broadcast. In the end Hilldring never assumed these duties.[30] Truman, worried about the Russian factor, told Rusk: 'Go and get a truce. There is no other answer to this situation.'[31] The American delegation to the United Nations attempted this, but the prospects of a truce in Palestine receded. On 4 May Washington proposed a ten-day ceasefire and the extension of the mandate for ten days. Bevin refused: only a deadline would force the Zionists and the Arabs to negotiate. In any case the British Parliament had already passed the Palestine Act.[32] B.A.B. Burrows of the Foreign Office did, however, show Douglas the British intelligence reports: these suggested that many Arabs favoured a truce; the difficulty was 'Jewish arrogance'. The Zionists' 'campaign of calculated aggression, coupled with brutality' was 'being carried through with thoroughness, and competence and with [a] close eye on British troop depositions'. The Zionists were reorganizing their administration, and reshaping their tactics to be ready for a possible war against Arab regular forces which they thought they would win. By 6 May the Foreign Office had reports of an estimated 50,000 Arab refugees who had fled from Palestine. It was felt that the Arabs would find it difficult to accept truce proposals while the Zionists were forcing them from their homes.[33] Douglas had difficulty in getting permission to pass on to the Foreign Office information Washington had about Irgun plans to bomb British ships after 15 May.[34] Britain, however, did take an initiative in the United Nations, and the American and British delegations worked on a compromise proposal. This, however, was described as an 'eleventh hour effort but too little and too late'.[35]

Truman was visited by the owner of the *New York Times*, Arthur Hayes Sulzberger, on 8 May. The President said that he was bitter about the New York Jews and the British. Sulzberger asked Truman to 'make that New York Zionists' (making the distinction between 'Zionists' and 'Jews'). Both Truman and Lovett were worried about the development of anti-Semitism in the United States as a result of Zionist activities. Sulzberger felt the President did not do much to offset that when he confused Jews with Zionists.[36] It was Truman's birthday, and that evening Marshall proposed the toast: 'I cannot recall that there has been a President in our history who has more clearly demonstrated courageous decision, and complete integrity in his decisions.'[37]

On 7 May Max Lowenthal, a White House consultant with Jewish Agency connections, and a close associate of Niles and Clifford, sent Clifford an eyes-only memorandum calling for the recognition of the Jewish state before 15 May. Such a move 'would free the Administration of a serious and unfair disadvantage' in the forthcoming November elections. The message was repeated five times over the next four days, sometimes through Clifford's assistant, George M. Elsey.[38] At a meeting on 12 May with Truman, Marshall, Lovett, Niles and others, Clifford, using a memorandum prepared by Elsey and Lowenthal, urged Truman to give prompt recognition to the Zionist state after the termination of the mandate. This should be done to pre-empt Russia. Truman should make a statement of this intention the following day at a press conference. Marshall reacted: 'This is just straight politics. "You wouldn't get my OK." ' Lovett objected that this was a transparent attempt to win the Jewish vote. The United States did not know what sort of state would be established, and there was no urgency. The Secretary of State argued that such a transparent 'dodge to win a few votes would seriously diminish the office of the president'. If the President followed this policy Marshall would vote against him in the forthcoming elections. Truman replied that he knew the dangers and the political risks he would have to run.[39]

Members of the British, American and Canadian delegations to the United Nations met in the Savoy-Plaza Hotel in New York and drew up a new plan for a truce, recommended to Washington by the American delegation. It was hoped this would be approved and formally introduced on the afternoon of 13 May. London authorized it that morning, but there was a delay on the American side. On 14 May the first committee adjourned to allow the General Assembly to meet at Flushing Meadows at 4.30 p.m.[40] Marshall prepared a statement on Palestine: the American representatives were using all their influence to secure a truce: a catastrophe could be avoided and there might be time to develop an acceptable solution.[41] Weizmann wrote to Truman on 13 May hoping that the United States 'which under your leadership has done so much to find a just solution, will promptly recognize the Provisional Government of the new Jewish State'.[42]

According to Clifford, Truman was convinced by the case of Marshall and Lovett, and agreed to postpone recognition. American sponsorship, the President thought, would increase American responsibility. It would also be a breach of propriety towards the United Nations. But then Truman thought there might be no government or authority of any kind in Palestine, and the title would be lying about for anyone to seize. The President began to think about recognizing the new state, but said he would have to wait for a request for recognition and for some definition of the boundaries. In the end, Truman refused to delay even for a day. In the repeated words of Clifford, the timing of the recognition was 'of the greatest possible importance to the President from a domestic point of view'. There was no time for consultation with other governments, or even a chance to inform them.[43]

Clifford worked with Epstein of the Jewish Agency on the afternoon of 14 May to ensure that the requisite request for recognition of the Jewish state was in front of Truman in good time.[44] Lovett sent the President a State Department memorandum reiterating the argument that had been accepted on 12 May. It appears that Clifford did not pass this on.[45] Throughout the afternoon Lovett argued against the recognition of Israel: the United States could 'lose the effects of many years of hard work in the Middle East with the Arabs'. But Clifford could not even accept that there should be a delay so that the United States' allies could be informed. Clifford was then in session with Truman until about 5.30 p.m. and could not be reached. Lovett finally contacted Clifford and pleaded for a delay, at least until the end of the General Assembly session around 10.00 p.m. A few minutes later Lovett was informed that the United States would recognize Israel immediately.[46]

Around 5.45 p.m. Clifford told Dean Rusk that the state of Israel would be declared at 6 p.m. The United States would recognize it immediately. Rusk objected: this cut across what the American delegation at the United Nations had been trying to accomplish under instructions. At Flushing Meadows, Warren R. Austin, the head of the American delegation, left the floor and took the telephone call from Rusk. Austin decided he could not inform the other member of the delegation and departed by car.[47] As the news came over the ticker tape there was pandemonium in the General Assembly. Marshall told Rusk to go to New York to stop the American delegation from resigning *en masse*. But tempers cooled.[48] Rusk complained that the recognition of Israel appeared to the General Assembly as a 'case of conscious duplicity'. The Americans had just pushed through the Security Council the truce commission proposal which provided for no recognition. There was a major effort to push through the General Assembly on 14 May the final truce and mediation proposal, 'everyone justifiably assuming that we had no intention of recognizing one party'.[49] Eleanor Roosevelt complained to Marshall about the procedure: it was unlikely that the United States could give a credible lead in the United Nations again. The Secretary of State replied that he was not 'free' to say much about it.[50] Truman explained to Mrs Roosevelt that since there was a vacuum in Palestine, and as the Russians were anxious to be the first to do the recognizing, together with Marshall, Lovett and Rusk, he had decided to recognize the Jewish government promptly.[51] Truman lied. The overwhelming evidence is that Marshall, Lovett and Rusk all opposed American recognition of Israel to the last: they saw the move as one made entirely for domestic political gains and a concern for the Zionist vote.

On 21 May the policy planning staff advised that American policy threatened 'not only to place in jeopardy some of our most vital national interests in the Middle East and the Mediterranean but also to disrupt the Unity of the western world and to undermine our entire policy towards the Soviet Union'.[52] From London Douglas warned of the widening crevasse between Britain and the United States: the Palestine issue could jeopardize the foundation-stone of American policy in Europe – 'partnership with a friendly and well-disposed Britain'.[53]

The British mandate over Palestine had ended on 14 May 1948. In the morning the Union flag was lowered at Government House, Jerusalem, to a tattoo of drums and a Highland lament on the bagpipes. Shortly after 11.30 that evening the seventh British High Commissioner, Sir Alan Gordon Cunningham, took the last salute on board HMS *Euryalus*. As the ship left Haifa Bay a band played 'Auld Lang Syne' and 'God Save the King'. At midnight HMS *Euryalus* left Palestinian waters. It marked the close of an episode in imperial history. Britain was no longer the paramount power over the Zionists.[54]

At 4 p.m. on the same day, in a museum in Tel Aviv, David Ben-Gurion, under a portrait of Theodor Herzl, proclaimed the establishment of a Jewish state in Palestine to be called Israel. He signed the black scroll on which the dedication was to be inscribed. No place was reserved for Weizmann's signature, a slight the gradualist never forgot. Concealed above, the Jewish Philharmonic Orchestra played the Hatiqva', the national anthem. Ben-Gurion noted in his diary that the fate of the new state rested in the hands of the defence forces. On 15 May various Arab armies entered Palestine: the Arab Legion went into the area allocated to the Arabs in Judaea and Samaria; the Egyptian army moved through Gaza and Beersheba; the Lebanese went into Arab Galilee; the Iraqis eventually went alongside the Arab Legion; the Syrians were held near the border.[55]

In effect the First Arab–Israeli War was already being fought. It had started in November 1947 with the proclamation of a *jihad* or holy war by the Mufti of Jerusalem on the announcement of the United Nations partition plan. The Arabs refused to accept the partition of Palestine as they felt such a move went against 1,800 years of Palestine's history. Furthermore, the partition gave most of the territory of the ancient Jewish states to the Arabs, and to the Jews most of the territory that had been non-Jewish. In 1947 the Jews owned less than 10 per cent of the land and were less than one-third of the population. Partition awarded them 55 per cent of the land area of Palestine.[56] The Zionists, however, regretted that the partition plan did not give them control of Jerusalem.

The Zionists had been preparing to fight for some time. In 1941 the Palmach (striking companies) were established under the Haganah, and in 1944 a naval company and air platoon were set up within the Palmach. During the Second World War 20,000 members of the Yishuv served with the Allied forces and were available afterwards in Palestine. By April 1948 the Zionists had about 30,000 men under arms, 10,000 others for local defence, with another 25,000 in a home guard. They were short, however, of heavy weapons, armour and aircraft. There were also 2,000 experienced terrorists in the Irgun by

November 1945, and 800 in the Stern gang. The combined Arab forces committed to the fight amounted to around 40,000 men, but only the 10,000 in the Arab Legion had training to an equivalent level of the Zionist forces. Though deprived by the arms embargo of easy access to weapons, the Zionists organized an efficient clandestine trade. The day after the partition vote, Ben-Gurion sent Ehud Avriel to Europe to establish the organization for the purchase and shipping of the secret purchases of arms. Many of these came through communist sources in Czechoslovakia, and were paid for by tax-free contributions from American citizens at the height of the Cold War. Freddy Fredkens, a former pilot in the Royal Air Force, assisted in organizing an airlift of arms to Palestine. Haim Slavine did similar work in the United States, and from 1945, with the assistance of American Zionist leaders who were later dubbed as the 'Sonneborn Institute', collected and shipped an armament industry to Palestine, which was waiting for reassembly in kibbutzim throughout the new state of Israel.

Fighting broke out between Arabs and Jews throughout Palestine early in December 1947. The British forces tried not to get involved. The Zionists complained that the occupation army did little to restore order. But there was little sympathy: over the previous two years 127 British soldiers had been killed and 331 wounded by Zionist terrorists and guerrillas. British troops, however, did try to maintain order, but it became increasingly difficult as both Arabs and Zionists resorted to terrorist atrocities against each other. When, however, an irregular Arab force from Syria attacked a Jewish village on 10 January 1948, British forces assisted the settlers to repel the invasion. By the end of March Arab terrorists assisted by some British deserters, Yugoslavs, Germans and Poles, had seriously hampered communications throughout Palestine. Each side had suffered at least 1,200 casualties. As hostilities increased in April, British forces at times arranged cease-fires to allow Zionist settlers to evacuate their children and wounded, at times helped Arab populations to leave some cities. On the whole the British commanders were even-handed and most interested in securing an orderly withdrawal of their troops. The Haganah utilized the information of one such withdrawal effectively to take control of Haifa, and under a British-arranged truce most of the Arab population of 100,000 left their homes. The Irgun, under Haganah's command, attacked the Arab city of Jaffa at the end of April. British forces intervened against the Zionists in an effort to maintain the status quo, but when Jaffa officially surrendered on 13 May only around 3,000 of the Arab population of 70,000 remained.

On 9 April contingents of the Irgun and the Stern gang, under Haganah command, encountered strong Arab resistance in the village of Deir Yassin, and slaughtered 245 men, women and children, most of the inhabitants of the town and seemingly all the terrorists they could find. The massacre of Deir Yassin was thought by the Arabs to have been perpetrated with the approval of Ben-Gurion and the Haganah leadership to terrorize the Arab population into fleeing from their land. Begin later spoke of the 'heroic' acts of his men at Deir Yassin, and attributed the Arab flight from the new state of Israel to this incident. The Arabs retaliated on 13 April, and besieged a convoy of mainly Jewish doctors and nurses on the road to Mount Scopus: seventy-seven were killed. The convoy expected to be relieved by British troops, but these never appeared. As the British troops evacuated Jerusalem on 14 May the Israelis and Arabs seized appropriate positions in the city and prepared for battle.[57] The Israelis had already secured a major strategic advantage: the face of the Samarian and Judaean mountains facing west.[58]

On the whole the Israelis fought the war with a united front. When, during the first cease-fire, the Irgun apparently defied the authority of the Israeli government and tried to bring in arms openly from the ship, *Altalena*, the official forces, initially led by Moshe Dayan, took action, and after a short engagement on 21 June, the Irgun withdrew. On 28 June the entire Israeli army took the oath of allegiance.[59] Generally, the provisional government controlled the activities of the Irgun and the Stern gang. The Arabs, however, were torn apart by old rivalries. King Farouk of Egypt probably would have preferred not to be involved. But his opponents at home, the Muslim Brotherhood, were fighting, and if he did not join battle they could consolidate their appeal to the Egyptian population. Farouk was also conscious that his old adversaries, the Hashemite kings of Transjordan and Iraq, could strengthen their position in the Arab world if they intervened and he did not. The leaders of Syria also had designs on at least the Arab areas of Palestine and wanted to keep them away from King Abdullah of Transjordan. Syria tended to side with Egypt. Abdullah did not like the idea of an Arab Palestine under the Mufti. Abdullah wanted the Arab area for Transjordan. He indicated this to Golda Meir (then Myerson) at a meeting in November 1947. During the negotiations for a new treaty with Britain in the spring of 1948 the Prime Minister of Transjordan, Tewfiq Pasha, told Bevin that after the end of the mandate the Arab Legion would cross the Jordan River with the limited objective of occupying the portion awarded to the Arabs by the partition resolution. Not only were the Arab armies without a unified command, but they faced serious logistic difficulties. On 14 May 1948 Abdullah claimed the title of commander-in-chief but it had no meaning.[60]

Even before the end of the mandate the morale of the Palestinian Arabs was seriously weakened with the death of its leaders including Abd el Kader el Husseini. Their organization in the vicinity of Jerusalem disintegrated, and individual Arab fighters returned to their villages. In the early stages of the war the main battle was for Jerusalem. Principally it was a war between the Arab Legion under

Glubb and an Israeli command under Yigal Allon who, together with an American West Point graduate, Colonel David Marcus, fought to secure Israeli access to the city.[61] At Lake Success Sir Alexander Cadogan proposed the appointment of a United Nations mediator. The Security Council endorsed this, and Count Folke Bernadotte of Sweden was chosen. He arranged a four-week truce starting on 11 June. During these weeks the Israeli army turned itself into an efficient modern fighting force. With an airfield provided by the Czechoslavaks, Israel was also able to prepare a shuttle of arms, bombs and fighters from Europe. These were often illegally obtained in Britain and the United States. France sold weapons in large quantities to Israel. Abdullah refused Glubb's request to make effective use of the truce, though other Arab leaders did something, and the number of regular Arab troops in Palestine grew to nearly 45,000. Bernadotte suggested a modification of the partition plan, but this was rejected by both sides.

When the Arabs started fighting again, the Israelis implemented a series of carefully planned offensives. These were largely successful. Bernadotte suggested further peace plans, the last being one prepared on the island of Rhodes and submitted to the United Nations on 16 September: Jerusalem was to be an international city under United Nations control; the Negeb would go to the Arabs together with Lydda and Ramle; in return Israel would get Galilee. Bernadotte stressed that the Arab refugees should have the right to return home. The following day Bernadotte was murdered in Jerusalem, apparently by members of the Stern gang. Ben-Gurion ordered the dissolution of the Irgun and the Stern gang. Over 200 were arrested, but eventually they were released without trial. Dr Ralph Bunche, an American, succeeded Bernadotte. London and Washington endorsed Bernadotte's report. Ben-Gurion became alarmed, and decided on new decisive military victories. These were largely achieved against the Egyptians and through the tactics of Allon. The Israelis were helped by further divisions in the Arab world. To the fury of Egypt and other Arab states, Abdullah organized a ceremonial conference at Jericho where Palestinian and Transjordanian delegates favoured the joining of Palestine and Transjordan as an indivisible Hashemite Kingdom of Jordan. This was on 1 December 1948, the day the cease-fire arranged by Dayan and Colonel Abdullah al-Tel, the commander of the Arab Legion in Jerusalem, came into effect. For the King of Jordan the war was over. As Israeli troops under Allon implemented the plans of Yigael Yadin and drove into Egypt, the other Arab countries stood aside. The Syrians and Iraqis had had enough. The Muslim Brotherhood rioted in Egypt. Finally, on 29 December, the Security Council ordered a cease-fire.[62]

London was disturbed as there were British troops in Egypt. Under the terms of the 1936 Anglo-Egyptian treaty Britain was obliged to assist Egypt in case of attack. On 30 December Sir Oliver Franks, the British ambassador in Washington, left a note with Lovett, then Acting Secretary of State, warning that unless the Israelis withdrew, Britain would fulfil its treaty obligations. There could arise out of this situation 'the gravest possible consequences, not only to Anglo-American strategic interests in the Near East, but also to American relations with Britain and Western Europe'. London hoped that Washington would place pressure on the Israelis so as to make this step unnecessary. Washington obliged.[63] Ben-Gurion gave Allon orders to withdraw.[64] But, in the end, Allon was allowed to take the heights above the border town of Rafa. On 7 January the Israelis shot down five Royal Air Force planes which they claimed had strafed Israeli troops. London argued the planes were over Egyptian territory and that the attack was unprovoked.[65] Britain sent troops to Aqaba, and alerted its Mediterranean ships. The Israelis threatened to place this 'intervention' before the Security Council.[66] Egypt demanded evacuation of the Rafa heights before starting negotiations. London reminded Washington of the Middle Eastern talks of November 1947, and the implied support offered by the United States to maintain Britain's position in the Middle East. Lovett warned that the position might arise whereby Britain would be arming one side in the dispute and the United States the other, with Russia the permanent beneficiary.[67] Ben-Gurion took a chance, and withdrew his offending troops. Aneurin Bevan attacked Bevin in Cabinet on 17 January: Britain could not maintain its position in the Middle East by supporting unstable and reactionary Arab governments. Britain should have relied on the friendship of the Jews. Bevin retorted, with the support of Attlee and the Cabinet, that the Commonwealth meant that Britain had a special position in the Muslim world: it had to support a fair deal for the Palestinian Arabs who had been in possession of the land for centuries.[68] On 24 February an armistice was signed at Rhodes between the Egyptians and Israelis. This was largely due to British efforts. Further agreements were soon signed with the Lebanon and Jordan, and finally with Syria. By these Israel gained 21 per cent more land than it had under the 1947 partition plan; indeed it covered almost 80 per cent of the area of the Palestine mandate. But it also acquired insecure frontiers. Britain, virtually the last Western country to do so, gave Israel *de facto* recognition after that country's national elections in January 1949.[69]

The Arab League split: Egypt argued with the Hashemites, Syria with the Iraqis. Each country blamed another for not providing enough for the war. The real victims were the Palestinian Arabs. In April 1946, according to the Anglo-American commission, there were 226,000 Jewish refugees in Europe of which 100,000 were in camps in Austria, Germany and Italy. In 1949 the legally certified number of Palestinian Arab refugees was almost 1 million. The American press hardly mentioned this new refugee problem.[70] The new stateless went to Gaza, Jordan, 100,000 to the Lebanon, 70,000 to Syria and smaller numbers to Iraq and Egypt. By the late 1960s it is estimated that they had grown to 2 million. On 16 June 1948 Ben-Gurion told his cabinet that the return of the Arabs should be prevented. They would have to bear the consequences of declaring war on Israel. When Bernadotte asked Ben-Gurion to allow the Arabs to return, the Israeli leader, on 1 August 1948, mentioned conditions that made any such event unlikely in the foreseeable future. Israeli encouragement for Jews in the Middle East to settle in their new homeland fired Muslim suspicion of those communities which for centuries had lived in their midst under the toleration of Islamic law. Between 1948 and 1957 567,000 Jews left Muslim countries in North Africa and the Middle East, and most settled in Israel. As a result the population of Israel rose from 1,174,000 in 1949 to 1,873,000 in 1956. Few American, or indeed European, Jews who were not refugees, settled in Israel. Rather the state was formed through a massive shift around of the population of the Middle East on religious lines.[71]

On 26 January 1949 there was a debate in the House of Commons. When Churchill interrupted Bevin's history of the Palestine problem he was told by the Foreign Secretary: 'over half a million Arabs have been turned by the Jewish immigrants into homeless refugees without employment or resources'. Bevin later went on to describe the tide of Arab nationalism that was 'running high' and had bitten deep into the ordinary young Arab: 'They consider that for the Arab population, which has been occupying Palestine for more than twenty centuries, to be turned out of their land and homes to make way for another race is a profound injustice.' The Foreign Secretary wondered how the British people would feel if they had been asked to give up a slice of Scotland, Wales or Cornwall to another race. He marvelled that the conscience of the world was so little stirred by the tragedy of the Arab refugees: 'I think that the driving of poor innocent people from their homes, whether it is in Germany by Hitler, or by anybody else, and making the ordinary working people of the place suffer, is a crime, and we really ought to join together to stop it if we can.' Bevin explained what he saw as having been one of the principal determining factors of the prevailing situation: American interests – 'the whole question of who should be elected to certain offices in the United States turned on this problem' of Palestine.[72] Churchill argued that the coming into being of a Jewish state had to be seen in the perspective of 2,000 or even 3,000 years.[73]

The creation of the state of Israel undermined British paramountcy in the Middle East. Until the end of the Second World War the story of the Palestine mandate was an episode of imperial history. Then a new determining factor emerged: American domestic politics. The Zionists utilized this. At the time of the joining of the Cold War Britain managed to isolate the Palestine issue from the deepening current of the Anglo-American special relationship, and even made Washington aware that it was in the interests of the West that Britain be helped to maintain its pre-eminent position in the Middle East. But Truman's concern for the Zionists' vote undermined this overall strategy. After the recognition of Israel, Marshall managed to secure a bipartisan approach to foreign policy in the run-up to the presidential election. Late in the campaign, however, Truman gave way to Zionist pressure. The President, after his unexpected victory, told Lovett: 'Haven't I just proved to you that you shouldn't pay any attention to the newspapers'; that also applied to the 'damned politicians' and the Palestine pressure groups.[74]

The state of Israel came into being because, in the end, two of the Great Powers, Russia and the United States, for conflicting reasons, strategic and domestic, thought it would be in their interests. Britain, concerned to maintain its paramountcy in the Middle East, opposed the move. British morale was eroded by a combination of Zionist terrorism, and a feeling that an American President dictated a policy in the interests of Zionism and his re-election, that led to the deaths of British troops. In any case this was the period of the twilight of the British Empire and the replacement of the *pax Britannica* by the *pax Americana*. After 15 May 1948 the situation in the Middle East was not determined just by Great-Power politics, but by a local fight for possession of land. Britain's imperial position there, established between 1917 and 1923, was eroded.

REFERENCES

1. *Joint Chiefs of Staff Leahy Records*, Folder 57, US/A/AC.21/13, Statement by the Jewish Agency for Palestine and the National Council of the Jews of Palestine, 23 March 1948.
2. See John Snetsinger, *Truman, the Jewish Vote and the Creation of Israel* (Stanford 1974), pp. 74–5, 169.
3. *New York Times*, 18 Feb. 1948; *RG 59*, Decimal Files 1945–49, Box 6749, 867N.00/31648, Jones to Merriam, 16 March 1948; Enclosing Memorandum of Conversation between Lewis Jones and Beeley, 16 March 1948.
4. *Clifford Papers* (Truman Library, Independence), Clifford to Truman, Memorandum on the Politics of 1948, 19 Nov. 1947; Snetsinger, op. cit., pp. 88–9.
5. *Policy Planning Staff* (National Archives Washington), PPS/23, Review of Current Trends in United States Foreign Policy, 24 Feb. 1948; Kenneth W. Condit, *The History of the Joint Chiefs of Staff. The Joint Chiefs of Staff and National Policy*, Vol. II, *1947–1949* (Marshall Library, Lexington) (Joint Secretariat Joint Chiefs of Staff, 22 April 1976), f. 93.
6. *Foreign Relations of the United States* (hereafter cited as *FRUS*), 1948

(5), pp. 545–54, Report by Policy Planning Staff, 19 Jan. 1948.
7. *Forrestal Diaries* (Princeton University Library, Princeton), Box 4, Vol. 9, f. 2026, Cabinet, 16 Jan. 1948; Walter Millis (Ed.), *The Forrestal Diaries* (London 1952), pp. 340–5, Diary, 6 Jan. –21 Jan. 1948.
8. *FRUS* 1948 (5), pp. 573–81, Kennan to Lovett, and Annex, 29 Jan. 1948.
9. Ibid., p. 633, Marshall to Lovett, 19 Feb. 1948.
10. Ibid., pp. 651–4, Statement of Austin, 24 Feb. 1948.
11. *FO 371*, E2773/1078/31, Inverchapel to Bevin, 21 Feb. 1948.
12. *FRUS* 1948 (5), pp. 666–75, Report by Central Intelligence Agency, 28 Feb. 1948.
13. Ibid., pp. 728–9, Marshall to Austin, 16 March 1948; p. 746, Notes dated 4 May 1948.
14. Ibid., pp. 687–9, Memorandum by Clifford, 6 March 1948.
15. Harry S. Truman, *Years of Trial and Hope* (New York 1956), pp. 160–1; Christopher Sykes, *Crossroads to Israel* (London 1965), pp. 410–12.
16. *FRUS* 1948 (5), pp. 742–4, Statement by Austin before Security Council, 19 March 1948.
17. *Cab 128*, 12, f. 107, Cab 24 (48) 6, 22 March 1948.
18. *FO 371*, 68648, E3726/1078/31G, Bevin to Inverchapel, 25 March 1948.
19. *FRUS* 1948 (5), pp. 756–7, Memorandum prepared in the Office of Near Eastern and African Affairs, undated.
20. Ibid., pp. 758–9, Gallman to Marshall, 24 March 1948.
21. *FRUS* 1948 (5), pp. 759–60, Marshall to Embassy in Egypt, 25 March 1948; *FO 371*, 68648, E3900/1078/31, Inverchapel to Bevin, 25 March 1948; Minute by Beeley, 27 March 1948.
22. *FO 371*, 68649, E4796/1078/31G, Bevin to Creech Jones, 16 April 1948; *FRUS* 1948 (5), p. 826, Douglas to Marshall, 16 April 1948.
23. *FRUS* 1948 (5), p. 837, Douglas to Marshall, 20 April 1948.
24. Ibid., p. 835.
25. Ibid., p. 838.
26. *RG 84*, Entry 59A543 part 5, Box 1032, 800 Palestine 4/20, Douglas to Marshall, 20 April 1948; Douglas passed this information on to Michael Wright at the Foreign Office.
27. *FO 371*, E5020/1078/31G, Bevin to Inverchapel, 21 April 1948 (draft); *FRUS* 1948 (5), p. 847, Douglas to Marshall, 22 April 1948.
28. *FO 371*, 68649, E5344/1078/31G, Cadogan to Bevin, 27 April 1948.
29. Ibid., E5751/1078/31G, Roberts to Inverchapel, 30 April 1948; *FRUS* 1948 (5), pp. 876–7, Douglas to Marshall, 29 April 1948.
30. *FO 371*, 68649, E5546/1078/31, Inverchapel to Bevin, Telegrams Nos. 2074–5, 30 April 1948; E5986/1078/31, Hadow to Mason, 2 May 1948.
31. *FRUS* 1948 (5), pp. 877–9, Memorandum by Rusk, 30 April 1948.
32. *FRUS* 1948 (5), pp. 896–7, Douglas to Marshall, 4 May 1948.
33. *RG 84*, Entry 59A543 part 5, Box 1032, 800 Palestine 5/11, Douglas to Marshall, Telegrams Nos. 2036 and 2052, 11 May 1948.
34. Ibid., 800 Palestine 5/5, Douglas to Marshall, 5 May 1948.
35. *FRUS* 1948 (5), pp. 970–1, Austin to Marshall, 10 May 1948.
36. *Arthur Krock Papers* (Princeton University Library), Box 1, Black Note Book, Book I, ff. 199–200, Memorandum by Sulzberger of Interview with Truman, 8 May 1948.
37. *George C. Marshall Papers* (Marshall Library, Lexington), Box 81,

Substance of a Toast by Marshall, 8 May 1948; Marshall to Mrs Truman, 10 May 1948.

38 *Clifford Papers* (Truman Library, Independence), Box 13, Lowenthal to Clifford, 7 May 1948; 9 May 1948; 11 May 1948; 12 May 1948; 12 May 1948.

39. *FRUS* 1948 (5), pp. 972–8, Memorandum of Conversation by Marshall, 12 May 1948; *Elsey Papers* (Truman Library, Independence), undated Notes on White House Meeting of 12 May 1948; Statement presented by Clifford at the White House Meeting of 12 May 1948, undated.

40. *CO 537*, 3924, The Last Days of the Palestine Mandate at Lake Success, undated.

41. *George C. Marshall Papers*, Box 158, File 32, Statement re Palestine and the United Nations, not used.

42. *FRUS* 1948 (5), pp. 982–3, Weizmann to Truman, 13 May 1948.

43. *FRUS* 1948 (5), pp. 1005–7, Memorandum by Lovett, 17 May 1948.

44. *Elsey Papers*, Notes on Events of Friday, 14 May, undated.

45. *Clifford Papers*, Box 13, Humelsine to Clifford, 14 May 1948; Memorandum by Ernest A. Gross, 13 May 1948.

46. *FRUS* 1948 (5), pp. 1005–7, Memorandum by Lovett, 17 May 1948. For Clifford's version see Clark M. Clifford, 'Factors influencing President Truman's decision to support partition and recognize the state of Israel' in Clark M. Clifford, Eugene V. Roston and Barbara W. Tuchman (Eds), *The Palestine Question in American History* (New York 1978), pp. 24–45; Clark M. Clifford, 'Recognizing Israel', *American Heritage*, XXVII (1977), 4–11; *Papers of Jonathan Daniels* (Truman Library, Independence), Notes for *The Man of Independence*, Part 1, ff. 46–7, Interview with Clark Clifford. See also Alfred W. Lilienthal, *The Zionist Connection* (New York 1975), p. 790, Lovett to Lilienthal, 3 Oct. 1977.

47. *FRUS* 1948 (5), p. 993, Rusk to Franklin, 13 June 1974; *Warren R. Austin Papers*, Box 69, Appointment Book 1948, 14 May 1948.

48. Jorge Garćia-Granados, *The Birth of Israel* (New York 1948), pp. 287–90; Philip C. Jessup, *The Birth of Nations* (New York 1974), pp. 290–1.

49. *RG 59*, Palestine Reference Book of Dean Rusk, Box 3, Rusk to Hickerson, 18 May 1948.

50. Ibid., Decimal Files 1945–49, Box 6, Eleanor Roosevelt to Marshall, 16 May 1948; Marshall to Eleanor Roosevelt 18 May 1948.

51. *Eleanor Roosevelt Papers* (F. D. Roosevelt Library, Hyde Park), Box 4560, Truman to Eleanor Roosevelt, 20 May 1948.

52. *FRUS* 1948 (5), pp. 1020–1, Kennan to Marshall, 21 May 1948.

53. Ibid., p. 1031, Douglas to Marshall, 22 May 1948.

54. *New York Times*, 15 May 1948; Bernard Postal and Henry W. Levy, *And the Hills Shouted for Joy* (New York 1973), pp. 3–27; Zeev Sharef, *Three Days* (New York 1972), pp. 256–67.

55. David Ben-Gurion, *Israel: A Personal History* (London 1971), pp. 92–3, Diary, 14 May 1948; Dan Kurzman, *Genesis 1948: The First Arab–Israeli War* (London 1972), pp. 250–1; John Glubb, *Britain and the Arabs. A Study of Fifty Years 1908 to 1958* (London 1959), p. 288.

56. For a map of the United Nations partition plan see Trevor N. Dupuy, *Elusive Victory: The Arab–Israeli Wars, 1947–1974* (London 1978), p. xxiv.

57. Dupuy, op. cit., pp. 3–40; Larry Collins and Dominique Lapierre, *O Jerusalem!* (London 1973), pp. 3–395; Kurzman, op. cit., pp. 3–258; Ben-Gurion, op. cit., pp. 65–93; Yigal Allon, *The Making of Israel's Army* (London 1970), pp. 1–29.
58. Glubb, *Britain and the Arabs*, pp. 287–8.
59. Shabtai Teveth, *Moshe Dayan* (London 1972), pp. 147–9; Moshe Dayan, *The Story of my Life* (London 1976), pp. 72–4.
60. John Bagot Glubb, *A Soldier with the Arabs* (London 1957), pp. 62–96; David Downing and Gary Herman, *War Without End. Peace Without Hope. Thirty Years of the Arab–Israeli Conflict* (London 1978), pp. 26–9; Howard M. Sachar, *Europe Leaves the Middle East* (London 1972), pp. 530–42.
61. Dupuy, op. cit., pp. 41–66; Allon, op. cit., pp. 30–7; Glubb, *A Soldier with the Arabs*, pp. 105–72; Kurzman, op. cit., pp. 343–443.
62. Dupuy, op. cit., pp. 67–111; Glubb, *A Soldier with the Arabs*, pp. 175–217; Kurzman, op. cit., pp. 444–678; Allon, op. cit., pp. 40–2; Pablo de Azcárate, *Mission in Palestine 1948–1952* (Washington 1966), pp. 80–135; Alec Kirkbride, *From the Wings: Amman Memoirs 1947–1951* (London 1976), pp. 67–9; Abba Eban, *An Autobiography* (London 1977), pp. 128–36; Ben-Gurion, op. cit., pp. 127–318.
63. *FRUS* 1948 (5), pp. 1701–3, Memorandum by Lovett, 30 Dec. 1948; Annex, Note Verbal by the British Embassy; p. 1704, Lovett to McDonald, 30 Dec. 1948; pp. 1705–6, McDonald to Lovett, 31 Dec. 1948.
64. *FRUS* 1949 (6), pp. 594–5, McDonald to Acheson, 1 Jan. 1949.
65. Ibid., p. 627, McDonald to Acheson, 7 Jan. 1949; pp. 627–8, Memorandum by Satterthwaite, 8 Jan. 1949.
66. Ibid., pp. 645–7, Memorandum by Lovett, 12 Jan. 1949.
67. Ibid., pp. 658–61, Lovett to Embassy in London, 13 Jan. 1949.
68. *Cab 128*, 15 Cab 3 (49), 17 Jan. 1949.
69. Sachar, op. cit., pp. 568–79.
70. William R. Polk, *The United States and the Arab World*, 3rd edn (Cambridge, Mass. 1975), p. 233; J. Rives Childs, *Foreign Service Farewell* (Charlottesville 1969), p. 152.
71. Sachar, op. cit., pp. 552–4; Harold Wilson, *The Chariot of Israel, Britain, America and the State of Israel* (London 1981), pp. 241–2.
72. *United Kingdom Parliamentary Debates House of Commons*, 460, cols. 933–5, 26 Jan. 1949.
73. Ibid., col. 952.
74. Snetsinger, op. cit., pp. 124–32; *George C. Marshall Papers*, Box 74, File 39, Lovett to Marshall, 8 Nov. 1948.

Chapter 8

REALIGNMENT AND CHANGE

After the signing of the armistice agreements between Israel and the Arab countries, the West tried to stabilize the situation in the Middle East with the Tripartite Declaration made by Britain, the United States and France on 25 May 1950. This acknowledged that the Arab states and Israel needed to maintain a certain level of armed forces for the purposes of legitimate self-defence of the area as a whole. The three powers agreed to consider all applications for arms or war materials by the countries of the Middle East in the light of these principles.[1] The United States, in particular, was concerned that its prestige had declined seriously in all Arab countries, and the State Department was anxious to convince the Arab states that it wanted the friendliest relations with both Israel and the Arab states on a strictly impartial basis. It was in the strategic interests of the United States that the Middle East be strengthened for defence against communist aggression, and that the countries in question obtain their arms from friendly sources.[2]

Initially the Arabs resorted to economic tactics: their boycott was consolidated by the closing of both the Suez Canal and the oil pipelines to Israel. The Iraq Petroleum Company transferred its headquarters from Haifa to Tripoli. Israel had to rely on oil imported by tankers, and started to explore for this commodity in the occupied territories. In 1949 Israel tried using the port of Eilat on the Gulf of Aqaba, but Saudi Arabia leased islands at the mouth of the gulf to Egypt, who then established shore batteries, in December 1950, at Sharm el Sheikh and Ras Nasrani on the southern tip of Sinai to close the gulf to Israeli shipping. In effect these moves did little damage to Israel, except psychologically; perhaps the most irritating consequence was the restriction placed on sea communications with the Zionists in South Africa who, together with their American counterparts, were Israel's most enthusiastic supporters. Britain repeatedly objected to Egypt, as British shipping was affected. For the Arabs, however, the principal benefit was a new interest in forming an independent Arab economic base in their own states. Arab economics were helped by the view held by many at that time that Europe was dependent on Arab oil, and that the oil lifeline of the West was the Suez Canal. In reality much of the oil for Europe passed through newly constructed terminals on the Mediterranean. But the Middle East's share of oil production did increase from 16.7 per cent in 1950 to 21.2 per cent in 1955, and its estimated share of the world's reserves from 45 per cent in 1950 to 75 per cent in 1956. In 1955 the Middle East supplied 79 per cent of Europe's oil; 45 per cent of this went through the Suez Canal, 33 per cent was carried by the Syrian pipelines and 4 per cent around South Africa. Much of Europe still relied on coal, but the United States, in 1955, depended on oil for 67 per cent of its energy needs. It was anticipated that the European demand for oil would increase.[3]

The First Arab–Israeli War, however, did not unify the Arab world. Rather it led to upheavals in individual Arab countries, often fomented by a new, young and disillusioned generation which had been nurtured on what was considered the injustice of Zionist dispossession of Arab land with the assistance of the Western powers. This emerging Arab nationalism found a common focal point in the hatred of Israel. But it also disliked what it saw as the reactionary influence of the old dynasties. Increasingly, Arabism was not just synonymous with the Islamic religion, the Arabic language and the geographic area of Arabia. The inhabitants of North Africa stressed their Arab identity. This Arab renaissance which had both cultural, political and economic manifestations was not always understood by leaders in the West. Some members of the British Establishment, including Anthony Eden, were inclined to identify the bedouin as Arabs, and to think of the Egyptians as something else. During the 1930s and 1940s Arab writers and thinkers developed the idea of the *ba'ath* or renaissance of the Arab nation. In 1942 Nuri el Said and Abdullal developed ideas of the Greater Syria into the Fertile Crescent which would be formed by the union of Transjordan, Palestine, the Lebanon and Syria, and to include in the end Iraq and Saudi Arabia. Britain was disturbed by the likelihood of an adverse reaction to this by Egyptian nationalists and the obvious consequences for the British base in Egypt. In the 1950s, however, Britain resisted what it saw as the claims of Gamal Abdel Nasser to be a Pan-Arabic leader. The young generation's dislike of Western imperialism was partly fomented by a scorn for the defeat of France and the subsequent division between Gaullist and Vichy officers in the Levant, by the crushing with Anglo-Indian troops in 1941 of the Rashid Ali government in Iraq, and by Lampson's forcing Farouk – with British tanks in the palace grounds – to appoint Nahas Pasha as leader on 4 February 1942.[4] Egypt also, unlike the other Arab countries, had experienced a British presence, rather like that based in India, which tended to isolate itself from the Egyptian community and conduct its own social life in the insular surroundings of Shepheard's Hotel or the Gezira Country Club.[5]

The revolutions in the Arab countries, brought about by the humiliating defeat at the hands of Israel, started in Syria on 30 March 1949. A series of coups and counter-coups meant in effect that that country was ruled by Colonel Adib Shishakly between 1950 and 1954. During this time the Ba'ath Party gained in strength, particularly when it united with Akram Hourani's Socialist Party in 1952. Syrian army officers, however, feared a union with Iraq in which they would not have the senior appointment in a combined army. In Jordan the Arab refugees from Palestine made up one-third of the population, and although given Jordanian citizenship they remained a discontented element. One of their number assassinated Abdullah on 20 July 1951 in the al-Aqsa mosque in Jerusalem. The throne first passed to a mentally unstable son, and in 1952, to the British-educated King Hussein, then only seventeen. Nasser invited the young King to Egypt, and both Syria and Egypt were critical of Hussein's British connections. He faced a difficult position as the Israelis mounted reprisal raids on frontier villages in retaliation for attacks by the Palestinian refugees in Jordan. Hussein was widely criticized for his reliance on Glubb, considered by some to be the real ruler of Jordan. As if to show his own independence, Hussein dismissed Glubb on 1 March 1956, and in October of that year elections returned a pro-Nasser government in Jordan. In Baghdad on 22 November 1952, what started as a demonstration by schoolchildren developed into arson and riots and military control. Similar outbreaks occurred until 1957. The country went through periods of martial law in between general elections. But from 1954 Iraq did embark upon a programme of social improvement. In the Lebanon Camille Chamoun became President in 1953 and for a while made overtures to Iraq and Egypt.[6]

Perhaps the most significant change occurred in Egypt. The conduct of the war against Israel convinced the younger officers that their rulers should be replaced. But initially the Wafd was returned to power and Farouk and Nahas Pasha reconciled. In 1950 Nasser was elected president of the Free Officers' Executive Committee. Following the Wafd's abrogation of the Anglo-Egyptian treaty moves were taken to isolate the Suez base. Britain tried to counter persistent guerrilla attacks by surrounding the Ismailia police headquarters on 25 January 1952. Resistance led to the deaths of fifty Egyptian police, and the next day, 'Black Saturday', a Cairo mob, instigated by the Muslim Brotherhood, destroyed British property. Nasser was in one of the units that helped to restore order and was encouraged by this demonstration of militant action. As governments came and went Nasser and his officers prepared for a coup scheduled for August 1952. Neguib was chosen as a figurehead, and the date was brought forward to 23 July. The coup was almost bloodless, and the next morning Anwar Sadat told the Egyptian people in the name of Neguib that the army had seized power to purge the country of the traitors and weaklings who had dis-

131

honoured Egypt. Farouk went into exile, and the revolution instituted social and land reforms which later came to be known as Arab socialism. The revolution took strong action against communist agitators and initially was largely nationalist rather than Pan-Arab. On 18 June 1953 Egypt was proclaimed a republic with Neguib as President and Prime Minister, and Nasser as his deputy. But Neguib was outmanœuvred by Nasser who replaced him in October 1954, at the same time as the repression of the Muslim Brotherhood. In a work published in 1954, *The Philosophy of the Revolution*, Nasser outlined his plans: Egypt was located at the coincidence of three circles: the Arab circle; the African circle and the Islamic circle. Egypt's wealth, size, population and religious and intellectual qualities made it the obvious leader of the Arab world, though Nasser did acknowledge that Egypt in the past had become somewhat detached from its Arab roots. The emerging Black African nations, struggling for their independence, would also look to Egypt which formed the link between Africa and the outside world. Cairo, with its ancient university, was also the major focal point in the Muslim world. It was obvious that to play the role envisaged by Nasser, Egypt would have to throw out Britain. Some British statesmen did not like Nasser's claims to be a grand Pan-Arabic leader, to say nothing of heading Africa, then largely still under the British Crown, and of the Muslim world with which Britain, because of its Commonwealth connections, felt a special identity. French strategists regarded *The Philosophy of the Revolution* as a revised edition of Adolf Hitler's *Mein Kampf*, and members of the French Ministry of Defence often drew the analogy between Nasser and Hitler. France, after all, had influence over most of North Africa.[7]

Following the First Arab–Israeli War, France was increasingly faced with demands for independence from the three Maghreb states in North Africa which also seemed to be wakening to a new Arab consciousness. In Tunisia, the Neo-Destour Party, under Habib Bourguiba, demanded autonomy and a parliament. Bourguiba was arrested, and later taken to France. There were acts of terrorism against the French police, and after various concessions Bourguiba returned in June 1955 to lead Tunisia with his gradualist tactics, and immediately won a campaign against an opponent who favoured a more violent approach. In Morocco the nationalist movement spread with the support of the Arab League, but was resisted by the French colony in that country. But French reprisals led to massive support for the Sultan, Muhammad V, and on 6 November 1955 France acknowledged the independence of Morocco, the transfer of power which acknowledged French interests taking place on 2 March 1956. In Algeria, France had granted an elected assembly in 1947 and acknowledged many Muslim rights, but the French community there prevented their practical application. An open Muslim rebellion started on 1 November 1954. By 1956 its headquarters were in Cairo.[8]

After 1949 Israel tried to consolidate its internal and international position. While maintaining a small regular army Israel introduced conscription for men and women: within forty-eight hours it could put into the field 200,000 soldiers. In November 1953, Moshe Sharett succeeded Ben-Gurion as Prime Minister. During the First World War Sharett had taken Ottoman citizenship and become an officer in the Turkish army. His approach was that of moderation and gradualism. Between February and September 1954 Egypt, anxious not to antagonize Britain and the United States, allowed shipping to and from Israel to pass through the Suez Canal. With the premiership of Pierre Mendès-France, Israel secured the sympathy of France. In August 1954 American Zionists tried to prevent the British evacuation of the Canal Zone, while at the same time attempting to secure Israel's use of the Suez Canal. Between 22 August and 3 September Israel mounted a number of reprisal raids in the Gaza strip, the first serious skirmishes since 1949. The *Bat Galim*, an Israeli-owned ship and the first to attempt the Suez passage since 1949, was seized by Egypt on 28 September for allegedly firing on Egyptian fishermen in the Gulf of Suez. The crew of the ship was finally released through Gaza on 1 January 1955. This test case confirmed the Egyptian boycott. Gradualism did not seem to achieve much.

Israel's image during these years was tarnished by several incidents. The Qibya raid of 14/15 October 1953, ordered by Ben-Gurion, achieved considerable international publicity. On that night Israeli soldiers killed sixty-six men, women and children of the village. Even sympathetic American newspapers compared the incident to the Nazi massacre of 185 men of the village of Lidice in Czechoslovakia on 10 June 1942 in reprisal for the assassination of an SS chief. Perhaps the worst Arab reprisal was the ambush of an Israeli bus on Scorpions' Pass, in the eastern Negeb, on 17 March 1954: 11 Isralis died. In retaliation, Israeli raiders hit the village of Nahhaleen, and killed 9 inhabitants. Britain threatened that Israel would have to fight both Britain and Jordan if it occupied any Jordanian territory. Henry A. Byroade, speaking for the State Department, warned Israel to drop the policy of force and retaliatory killings. In July 1954, possibly at the instigation of Ben-Gurion, a group of rather amateur Israeli agents tried to sabotage British and American property in Egypt in the hope of giving the impression that violent elements in Egypt opposed the *rapprochement* with Britain and the United States, and that the Egyptian government could not control these dissident elements. The operations failed, and the Egyptians later released details of the ring, and hanged two members on 31 January 1955. The Israeli Defence Minister, Pinchas Lavon, was seen by some as being responsible, but he tried to blame the affair on Shimon Peres, the Director-General of the Ministry of Defence, Moshe Dayan, and General Benjamin Givly, the chief of intelligence.

A consequence was the return of Ben-Gurion as Minister of Defence on 17 February 1955. Ben-Gurion had a special attachment to the Defence Ministry and had maintained that during his sojourn on a kibbutz as a shepherd. It was hoped that Ben-Gurion would be able to restore the Mapai Party's sagging fortunes for the forthcoming election. Ben-Gurion returned with his activist policies. Perhaps, even during Sharett's premiership, activism had been independently pursued through Ben-Gurion's cohorts, Peres and Dayan, in the Ministry of Defence. Sharett had complained to Lieutenant-General E. L. M. Burns, the United Nations commander, that he needed help from the United Nations against the Arabs on the border incidents so that he could win against that powerful bloc in Israel who wanted to retaliate with force. Ben-Gurion brought with him a philosophy that the only way to secure Israel was to force the Arabs, probably by military measures, to accept peace with Israel. Great Power and United Nations intervention were to be avoided, and the Arabs should be made to sue on Israel's terms. In doing this Israel might also add to its territory. For Ben-Gurion the Gaza strip was seemingly an obvious target: it was after all populated not by Egyptians, but by Palestinian refugees. On 28 February 1955 two Israeli platoons of paratroopers stormed an Egyptian encampment at Gaza and killed thirty-eight. The Israelis lost eight men. The United Nations Mixed Armistice Commission and the Security Council condemned Israel for a 'prearranged and planned attack ordered by Israeli authorities'. Ben-Gurion's policy of direct confrontation was under way.[9]

Israel returned to its policy of activism knowing that it had at least the support of France. Many French officers and members of the Ministries of the Interior and Defence disliked both Britain and the Arabs. Not only had the Israeli army earned their sympathy with its defeat of the Arabs, and in effect earlier of Britain, but Israel's victories over the Arabs were seen as having delayed the rebellions in North Africa. Some sections of the French Right also saw developments in the Middle East in terms of communism and identified Arab nationalism with Russia. Backing Israel was a means of countering this. The military and the Right were, however, often at odds with a diplomatic corps concerned to preserve France's relations with the Arabs, and particularly Syria. But, as Egypt and not Syria emerged as Israel's principal enemy, this opposition eased. When Ben-Gurion embarked on his policy of developing Israel's nuclear option, securing aircraft and an armaments industry, he turned to France. In January 1955 Paris overrode British objections, and agreed to sell Mystère aircraft to Israel. There was only a mild reaction in France to the Gaza raid. Ben-Gurion explained to the French Ministry of Defence that he had decided to use French equipment. France became Israel's principal source of weapons before the Suez–Sinai War of 1956 and the country where Israel's nuclear researchers learnt their trade.[10]

In effect, France replaced the United States as Israel's sponsor. The presidential election of November 1952 had returned Dwight D. Eisenhower and a Republican administration. Eisenhower chose as his Secretary of State, John Foster Dulles. Throughout his life Dulles had been preparing for this office. Anthony Eden told Eisenhower that he hoped the President would appoint someone else, but was informed that Eisenhower knew of no one so well qualified. Fairly late in life, Dulles had been a convert to fundamentalist Christianity, and was thus inclined to see the world in terms of good and evil, black and white with no greys. The emerging philosophy of neutralism was peculiarly abhorrent to the new Secretary of State. While at Versailles at the end of the First World War Dulles had acquired a suspicion of what he saw as British machinations. In the negotiations leading up to the signing of the Japanese peace treaty Dulles had dealt with Herbert Morrison, and the British Foreign Secretary had paid tribute to Dulles's helpful attitude when he urged the Cabinet to accept the terms. Eden, however, did not get on with Dulles. Indeed the new Republican administration reviewed the special relationship, and at Bermuda, in December 1953, Eden and Churchill learnt that Britain was no longer the special ally, but only one among a number of allies. At the Geneva Conference of 1954 Britain went its own way and Eden triumphed over Dulles. The special relationship was only revived again, at American instigation, when the leaders of the two countries met at Bermuda in early 1957 in the aftermath of the Suez crisis.[11]

Dulles had been a member of the American delegation to the United Nations in 1947–48 when the partition of Palestine was considered. He did not take much part in discussions, and had confined himself to legalistic niceties. Perhaps it was the lack of an over-enthusiasm for Zionism that led to accusations in 1949 that he was anti-Semitic.[12] Shortly after becoming Secretary of State, Dulles undertook a tour of the Middle East and gave the impression of American neutrality and impartiality in the Arab–Israeli dispute. Dulles's principal concern, as he told the American people when he returned in June 1953, was to encourage the area to strengthen itself against communism: the members of the Arab League seemed so engrossed in their quarrels with Britain, France and Israel that they did not seem to notice Russia. Israel felt betrayed. When Byroade, as Assistant Secretary of State, campaigned for the 'de-Judaization' of Israel, Abba Eban, the Israeli ambassador to the United States, protested officially. Eban also felt that the United States showed a reluctance to redress what he saw as the growing imbalance of arms in the Middle East.[13]

At the time of the Cold War, however, Washington's main preoccupation in the Middle East was to prevent Russian penetration, and even to secure a defence organization to fulfil the same role in the area as NATO did in Europe. Eisenhower, perhaps, saw Britain as the country best able to take the lead in this: Britain, after all, had considerable experience of the Arab world. Defence discussions between Washington and London in the early 1950s concluded that the Middle East would be largely a British responsibility. It was official American policy – though Britain at times doubted some of the manifestations of this – to help Britain to secure and consolidate its interests in the Middle East.[14]

British paramountcy in the Middle East was undermined by the birth of Israel. At the end of the First Arab–Israeli War Britain's military foothold in Arabia proper was restricted to the use of two air bases in Jordan, and two in Iraq. Britain's share of Middle East oil was also cut when Dr Mohammed Mossadeq secured the passage through the Iranian parliament (Majlis) on 1 May 1951 of a bill nationalizing the Anglo-Iranian Oil Company. The British Cabinet considered military action, but Washington approved of nationalization, urged restraint and sent a mediator to Tehran, Averell Harriman, who, *en route*, assured Hugh Gaitskell in Paris that he would do his best to sustain the British position. Just before handing over to Churchill, Attlee told his colleagues that Britain could not afford to break with the United States on an issue like this.[15] In the end the United States was convinced that Mossadeq was not the only alternative to communism in Iran. The Central Intelligence Agency arranged the overthrow of Mossadeq and the return of the Shah. The American ambassador, Loy Henderson, worked with his British counterpart, Sir Roger Stevens, to secure a satisfactory arrangement over oil. But it meant that the share of British capital invested in the oil industry of the Middle East dropped from 49 to 14 per cent, and the British share of oil production from 53 to 24 per cent. The American share increased from 44 to 58 per cent, and the American companies controlled 42 per cent of the capital. The image of British power faded in Arab eyes.[16] Saudi Arabia, furthermore, made moves towards the British-protected sheikhdoms in the Persian Gulf, and in August 1952 a Saudi expedition seized the Buraimi oasis. Relations between Britain and Saudi Arabia were strained. The attempted annexation had been arranged by Kim Roosevelt of the Central Intelligence Agency: the Saudis had tempted the Americans with the offer of oil concessions. But British-led Omani scouts drove the Saudis out. Roosevelt then attempted to bribe people in Abu Dhabi to cede the oasis to King Saud to open the way to the American firm Aramco, and to close it to the British-controlled Iraq Petroleum Company. But Britain was informed, and took the dispute to an international court where the Central Intelligence Agency tried to bribe the arbitrators.[17]

Britain's power in the Middle East, however, depended on its success in renegotiating the Anglo-Egyptian treaty of 1936. With the onset of the Cold War British ministers' and military officials' concern extended from just securing the Canal Zone to the defence of the Middle East as a whole. During 1946 talks with the Egyptians resulted in consideration being given by both sides to a draft treaty, but the whole issue foundered on Cairo's insistence on the unity of the Sudan with Egypt under the Egyptian Crown. Negotiations were broken off at the beginning of 1947, at a time when the Cabinet was considering throwing the Palestine question to the United Nations. The chief of the air staff warned that although Palestine was of special importance in the general scheme of defence, in war Egypt would be Britain's key position in the Middle East. With the formation of NATO Britain's responsibility for the defence of the Middle East remained, and London tried to interest Commonwealth countries, particularly Australia, New Zealand and South Africa, in playing a part. But in July 1950 Sir Robert Menzies, the Australian Prime Minister, failed to interest Cairo in the idea of a Commonwealth force to assist in Egyptian defence. In British eyes Egypt remained more concerned over Israel than the threat of Russia. In the Egyptian view Britain had exceeded the provisions of the 1936 treaty. As Morrison reported to the Cabinet, just before the Labour government was voted out of office, Cairo was determined to rid Egyptian soil of British troops irrespective of the consequences for Middle East security.[18]

On 16 October 1951 the Egyptian parliament, in a unanimous vote, abrogated the 1936 treaty with Britain. The new Conservative government sent reinforcements to the Canal Zone. The conflict escalated and strained Britain's military reserves. In January 1952 Churchill asked for token forces from the United States, France and Turkey, but met with a stony response. At the end of the month clashes in Ismailia resulted in about fifty Egyptians dead. This probably precipitated the riots of 26 January, 'Black Saturday', in which the Muslim Brotherhood, socialists and students, probably assisted by the police angered over the sacrifice of their fellows by the government at Ismailia, attacked the European quarter of Cairo with cries of 'Allah akbar' and 'We want arms to fight for the Canal'. The symbols of the British in Egypt, Shepheard's Hotel, Thomas Cook's and BOAC, were ravaged, together with 400 other buildings, and 17 British subjects killed. Farouk dismissed Nahas and the Wafd, and the new government worked for cordial Anglo-Egyptian relations. But Nasser and his officers advanced the date of their coup. Britain revived the idea of a Middle East defence organization in September 1952: the suggestion was dismissed by Neguib as 'hateful and horrible'. The officers were determined to get Britain out, and were prepared to risk the Sudanese question to do this; they probably hoped Sudan would voluntarily choose association with Egypt. On 6 February 1953 London and Cairo agreed terms for the liquidation of the Condominium and self-determination for the Sudan. The next month Eden secured the agreement of Washington – which had previously backed Egypt on the Sudan question – to a new approach for securing a workable British base in Egypt, and one which could be reactivated in time of war.

Washington helped London in the subsequent negotiations by dropping hints to the Egyptians of possible economic aid if a fair solution were achieved. But negotiations reached deadlock. To Eden, however, it seemed that Washington and its ambassador, Jefferson Caffrey, were encouraging Egyptian beliefs that Cairo was the victim of British 'colonialism'. The United States and Egypt, under Caffrey's guidance, entered into technological and economic agreements which disturbed Israel as well. But the possession of the nuclear deterrent was changing Britain's thinking. In any case the Anglo-Egyptian treaty was due to expire in 1956 and it seemed important to try to salvage something.

In December 1953 Britain decided to transfer the headquarters of the Middle East forces from the Canal Zone to Cyprus. By the middle of December, forty-one Conservative Members of Parliament had formed the Suez group. Led by Captain Waterhouse they fought to stop what they saw as a retreat from empire that had been uninterrupted since 1945. The Suez group felt that under Egyptian and American pressure the government had lost touch with British opinion: they fought to restore Britain's mission and won the emotional sympathy of Churchill. They were also supported by Zionists who suddenly found the Suez Canal the corner-stone of the Commonwealth. But the government became more conscious of air transportation and the Cape route: in 1952 the Comet service was started to Johannesburg; Union Castle Lines sailed between Cape Town and Southampton in under twelve days. As the terms were being negotiated Zionist sympathizers urged the transfer of the British base to the Negeb instead of Cyprus. Under the agreement of December 1954 which was to last for seven years, British troops were to withdraw within twenty months, the base would be maintained by 1,200 civilian technicians, and could be remilitarized in the limited emergency of an attack by a foreign power excluding Israel. Britain had rights of re-entry in the event of actual war within limitations. The Suez Canal was acknowledged to be an integral part of Egypt. The Suez group protested at this 'evacuation' of 'the linch-pin of the British Commonwealth': twenty-six members defied the government in the House. The British Empire lost an area the size of Wales: it was seen as the biggest retreat from empire since the division of the Indian subcontinent. The Anglo-Egyptian agreement of 1954 marked a significant decline in British power in the Middle East. British forces moved to Cyprus and had to contend with mounting terrorism on the Mediterranean island.[19]

At the time the Anglo-Egyptian agreement was being initialled Nasser started implementing one of the concentric circles of his Philosophy of Revolution; that of leading Black Africa. Nasser's nationalism had been founded on a hatred of British imperialism represented by Lampson's treatment of Farouk and British troops calling the

Egyptians 'wogs'. In July 1954 Nasser instigated wireless broadcasts in Swahili supporting Mau Mau terrorism and inciting Black British subjects in East Africa to rebellion. As British settlers were being savaged, Eden started to look to the Iraq controlled by Lawrence's old comrade, Nuri, as an alternative base for British influence. Dulles was also concerned about the gap in Western defences on the 'northern tier'. With his encouragement Turkey was trying to establish a northern alliance, and on 2 April 1954 Turkey and Pakistan formed the nucleus of this with a pact. The Secretary of State also sent a new ambassador, Waldemar Gallman, to Baghdad in September to investigate the possibilities of a defence arrangement including Iraq. Britain had some hesitations about allying with Pakistan, because of possible reactions in India. Nuri had ideas about using the alliance to revive his old ideas of a united Iraq, Syria, Lebanon and Jordan. He bitterly resented the rejection of his Fertile Crescent scheme in the early 1940s in favour of the Arab League centred on Cairo. Having secured his home base with rather dictatorial tactics, Nuri hoped to counter Nasser's claim to lead the Arab world. Nuri's policy reflected the historical rivalries between Iraq and Egypt. To achieve his aims Nuri accepted American arms on American terms, and told Nasser in Cairo in September 1954 that while he could accept Western help to counter the Russian threat, his commitments to the Arab League's collective security pact would prevent him from joining formal Western defence pacts. Nuri then went on to London and Ankara to lay the foundations of what emerged as the Baghdad Pact. Eden saw this arrangement as a means of reasserting British influence in the area. In the tradition of Bevin he was perhaps not especially keen to encourage American participation. Using Nuri, Eden possibly also hoped to isolate Nasser in the Arab world. Dulles did not expect the announcement of the agreement between Iraq and Turkey on 12 January. Iraq hoped that Britain would accede to the pact as soon as possible. Eden anticipated that Iran and Jordan might become members as well and that the pact might grow into a NATO for the Middle East. He does not appear to have included the United States in his calculations. The Foreign Secretary perhaps hoped for a reassertion of British paramountcy in the Middle East.

Eden travelled east. On the way he saw Nasser who, despite Eden's greeting in flawless Arabic, remained hostile to the envisaged pact. Nasser was increasingly attracted to philosophies of neutralism, and did not want the Arab world dragged into a conflict between East and West. Eight days after the meeting with Eden, Israel attacked Egypt with the raid on Gaza. Nasser decided immediately that it was necessary to increase Egypt's armaments. On 25 February, Iraq and Turkey formalized the pact. Dulles was taken by surprise; Byroade thought it an unfortunate development but said that the United States had no option other than to give its cautious approval. On his return from the

East, Eden dropped in to see Nuri in Baghdad to discuss Britain's accession. The Labour opposition was worried about the effect on Israel of the pact, but did not divide the House, and on 5 April 1955 Britain acceded formally to the pact. Pakistan joined in September, and Iran in November. Early in 1956 Harold Macmillan as Foreign Secretary worked for its extension to Jordan: the United States wanted Jordan in so as to relieve pressure on Iraq which was criticized for being the only Arab member. Eden's actions placed Dulles in a difficult position. The form the Baghdad Pact took, as the Near Eastern affairs section of the State Department warned, would antagonize Nasser and most other Arab leaders who shared his anti-British views. Dulles's principal concern was to block Russian expansion into the Middle East. The Baghdad Pact emphasized a division in the Arab world that could prevent overall Arab participation in this enterprise. Eden wanted to reassert British power and prestige in an area where Britain had been paramount for three decades. Increasingly, Eden also wanted to isolate Nasser who, through his propaganda, was setting out to challenge Britain's position in Africa. Dulles did allow Gallman to be an observer to the new pact organization in Baghdad, and by February 1956 it was apparent that the United States would give Britain support over the pact, moral and material, and possibly, after the presidential election of November 1956, might even join.[20]

Nasser, threatened both by the Baghdad Pact and the Gaza raid of 28 February 1955, needed money and arms to build his new Egypt that would form the centre of the three circles. He tried for arms from the West. Britain stalled: it was backing another part of the Arab world and was reluctant to arm a man inciting British subjects to rebellion elsewhere on the African continent. The Americans hesitated as well. Initially the Americans had refused: Churchill had told Eisenhower that it would be inappropriate for the Americans to give the Egyptians arms to kill British soldiers who had fought alongside American troops during the war. There was also another important factor: in the 1954 congressional elections the Republican share of the vote had dropped. Political analysts explained this in terms of Zionist displeasure with the Dulles policy of courting Egypt at the expense of Israel. Then, in April 1955, Nasser actively furthered his neutralist activities and departed for the conference of non-aligned nations at Bandung. *En route*, in Rangoon, Nasser spoke to Chou En-lai, Communist China's delegate about the aggressions of Israel. Chou agreed to place Nasser's difficulties over arms supplies to the Russians. Dulles was furious: the Communist Chinese were threatening Quemoy and Matsu. The Russians made the necessary overtures in Cairo between April and July, and then, on 20 July, explained to Nasser that as talks with the Americans were progressing well at the Geneva summit, the arms would have to come through Czechoslovakia. The Central Intelligence Agency uncovered what had happened and its head, Allen Dulles, urged his brother to get Byroade, then ambassador in Cairo, to put pressure on Nasser. John Foster had lost faith in Byroade's attempts to keep Nasser in the Western camp, and flew Kim Roosevelt there instead. When Nasser learnt this, he publicly announced Egypt's arms deal with Czechoslovakia before Roosevelt even arrived. Roosevelt was followed by Eric Johnson, the President's special representative, and George V. Allen, the Assistant Secretary of State. All to no avail. Eisenhower was not especially close to John Foster: the President preferred the company of George Humphrey, the Secretary of the Treasury, and his golfing cronies. But in September he had a heart attack while on holiday in Colorado, and Dulles, under the guidance of Vice-President Richard Nixon, took charge.

While Eisenhower was convalescing, Washington learnt of the scheme for which Nasser needed money: the Aswan dam. This Nasser felt would move Egypt into the modern age: harnessing the waters of the Nile would provide the energy. Earlier British feasibility studies had correctly predicted that this would ruin the Egyptian ecology and economy. But the World Bank, under the American, Eugene R. Black, concluded otherwise in its studies in 1953 and 1954. Nasser, after the Czechoslovak arms deal, let Washington know that he would prefer to finance the dam with American money, and so maintain his neutral posture. The American response was slow: Eisenhower was being protected from difficult matters; Humphrey saw the scheme as a British plot and Humphrey did not like Britain; one of Humphrey's closest friends, Herbert Hoover Jr, whom Dulles placed in charge of the negotiations saw it as a greedy ploy mounted by British manufacturers and construction companies. Discussions took place in Washington between Black, the Egyptian Finance Minister, Abdel Kaissouni, and the British ambassador, Sir Roger Makins, between 21 November and 16 December. The United States would provide $56m. and Britain $14m. for the first stage of the construction, and consider later grants up to $200m. Contingent on the Anglo-American grants, the World Bank would lend $200m. The American Zionists disliked the scheme as did the 'cotton' senators who felt their industry in the south would be damaged. Early in December Dulles secured Eisenhower's approval for a scheme that would lessen their domestic risks. An American emissary, Robert B. Anderson, would try to persuade Nasser that with a strengthened domestic position the President could negotiate a peace with Israel. But shuttle diplomacy between Cairo and Tel Aviv was fruitless: Nasser felt he could not speak for other Arab states; Ben-Gurion did not think the Aswan dam good for Israel. Dulles perhaps hoped that American financing would mean control of the Egyptian economy and thus no more arms from Czechoslovakia. But the Secretary of State became disillusioned with the domestic opposition, probably partly engineered by the anti-British alliance of Hoover and Humphrey.[21]

Relations deteriorated all around early in 1956. Nasser's suspicions of Eden were confirmed by the British efforts to secure Jordanian accession to the Baghdad Pact. Eden, possibly thinking that Macmillan was taking too independent a line as Foreign Secretary, moved him to the Exchequer, but the older man, reputedly bitter that Eden's accession to the premiership had destroyed his chances, only went on the understanding that as Chancellor he would still be the number two. Selwyn Lloyd, more amenable to Eden's interference in foreign affairs, replaced him. Lloyd was with Nasser in Cairo when Hussein dismissed Glubb on 1 March 1956. Nasser congratulated him on Britain's removing Glubb to improve relations with Egypt. Eden initially thought Nasser was behind Glubb's dismissal, but the former head of the Arab Legion probably persuaded the Prime Minister otherwise. But Eden had made his reputation as an opponent of Neville Chamberlain's policy of the appeasement of Europe. He saw the 1950s through the spectacles of the myths created largely for political ends, about the conduct of British policy in the 1930s. Eden was a finely charged thoroughbred. He was also sometimes on the drug benzedrine, as a result of three operations on his bile duct of which only the last one in Boston had been partially successful. Eden concluded that Nasser had to go.[22]

Dulles was wary about the visit of Nikita Khrushchev and Nikolai Bulganin to Britain in April. There, on 27 April, Khrushchev spoke about Russia preferring an arms embargo in the Middle East and offered Russian participation in this if it were organized by the United Nations. Nasser thought this threatened his arms supply from Russia and hastily recognized Communist China. Dulles was furious. Eden initiated meetings between the Foreign Office and the State Department to consider a coup against Nasser. British external intelligence, MI6, and the Central Intelligence Agency investigated the matter, but Dulles prevaricated. Dulles and Eden, however, were in agreement about the overall objective of Anglo-American policy from this point and throughout the Suez crisis: the removal of Nasser.[23]

Initially, Britain had pursued the Aswan dam loan as a way of maintaining some influence in Egypt at a time when Russian penetration was evident. But when Lloyd returned from the Middle East in March 1956 opinion was shifting. The Foreign Secretary feared that Nasser intended to undermine the government of Libya which was friendly to the West, and queried whether Britain should pursue the loan. On 12 March Eden spoke to Guy Mollet, the French Premier, and discussed the possibility of an Anglo-French alignment against Nasser. A Cabinet meeting of 21 March suggested that Nasser could be isolated by Anglo-American action: Britain could use Iraq to overthrow a regime sympathetic to Nasser in Syria, while the United States could use Saudi Arabia. Action could also be taken against Nasser, including the cancellation of the loan. Eisenhower, too, was thinking of isolating Egypt in the Arab world and winning over the Saudis. The President was depressed that Nasser had not responded to the Anderson mission and evidently did not intend to make peace with Israel. Britain, however, would have to make concessions to Saudi Arabia. The Foreign Office prepared a scheme on these lines, but Eden rejected it: he did not like American influence in Saudi Arabia. At the end of March, Lloyd warned Makins that Nasser would not get the money unless Egypt acknowledged Western interests in the Middle East. Early in May, at a NATO meeting in Paris, the Foreign Secretary and the Secretary of State agreed to let the Aswan dam project 'wither on the vine'.[24]

Nasser was warned of this decision through his intelligence agents. Cairo tried to let London know that it would nationalize the Suez Canal to find an alternative source of revenue. Hints were passed to the oriental counsellor to the British embassy, Trefor Evans, but, as he later admitted, he failed to put two and two together and went home on leave. It seems that neither the Foreign Office, nor the State Department anticipated Nasser's actions. Nasser, envisaging the possibility of a Russian loan, decided to force the issue. Suddenly he accepted the conditions that had been imposed: Black and Byroade had done their utmost to persuade him. The last British troops withdrew from the Canal Zone on 13 June: London decided that it could not renege on the agreements of 1954. Against this background Nasser sent his ambassador, Ahmed Hussein, to Washington. Dulles was having trouble with Congress. He summoned his staff and they decided that it was not worth fighting every clause of the loan through that body. There was some opposition to a sudden cancellation, but that was what was agreed. On 7 June Eisenhower had been stricken with an attack of ileitis and had undergone major surgery; for a while the President lost control of his faculties. He was still recovering in Gettysburg when Dulles informed him on 13 July of the new developments. Having decided to run again as President, Eisenhower resented having to take any political risks domestically for Nasser. But it seems that Eisenhower left the handling of policy to Dulles. Britain was informed but not consulted about Dulles's decision: the British tactic was to 'play this long'. The press releases were prepared before Dulles, accompanied by Hoover and Allen, saw Hussein on 19 July 1956. Hussein gave Dulles the opportunity for a staged show of temper when he patted his pocket in agitation at the drift of Dulles's statement and said that he had there a Russian promise of finance. Probably Hussein did not want Russian finance: the ambassador was pro-American and wanted American aid. But Dulles apparently retorted that anyone who built the dam would earn the hatred of the Egyptian people because the burden would be crushing: the United States was leaving that pleasure to Russia. Dulles seemed to doubt whether Russia would offer the money anyway. The British Cabinet decided on 20 July that it also had to withdraw from the dam project. Sir Harold Caccia told the Egyptian ambassador that the decision had been an economic one: Egypt was indulging in other expenditures which would prevent it from giving priority to the Aswan dam. Britain still wanted good relations with Egypt.[25]

All this Great-Power diplomacy that was to culminate in the Suez–Sinai confrontation in October 1956 took place against a background of renewed Israeli preparations for war against Egypt. These were partly prompted by the fedayeen, the special unit of 'self-sacrificers' who raided Israel from the surrounding countries. Established in April 1955 by Egyptian general headquarters, the fedayeen increased their activities in September. Opinion in Israel was particularly sensitive to the deaths of its citizens. Egypt also blockaded the Straits of Tiran in September, effectively stopping the movement of ships from the Red Sea to Eilat, and flights of the Israeli airline, El Al, to South Africa. On 29 September Cairo radio threatened that Israel's defeat was at hand. Dayan, holidaying in France, was summoned home by Ben-Gurion and told to make preparations for the capture of the Straits of Tiran to ensure the passage of shipping through the Gulf of Aqaba. The general elections of 2 November meant that Ben-Gurion became Prime Minister as well as retaining his portfolio as Minister of Defence. The new cabinet, however, opposed the scheme to take the straits by force. Ben-Gurion warned the Israeli parliament, the Knesset, on 2 January 1956 that Nasser's Czechoslovak arms deal had changed the balance between Egypt and Israel in a most serious and dangerous manner. Israel pursued the French connection as it emerged that Egypt was acquiring up to 250 modern aircraft, armoured vehicles and cannons. France was also worried: Nasser could send his obsolete weapons to the Algerian rebels. But changes in French ministries resulted in delays in furthering agreements on the supply of Mystère IVs, tanks and artillery to Israel in terms of the discussions between Shimon Peres and Maurice Bourgès-Maunoury in October 1955. Elements in France were also worried about the publicity in the Arab countries given to earlier French sales to Israel, and annoyed over Israeli exhortations to Jews in North Africa to emigrate to Israel. American approval was also necessary for the transfer of Mystère IVs as they were being manufactured for NATO. Early in 1956, however, Mollet's ministry came to power, and after talks between Peres and Bourgès-Maunoury, now Minister of Defence, and Christian Pineau, the Foreign Minister, Paris tried for American consent to the sale of the Mystères. Eisenhower, in February, had no objection to Israel acquiring twelve: he later observed that these twelve multiplied like rabbits. The first eight Mystères arrived in Israel on 11 April 1956. At the same time Israel was negotiating for the purchase of aircraft and Centurion tanks from Britain who agreed to sell six Meteor night-fighters. The United States, however, maintained its arms embargo. On 17 June Dayan and

Peres met members of the French secret service and learnt that Paris was prepared to provide Israel with what it wanted. Mollet and Pineau were informed about the discussions. It seems that the Israelis had hints of the possibility of an Anglo-French action against Egypt. Perhaps Dayan and Peres also were told, or surmised, that France was thinking of action in concert with Israel. At any rate Israel knew that it had a source of weapons to balance Nasser's supply from Czechoslovakia, both in quantity and quality.[26]

Sharett, the gradualist, had to go. He resigned as Foreign Minister on 18 June and was replaced by the activist, Golda Meir. On 20 June two destroyers bought in Britain, with crews trained by the Royal Navy, sailed into an Israeli port. Large quantities of arms were arriving in secret from France. Ben-Gurion who, unlike Dayan, had had doubts about the likelihood of an Israeli victory over the Arabs, acquired a new confidence.[27]

The origins of the Suez–Sinai War of 1956 can be found in the realignment of power in the Middle East that followed the First Arab–Israeli War of 1948–49. Changes of governments in the Arab states, humiliated by the recent defeat, meant that a new Arab nationalism was able to take root across North Africa and Arabia. This was largely motivated by what many Arabs saw as the existence of an aggressive, expansionist and alien state in their midst. Britain had lost its paramountcy over the Zionists in 1948. Between 1949 and 1956 British influence in the Arab world, as had been predicted by Bevin and the Foreign Office and their counterparts in the 1920s and 1930s, was shattered with the creation of the Zionist state. London did try to reassert its position with the formation of the Baghdad Pact, but in effect this constituted working with the old ruling houses and not the new nationalists. In a major retreat from empire, Britain lost what had been considered in the prenuclear age the essential base for Middle Eastern security, Egypt. This transfer of power invited Russian penetration. The United States, despite domestic opposition, tried a policy of even-handedness. Washington's priority was to close a gap in the West's security system; London's was considerations of imperial policy. France, too, was drawn in with the Algerian rebellion. By 1956 the Middle East was an area of Great-Power politics. And it was this power politics that made Israel's pre-emptive war against Egypt possible. Nasser's claims to be a great Pan-Arabic leader, his vision of Egypt as the centre of three concentric circles, challenged Britain's position not only in the Middle East but in Africa, and its special relationship with the Muslim world; it threatened France's base in Algeria; it offended American susceptibilities about neutralism. By the middle of 1956 those who saw the 1950s through an erroneous interpretation of the 1930s were increasingly making comparisons between Nasser and Mussolini and Hitler: even the Secretary-General of the United Nations, Dag Hammarskjöld, told Lloyd in April 1956

The origins of the Arab–Israeli Wars

that Nasser was comparable to Hitler in 1935.[28] Nasser's policies and propaganda effectively killed the tripartite agreement of 1950 by which the Western powers had tried to stabilize the Middle East. Nasser replaced Zionism as the threat to the British power base: the Philosophy of Revolution resulted in Britain and France arming Israel against Egypt. All three Western powers were in agreement: Nasser had to go. Where they differed was on the means and timing. Israel was the beneficiary: the Sharett policy of gradualism was finally eclipsed by Ben-Gurion's determination to force a peace on the Arabs on Israel's terms. But it was Great-Power politics that made this possible.

REFERENCES

1. *Department of State Bulletin*, Vol. 22, p. 886.
2. *Foreign Relations of the United States* 1950 (5), pp. 895–9, Department of State to Truman, sent 18 May 1950; pp. 913–15, Webb to Johnson, 25 May 1950.
3. D. A. Farnie, *East and West of Suez. The Suez Canal in History 1854–1956* (Oxford 1969), pp. 660–90.
4. Peter Mansfield, *The Arabs* (London 1978), pp. 1–154, 261–7; Jon Kimche, *The Second Arab Awakening* (London 1970), pp. 148–53; Howard M. Sachar, *Europe Leaves the Middle East* (London 1972), pp. 176–334.
5. See Trefor E. Evans (Ed.), *The Killearn Diaries, passim*; *contra* Lawrence Durrell, *The Alexandrian Quartet* (London 1957–60); *Monsieur* or *The Prince of Darkness* (London 1974).
6. John Glubb, *A Soldier with the Arabs* (London 1957), pp. 285–428; *Britain and the Arabs. A Study of Fifty Years 1908 to 1958* (London 1959), pp. 295–305; Mansfield, op. cit., pp. 305–10.
7. Anthony Nutting, *Nasser* (London 1972), pp. 12–73; R. Hrair Dekmejian, *Egypt under Nasser. A Study in Political Dynamics* (London 1972), pp. 82–118; Gamal Abdel Nasser, *The Philosophy of the Revolution* (Buffalo, New York 1959), *passim*; Sylvia K. Crosbie, *A Tacit Alliance. France and Israel from Suez to the Six Day War* (Princeton, NJ 1974), p. 18.
8. Mansfield, op. cit., pp. 310–16; Edgar O'Ballance, *The Algerian Insurrection, 1954–62* (London 1967), pp. 19–69; David C. Gordon, *The Passing of French Algeria* (London 1966), pp. 49–69; Jamil M. Abun-Nasr, *A History of the Maghrib* (Cambridge 1971), pp. 313–92.
9. Kennett Love, *Suez. The Twice-Fought War* (London 1970), pp. 1–80; E. L. M. Burns, *Between Arab and Israeli* (Toronto 1962), pp. 7–68; David Ben-Gurion, *Israel: A Personal History* (London 1971), pp. 378–443; Shablai Teveth, *Moshe Dayan* (London 1972), pp. 180–243; Moshe Dayan, *The Story of My Life* (London 1976), pp. 119–50; Farnie, op. cit., pp. 712–16; David Ben-Gurion, *Israel: Years of Challenge* (London 1964), pp. 45–70.

10. Crosbie, op. cit., p. 29–57.
11. Dwight D. Eisenhower, *Mandate for Change* (London 1963), p. 142; Townsend Hoopes, *The Devil and John Foster Dulles* (Boston 1973), pp. 3–328; Leonard Mosley, *Dulles: A Biography of Eleanor, Allen, and John Foster Dulles and Their Family Network* (London 1978), pp. 3–301; Victor Bator, *Vietnam: A Diplomatic Tragedy* (London 1967), pp. 19–23; *Cab 129*, 46, ff. 89–96, CP (51) 166, Memorandum by Morrison on Japanese Peace Treaty, 19 June 1951.
12. *Dulles Oral History* (Princeton University Library), Loy W. Henderson (7 Nov. 1963), ff. 1–3; Jacob J. Javits (2 March 1966), f. 3; *John Foster Dulles Papers* (Princeton University Library), Box 34, Dulles to Irving M. Ives, 28 Feb. 1947; Box 37, Dulles to Austin, 9 March 1948; Box 38, Silver to Dulles, 30 June 1948.
13. Robert W. Stookey, *America and the Arab States: An Uneasy Encounter* (New York 1975), pp. 136–7; Abba Eban, *An Autobiography* (London 1977), pp. 179–83.
14. Dwight D. Eisenhower, *Waging Peace* (London 1966), pp. 22–3; Ritchie Ovendale, 'The South African policy of the British Labour government, 1947–1951', *International Affairs*, **59** (1982–3), pp. 44–50.
15. *Cab 128*, 19, Cab 28 (51) 3, 16 April 1951; Cab 30 (51) 3, 23 April 1951; Cab 33 (51) 7, 10 May 1951; Cab 37 (51) 3, 28 May 1951; Cab 44 (51) 5, 21 June 1951; Cab 50 (51) 2, 9 July 1951; 20, Cab 60 (51) 6, 27 Sept. 1951; 21, Cab 52 (51) 1, 16 July 1951.
16. Eisenhower, *Mandate for Change*, pp. 159–66; Anthony Eden, *Full Circle* (London 1960), pp. 198–219; Mosley, op. cit., pp. 325–7, 347; Farnie, op. cit., pp. 678–9; H. G. Nicholas, *Britain and the United States* (London 1963), pp. 113–15.
17. Elizabeth Monroe, *Britain's Moment in the Middle East*, 2nd edn (London 1981), p. 172; Mosley, op. cit., pp. 348–9.
18. *Cab 129*, 43, CP (50) 283, Nov. 1950; *Cab 128*, 11, Cab 6 (47), Confidential Annex, 15 Jan. 1947; Ovendale, 'South African policy of the British Labour government', pp. 44–50; *Cab 129*, 45, CP (51) 140, June 1951.
19. Eden, op. cit., pp. 224–61; Lord Moran, *Winston Churchill, The Struggle for Survival 1940–1965* (London 1968), pp. 610–18; Eisenhower, *Mandate for Change*, pp. 150–9; Mosley, op. cit., pp. 349–50; Farnie, op. cit., pp. 691–717; Sachar, op. cit., pp. 580–618.
20. Eden, op. cit., pp. 219–23; Harold Macmillan, *Tides of Fortune* (London 1969), pp. 631–55; *Riding the Storm* (London 1971), p. 91; Love, op. cit., pp. 193–206; Hoopes, op. cit., pp. 320–3; Nutting, *Nasser*, pp. 74–90; Robert Stephens, *Nasser. A Political Biography* (London 1971), pp. 145–53.
21. Mosley, op. cit., pp. 379–400; Love, op. cit., 297–314; Hoopes, op. cit., pp. 323–36; Eisenhower, *Mandate for Change*, pp. 535–46; Nutting, *Nasser*, pp. 91–139.
22. Macmillan, *Riding the Storm*, p. 1; Selwyn Lloyd, *Suez 1956* (London 1978), pp. 32–48; Anthony Nutting, *No End of Lesson. The Story of Suez* (London 1967), pp. 28–35; Ovendale, *Appeasement and the English Speaking World*, *passim*; Eden, op. cit., Foreword, pp. 51–2, 518.
23. Hoopes, op. cit., pp. 336–7; Love, op. cit., p. 216.
24. Humphrey Trevelyan, *The Middle East in Revolution* (London 1970),

pp. 48–55; Lloyd, op. cit., pp. 32–72; Love, op. cit., pp. 308–10.
25. Nutting, *Nasser*, pp. 138–41; Stephens, op. cit., pp. 191–4; Eisenhower, *Waging Peace*, p. 9; Eden, op. cit., p. 422; Love, op. cit., pp. 314–22; Lloyd, op.cit., pp. 70–2; Mosley, op. cit., pp. 400–4; Hoopes, op. cit., pp. 340–2; Trefor Evans, Lecture on Suez at University College of Wales, Aberystwyth, 1971; Herbert Finer, *Dulles over Suez: the Theory and Practice of His Diplomacy* (New York 1964), p. 46.
26. Shimon Peres, *David's Sling. The Arming of Israel* (London 1970), p. 185; Dayan, op. cit., pp. 145–50; Crosbie, op. cit., pp. 57–67; Teveth, op. cit., pp. 237–50; Eisenhower, *Waging Peace*, p. 29; André Beaufre, *The Suez Expedition 1956* (London 1969), pp. 23–5.
27. Ben-Gurion, *Israel: A Personal History*, pp. 494–6.
28. Lloyd, op. cit., p. 66.

Chapter 9

THE SUEZ–SINAI WAR OF 1956

After the Anglo–American withdrawal from the Aswan dam venture, Nasser was probably left without any secure means of financing his scheme to bring Egypt into the modern age. But he was in a strong position domestically: an alleged 99 per cent of Egyptian voters had just elected him President. The nationalization of the Suez Canal Company had been considered earlier as a source of revenue, but even that would not provide all the necessary foreign exchange. It would, however, be something. And, probably, during the diplomatic consultations between Cairo and Moscow that immediately followed Dulles's interview with Hussein, Russia agreed in principle to help. In any case Nasser felt that his new Egypt had been slighted. He had heard the news of the renege in the company of his fellow neutralist, Jawaharlal Nehru, with whom he had had discussions in Yugoslavia together with Marshal Tito on such subjects of interest to the three non-aligned leaders as the war in Algeria and relations between the Third World and the power blocs. Nehru had commented on the arrogance of people in the West. Nasser made secret plans to seize the Canal Company's offices. On 26 July, Nasser, speaking in Alexandria, referred to his revolution restoring Egypt's sense of dignity: no longer were Eygptian leaders left waiting in the offices of the British High Commissioner; in Egypt the Russian arms became Egyptian arms. He gave a history of Palestine and accused Britain, erroneously, of promoting Zionism to combat Arab nationalism. The West's terms for the Aswan dam loan were 'imperialism without soldiers': with Eugene Black Nasser had felt he was sitting in front of Ferdinand de Lesseps. That was the signal for the seizure of the company's premises. Nasser concluded by declaiming that the days of alien exploitation were over: the Suez Canal and its revenues would belong to Egypt. Nasser's military experts had assured him that it would take Britain and France at least a month to send a military expedition.[1]

Eden heard the news at a dinner at Number 10 given for Feisal and Nuri, Nasser's rivals in the Middle East. Apparently the guests encouraged the Prime Minister to respond with resolution, but warned him of the danger of allying Britain with France and Israel to destroy Nasser because of the effect that would have on Britain's relations with the Arab world. The leader of the opposition, Hugh Gaitskell, was also there. After the guests had departed those members of the Cabinet, Eden, Lord Salisbury, Lord Kilmuir, Lord Home and Lloyd, together with three of the service chiefs, Lord Mountbatten, Field Marshal Sir Gerald Templer and Sir Dermot Boyle, discussed the matter. The American chargé d'affaires, Andrew Foster, and Jean Chavel, the French ambassador, were present as well. Jacques Georges-Picot, the director-general of the Canal Company, was kept waiting outside. The Prime Minister and his colleagues rejected recourse to the Security Council: the issue would just be delayed there. Their concern was how far the United States would support economic sanctions against Nasser and, if necessary, military action. The chiefs of staff were instructed to produce a study of the forces needed to seize the canal and how they would be disposed if military action were necessary. Lloyd told Foster that he inclined to the view that the only solution would be for a Western consortium to take over and operate the canal, establishing itself by military force if necessary.[2]

Initially, London wanted to act together with Washington and Paris. But most of the British leaders failed to appreciate the significance of American elections. In 1949 the Permanent Under-Secretary's committee at the Foreign Office, headed by William Strang, had pointed to the dangers of this factor for Anglo-American relations. Bevin had had bitter experience of it. Eisenhower wanted to be re-elected President: this time on the platform of peace. It was his main preoccupation. He could not afford to have the principal allies of the United States fighting what the American public would probably regard as an imperial war. His administration had, after all, avoided allying itself with Britain and France in the Middle East, and had tried to pursue a policy of even-handedness towards the Arabs and Israelis at the cost of Zionist discontent in the United States. Eisenhower wished to project the image of the United States as an anti-colonial power. Dulles understood this. But the Secretary of State during the previous year had had considerable control of policy towards the Middle East during Eisenhower's illnesses. Nasser had offended Dulles, and John Foster agreed with Eden that the President of Egypt had to go. The only way of reconciling Eisenhower's election preoccupation with their objective was to delay any military action until after the presidential elections. As a lawyer, Dulles was also conscious of the possible consequences of Nasser's nationalization for the American-operated Panama Canal.[3]

On 27 July Eden told the House of the serious situation Nasser's action had created. Immediately afterwards the Cabinet met together with some of the chiefs of staff. It was told that the canal was vital to Western Europe: two-thirds of the oil supplies for that area passed through it. The Cabinet decided unanimously that if economic and political pressure failed, then Britain would have to be prepared to use force. The threat might be enough. But as all British interests in the Middle East were threatened, Britain should be prepared to act on its own. This would be a last resort. The chiefs of staff were ordered to make the necessary military preparations. Eden informed Eisenhower that same day that firm action was necessary otherwise Anglo-American influence in the Middle East would be destroyed. Economic pressures on their own were unlikely to be successful, and Britain was, in the last resort, prepared to use force. But the Prime Minister thought that the first step should be for France, the United States and Britain to align their policies, and put maximum pressure on Cairo.[4]

Eisenhower knew the British position both from Foster and Eden. Dulles was in South America, so the President consulted with Hoover and they decided to send Robert Murphy, the Deputy Under-Secretary, to the proposed meeting in London. The President was also told that Pineau had compared Nasser's action to Hitler's seizure of the Rhineland: the Foreign Minister argued that the West should act immediately and in strength otherwise Europe would find itself dependent on the goodwill of the Arab powers. On 30 July Murphy met Pineau in London and learnt about American naïvety. Macmillan, with Eden's acquiescence, impressed on Murphy that Britain and France were prepared to participate in a military operation. Lloyd told the Under-Secretary that Nasser would be unimpressed by economic and political pressures unless there were military preparations in the background. Significantly, Murphy advised that American public opinion was not prepared for the use of force: the possibility of military intervention should be kept in the background. Murphy appreciated Eisenhower's anti-colonialism and the influence of Hoover who disliked Britain and that country's oil interests in the Middle East – the Central Intelligence Agency had constantly tried to undermine the latter, presumably with presidential approval. Murphy saw Lloyd and Pineau on 31 July; that day Paris accepted British command of forces that might be used. Dulles, just back from Peru, met Eisenhower to discuss reports from Murphy that Britain had decided to 'break Nasser': it would take six weeks to mount the military operation. The President immediately despatched his Secretary of State with a message for Eden asking for a conference of maritime nations before corrective measures were taken: that would have 'a great educational effect throughout the world'. Initial military successes might be easy, but the eventual price would be too high. If American forces were to be used it would be necessary to show that every way of resolving the matter peacefully had been tried. Should such efforts fail, then world opinion would understand that 'we simply could not accept a situation that would in the long run prove disastrous to the prosperity and living standards of every nation whose economy depends directly or indirectly upon East–West shipping'.[5]

In London Dulles saw Lloyd and Pineau on 1 August. The Secretary of State reiterated Eisenhower's policy: what was needed was a conference of the users of the canal. Washington did not exclude the use of force, but it needed to be backed by world opinion. Lloyd explained that Britain might have to use force in the end. Dulles ceded that Nasser would have to be made to 'disgorge'. But Dulles was obviously playing for time: he thought it would take three weeks to prepare for the envisaged conference, but 16 August was the compromise date agreed. Dulles was cheered by a crowd in Downing Street and was pleased. He also saw Macmillan and was told that the question for Britain was one of survival. The Secretary of State met Eden privately the next day. In view of their clash at Geneva in 1954 the two men appear to have had a friendly talk. Dulles was particularly flattered by the Prime Minister's suggestion that he would go down in history as one of the great foreign ministers. It appears he gave Eden the assurance that he understood the Anglo-French position, and that Britain could always count on the moral support and sympathy of the United States. Eden offered the details of the Anglo-French military preparations, but Dulles interrupted to say that it would probably be better if Washington did not know. Presumably Dulles had possible domestic complications in mind; and the Central Intelligence Agency's activities were such that it would find out anyway; friendly exchanges between American and British military officials would also keep Americans apprised. After this warm talk both London and Washington were relieved and pleased.[6]

On 2 August Gaitskell, a friend of Israel, told the House that Nasser's aggressive intentions were clear: the Egyptian President intended to destroy Israel, subvert Jordan and other Arab states and create his own Arab empire from the Atlantic to the Persian Gulf. The Suez episode was part of the struggle for the mastery of the Middle East. Nasser's speeches were reminiscent of those of Hitler. In the Shadow Cabinet Gaitskell's pro-Israeli stance was countered by George Brown. The Shadow Cabinet later veered away from supporting the government's position. Though admittedly not fully informed of the Cabinet's preparations for the possible use of military force, the opposition mounted an attack on government policy virtually without precedent in the post-war era of bipartisan foreign policy.[7]

Eisenhower became increasingly involved in his election campaign. He wanted to delay the use of force until after its successful conclusion, and was probably disturbed by Eden's letter to him of 5 August. The Prime Minister did not think Nasser a Hitler, but the parallel with Mussolini was close. Thus Nasser's removal, and the installation of a regime less hostile to the West, was important. If the forthcoming conference ensured that Nasser disgorged his spoils, he would be unlikely to maintain his internal position. Eden concluded that

London was determined that Nasser should not get away with it, because if he did the British people's existence would be at Nasser's mercy.[8]

Britain and France prepared for the possible use of force.[9] At the meeting of the maritime nations in London between 16 and 23 August Dulles, in line with Eisenhower's thinking, suggested an international Suez Canal Board, and it was agreed that Sir Robert Menzies, the Australian Prime Minister, would take the suggestion to Nasser. On 24 August Macmillan again told the Secretary of State that Britain and France were determined that if diplomatic pressure did not work, they would have to use force.[10] Eisenhower wrote to Eden on 2 September reiterating that American public opinion flatly rejected the use of force: the President doubted that he could get congressional support for the lesser support measures Britain might want. Peaceful means had to be exhausted first.[11] On Duck Island Dulles devised another delaying tactic, what later became known as the Suez Canal Users' Association: the users should manage the canal themselves and prevent Nasser from making a profit. Lloyd received the plan just before leaving for Paris: he told Pineau that he was worried that Dulles intended to delay matters and so make a military operation impossible.[12] Eisenhower stressed the need for delay in another letter to Eden on 8 September: American public opinion was not yet ready for the use of force; though there should be no capitulation to Nasser, slower and less dramatic measures should be explored. But the President implied that force might in the end be necessary if Nasser resorted to violence. Then it would be Nasser and 'not we' who were violating the United Nations charter. This policy tied in closely with Eisenhower's election campaign on the platform of peace.[13] Macmillan favoured the Users' Association, and London decided Dulles was acting in good faith. But the government's precarious position in the House was undermined when Dulles, during a debate on the 12/13 September, said that the United States did not intend to shoot its way through the canal. Britain took the affair to the United Nations, and revised the military plans with France to allow for more time.

Between 20 September and 1 October Macmillan was in the United States. He saw Eisenhower on 24 September and found the President very keen to win his election. Eisenhower was sure that Nasser had to go. The question was how to achieve this. Macmillan made it clear that Britain could not play it long without aid on a large scale. When he returned the Chancellor assured Eden that Eisenhower was determined to stand up to Nasser. Macmillan also saw Dulles who was angry about the reference to the United Nations. In any case the Secretary of State hoped that nothing serious would happen until the presidential elections were over. Dulles gave no indication that he did not recognize Britain's right to use force. Macmillan acknowledged later that he should have attached greater weight to the date of the presidential election. The Chancellor arrived back in Britain to Dulles's statement that he did not know of any teeth in the users' association.[14] Eden felt that Dulles had placed him in an impossible situation. Under criticism from sections of his party for not taking more resolute action and from others who opposed force, threatened by the French that the weather would preclude military action after the end of October, and believing that Pineau did not want a settlement at all, and faced with an opposition determined to undermine national unity, Eden's health deteriorated. The Prime Minister collapsed on 5 October, and had to resort to benzedrine.[15]

In New York Lloyd was encouraged by the attitude of the Egyptian Minister for Foreign Affairs, Dr M. Fawzi, who went some way to agreeing on the principles governing the operation of the Suez Canal, but was vague on the important aspect of application. Lloyd warned the Security Council on 12 October against exaggerated optimism. That day Eisenhower undermined Britain's position with a statement about these developments: 'it looks like here is a very great crisis that is behind us'. Even Dulles appeared shocked, and murmured to Lloyd that the Foreign Secretary should not pay too much attention to what people said in the middle of an election campaign. That evening the Secretary of State suggested to Lloyd that the Users' Association should give 90 per cent of the dues to Nasser. Lloyd did not consider this a way of securing reasonable counter-proposals from Egypt. On 13 October the Foreign Secretary warned Eden that Egypt might feel that the critical phase was over: Eisenhower's naïve statement had shown the danger of excessive optimism. That weekend the Conservative Party appeared to achieve a united front at its Llandudno conference. Eden told the delegates that he agreed with Eisenhower's dictum that peace needed justice or it was not peace: force was the last resort but it could not be excluded.[16]

During August and September Paris, in General André Beaufre's words, 'obsessed by Israel', had been increasingly concerned over what it saw as London's attempts to delay possible military operations – 'the hesitation waltz'.[17] The situation was to Israel's advantage as that country's leaders, since early 1955, had been working towards a pre-emptive strike against Egypt. As Dayan later observed the Sinai War was the joint product of a sharpening of the conflict between Israel and its Arab neighbours and of the Anglo-French decision to use force to take control of the Suez Canal Zone; but for the Anglo-French action Dayan doubted whether Israel would have been able to launch the campaign.[18]

As early as 29 July 1956 French defence officials started to draw up contingency plans for a possible operation with Israel, independent of any military moves with Britain: ten officers, Pineau, Mollet and Bourgès-Maunoury were involved. During August Bourgès and a few of the military planned for a joint attack with Israel on the canal.

Deliveries of weapons to Israel were accelerated, and defence contacts between the two countries increased. According to André Martin, the chief of the air force, the Israelis were not then apprised of the Anglo-French plans. Until September, when Dulles made it clear that Washington opposed force, the Americans were kept informed.[19] On 1 September Dayan was told of the Anglo-French plans and that Admiral Pierre Barjot thought that Israel should be invited to take part. Barjot met an Israeli emissary in Paris on 7 September: soundings were taken as to Israel's likely attitude. Later that month Peres went with instructions that he was to ensure that in any conflict Britain would not go to Jordan's assistance. He reported to the Israeli cabinet on 25 September: Paris had invited discussions on joint military action against Egypt. Ben-Gurion was determined that this should be a co-operation of equals, and that Britain should ensure Jordan's neutrality. The Prime Minister hoped to gain control of the Straits of Tiran so that Eilat could become a large port and the Negeb flourish. He sent Golda Meir, Peres, Dayan and Moshe Carmel to France on 28 September. Pineau told the Israelis that he wanted action before the American presidential elections: Eisenhower would not want to appear to the electorate as one prepared to accommodate the Russians and sacrifice Britain and France. The discussions revealed that France did not have the bombers to take out the Egyptian aircraft that could bomb Israeli cities. British participation would be decisive. Joint talks continued in Jerusalem from 1 October. Ben-Gurion, after discussions with members of his government, emphasized the need for British participation – otherwise Israeli cities could be bombed. Before the French visitors left contingency decisions were taken. Ben-Gurion gave instructions for urgent preparations. During these there were reprisal raids against Jordan. On 5 October London warned Ben-Gurion that an Iraqi division was going to enter Jordan: Britain would go to Jordan's aid if that country were attacked.[20]

Barjot and General Paul Ely developed plans for Franco-Israeli action based on the assumption of British and American neutrality. Conferences with the Israelis were held in Paris from 12 October under General Gazin. It was clear that Israel would only attack if guaranteed Britain's neutrality. Israel's action near the canal would be token: its operation would concentrate on securing the Straits of Tiran.[21] On 3 September Lloyd had mentioned to Lester Pearson, the Canadian Minister of External Affairs, that Israel could take advantage of the situation and make an aggressive move against Egypt; that could help Britain out of immediate difficulties.[22] But, in effect, it was France that asked Britain to help it out of its difficulties with Israel. On 14 October Albert Gazier and Maurice Challe met Eden and Anthony Nutting at Chequers. Eden agreed to ask Nuri to suspend Iraqi movements into Jordan. When reminded by Gazier that Egypt had claimed that it was not bound by the Tripartite Declaration, Eden concluded that Britain was under an obligation to stop Israel from attacking Egypt. After this, Challe outlined a plan for Britain and France to gain physical control of the Suez Canal. Israel should be invited to attack Egypt across Sinai. Once Israel had seized all, or most of the area, Britain and France would then order Egypt and Israel to withdraw from the canal and allow an Anglo-French force to occupy it to safeguard it from damage. This pretext of separating the combatants would restore the canal to Anglo-French management and place the terminal ports, Port Said and Suez, in Anglo-French hands. Britain and France would then be able to supervise the shipping and break the Egyptian blockade of Israel. Gazier and Challe did not say that the Israelis had agreed to this, but it was clear that France had made preliminary soundings. Eden's response was non-committal: he would give the suggestions careful thought.[23] The Prime Minister summoned Lloyd back to London. Nutting briefed the Foreign Secretary who thought the French plan a poor one. The Cabinet, including Home, Macmillan, Kilmuir and Nutting, had an indeterminate discussion and Eden decided that he and Lloyd should go and see Mollet and Pineau in Paris.[24] On 16 October the four met in Paris. Mollet and Pineau gave no indication of the state of their planning with Israel: Lloyd thought it was limited to France's supplying aircraft. Pineau said he believed that the Israelis would attack soon. The Prime Minister agreed that, subject to the approval of their cabinets, Britain and France would implement the Anglo-French military plan (Musketeer Revise), to safeguard the canal and stop the spread of hostilities. In conclusion the French asked if Britain would fight to defend Nasser. Eden thought not, but that Britain would intervene to safeguard the canal. Back in London, Lloyd told Nutting that there would be further consultations in Paris between French and Israeli representatives: the Foreign Secretary hoped that Britain would not be directly associated with these talks, but the possibility could not be ruled out.[25] On 18 October the British Cabinet assembled: before it met Lloyd saw R. A. Butler and mentioned Anglo-French intervention to separate Israel and Egypt in the canal area. The Cabinet agreed that Britain and France should intervene to protect the canal if Israel attacked Egypt.[26]

The same day Mollet invited Ben-Gurion to Paris. France toughened its Algerian policy: Ben Bella and four of his nationalist associates were arrested. On 19 October Israel received from France a document, signed by Eden, stating that Britain would not aid Egypt if there were war with Israel; Britain would, however, defend Jordan if it were attacked; Britain and France would intervene to ensure the operation of the canal if either Egypt or Israel did not withdraw. Paris probably transmitted this without Eden's authorization. Indeed, French emissaries arrived in Israel on 21 October and tried to negotiate on this 'British proposal'. It was a French proposal, originally made at Chequers on 14 October by Challe. Paris was probably using

London as a stooge. That evening an Israeli delegation including Ben-Gurion, Dayan and Peres flew to Paris.[27] That same day a government opposed to the West was elected in Jordan. At Chequers a group of Cabinet ministers including R.A. Butler and Macmillan decided it was important that Britain be represented at the Franco-Israeli meeting scheduled for the next day. Lloyd and one of his private secretaries, Donald Logan, were despatched incognito.[28]

On the afternoon of 22 October in a villa in Sèvres, Mollet, Pineau, and Bourgès-Maunoury talked to Ben-Gurion, Peres and Dayan. Ben-Gurion outlined a comprehensive plan for the Middle East: Jordan should be divided between Iraq and Israel; Lebanon should give up some of its Muslim districts and become a stable state based on the Christian areas. Britain would exercise influence over Iraq and the southern parts of the Arabian Peninsula; France's sphere would be the Lebanon, possibly Syria, and France would also have close relations with Israel. There would be international status for the Suez Canal, and the Straits of Tiran would be Israel's. The French shifted the conversation to the military campaign: it had to be launched within a few days. Pineau suggested a timetable claiming it as being British, whereas in reality it was French. Indeed, French duplicity was apparently evident in the separate talks with both the Israeli and the British representatives. Lloyd was told that Israel had decided to attack Egypt. The French might have decided that, but at that stage Israel had not: Ben-Gurion did not want to hurry the military campaign, but instead to take time to clarify the political possibilities. Lloyd was not informed before he went into the Franco-Israeli meeting of the extent of the latter's joint military plans. Ben-Gurion said that Israel would not start a war with Egypt, but would only respond if attacked. Dayan, however, said that Israel would take reprisal action which could be in the vicinity of the canal. Britain and France could then demand that Egypt evacuate the zone, and that Israel should not advance beyond the canal. If Egypt refused, Anglo-French bombing raids on Egyptian airfields could start the next morning. Lloyd refused to agree to French planes operating from Cyprus, and insisted that the Israeli action would have to be a 'real act of war'. Dayan assured him that Israel would do this. Lloyd warned Ben-Gurion of the dangers inherent in this sort of military operation: the uniting for peace procedure could be invoked in the General Assembly to override the British and French vetoes; the American attitude was uncertain; Canada would probably oppose what had happened. The military operation might have to be stopped after a few days. The British Foreign Secretary tried to make it clear that an agreement between Israel, France and Britain to attack Egypt was impossible: it could result in the slaughter of British subjects in Arab countries. There was some discussion as to whether it would be possible for Britain and France to intervene within thirty-six hours of the start of the Israeli campaign. Nothing was agreed at Sèvres: Lloyd left at midnight to report to his colleagues.

On 23 October Lloyd saw his senior colleagues and then the Cabinet: the Foreign Secretary doubted whether Israel would launch an attack in the immediate future. Eden felt that Britain could not keep its forces in a state of readiness for much longer. Lloyd was doubtful about the prospects for a negotiated settlement, and what was possible would not diminish Nasser's prestige. Macmillan appears not to have mentioned the crucial factor: the timing of the American presidential elections. The Cabinet then adjourned so that Lloyd and Eden could see Pineau who was flying to London. The meeting of the three over dinner that evening concentrated on defining the actions Britain and France would take if Israel attacked Egypt. Lloyd wrote to Pineau afterwards making it clear that Britain had not asked Israel to take action: London had only stated its reactions in the event of certain things happening. It was decided there should be another meeting at Sèvres. Lloyd had to answer questions in the House. He and Eden agreed that Patrick Dean, a deputy Under-Secretary at the Foreign Office, accompanied by Logan, should go instead. The next morning Eden told Dean that the discussions were only to be about actions which might be taken in certain contingencies: British forces would not go in unless there were a threat to the canal. The Cabinet then met and was told of the military dilemma; it was agreed that the objectives of any military operation would be to secure control of the canal and defeat Nasser. Eden agreed that unless Anglo-French action led to the speedy collapse of Nasser the effect in other Arab countries would be serious. The greater risk was that Nasser's influence would grow: he was plotting coups in many Arab countries and the seizure of the canal gave Britain a reason for intervention that might not recur. But the action had to be quick and successful.[29]

In Paris, on 23 October, Ben-Gurion had to be stiffened. Peres and Dayan tried, and in the end Dayan proposed a military schedule to Pineau and explained that it had not been authorized by Ben-Gurion. It was this that Pineau had taken to London, and presumably discussed with Lloyd and Eden. Dayan's scheme envisaged only localized fighting by Israel on the first day: Israeli forces would operate at Mitla, about 30 miles (50 km) from Suez, and would be large enough to commit what Britain called a 'real act of war'. Britain, however, would not be told of the Israeli dispositions, and would be misled into thinking that the operation was in the north and not the south.[30]

Ben-Gurion still hesitated: he wanted to delay the campaign until after the American presidential elections and secure American support. But by the morning of 24 October Ben-Gurion was talking to Dayan about 'when' and not 'if'. Dayan set D-Day for the Israeli army at 5 p.m. on Monday 29 October; for Britain and France it would be the Wednesday. Israel would secure the Straits of Tiran. Ben-

Gurion told the French this before Dean and Logan arrived. Clearly, as Dayan noted, Israel would act on its own and not in partnership with Britain and France. This was his assessment of the conclusions of the meeting of the representatives of the three countries that afternoon. Dayan refused to give details of Israel's operational plan to the French and the British. While the discussions were in progress a document was typed on plain paper in an adjoining room outlining the contingency plan and anticipated action in given circumstances. This outlined a 'large-scale' Israeli attack on Egyptian forces on 29 October with the aim of reaching the Canal Zone the following day; an Anglo-French ultimatum followed by an attack on Egypt early on 31 October; Israeli occupation of the west shore of the Gulf of Aqaba and the islands in the Straits of Tiran; provided Israel did not attack Jordan, Britain would not go to its ally's aid; all parties were enjoined to the strictest secrecy. Dean and Logan did not expect anything to go on paper. They discussed the matter, and decided that Dean should sign the document merely as a record of the discussions. Pineau had suggested that the document provided for ratification by the three governments but, as yet, there is no evidence to corroborate his claim.[31]

Dayan immediately ordered his chief of operations to mobilize Israeli units in secrecy, and to give the impression that this was aimed against Jordan. Dean reported that evening to Eden, Lloyd, Macmillan, Butler and the Secretary for Defence, Anthony Head. Earl Mountbatten was also present. The contingency plan was referred to the full Cabinet on 25 October. The Prime Minister said that Israel was likely to attack Egypt on 29 October. There should be an Anglo-French ultimatum so that the two countries would seem to hold the balance between Egypt and Israel. Lloyd supported him: unless prompt action were taken to check Nasser's ambitions Britain's position would be undermined throughout the Middle East. The Cabinet considered whether such action would offend the United States. Disapproving noises were anticipated, but it was thought that, in view of American behaviour, Washington would have no reason to complain. The significance of the date of the presidential elections does not seem to have been considered. The Cabinet decided, without dissent, to act as Eden had suggested in the event of an Israeli attack on Egypt. Eden wrote to Mollet affirming that, in the situation envisaged in the talks at Sèvres between 22 and 24 October, Britain would take the planned action. Britain did not, it appears, communicate this to Israel. Mollet, however, saw fit to send Ben-Gurion a copy.[32]

On the available evidence it seems that Paris concealed from London the extent of prior Franco-Israeli planning. In effect the contingency plan typed at Sèvres on 24 October was in origin French, and modified by Dayan to overcome Ben-Gurion's objections. As Dayan had observed it preserved Israel's independent action, and enabled that country to fight its own war to secure the Straits of Tiran. Where the British Cabinet miscalculated was on the importance of the timing of the presidential election. Macmillan failed to emphasize Dulles's warnings on this. It seemed that as military action appeared likely – and the Americans knew this both from Central Intelligence Agency sources and through military exchanges between both joint chiefs of staff – Eisenhower specifically asked Eden to delay the operation until after the presidential election of 6 November. Provided this were done, the President agreed to form a common front with Britain and France. Eden communicated this to Pineau.[33]

Dayan's forces, on 29 October, mounted an attack 30 miles (50 km) from the Suez Canal. Israel maintained its independent action: it merely used the dispute over the Suez Canal to secure the Straits of Tiran. Israel's campaign plans, withheld from London and Paris, made a nonsense of the Anglo-French ultimatum when it was issued: Israel could hardly withdraw 10 miles (16 km) from the canal when it was still 30 miles (50 km) away. By 3 November, when the United Nations was demanding a cease-fire, Israel had occupied nearly all of Sinai except Sharm el Sheikh. Israel's lack of interest in the Anglo-French operation could be attributed to the British delay in bombing the Egyptian airfields owing to the American evacuation in progress. On 14 November the Knesset agreed to withdraw from the territories captured in the Sinai campaign, provided there was a satisfactory arrangement with the United Nations Emergency Force (UNEF). Eban, working with Murphy, assisted by the party leaders in the Senate, Lyndon B. Johnson and William K. Knowland, and Abba Hillel Silver who synchronized the Zionist pressure groups, secured freedom of passage through the Straits of Tiran: on 24 April 1957 an American ship, the *Kernhills*, docked in Eilat carrying a cargo of crude oil. An Egyptian administration, but not an Egyptian army, returned to the Gaza strip. The pre-emptive strike by Israel in the Suez–Sinai War of 1956, largely planned by Dayan, achieved its objectives.[34]

Dulles was angry over the Anglo-French ultimatum. At a time when Russia was taking repressive action against Hungary he denounced Britain and France in the United Nations. The uniting for peace resolution was used to overcome the veto. But Dulles then entered hospital for a cancer operation. Perhaps he was annoyed as well about London's ignoring his warnings over the importance of the presidential election. In the middle of November he protested from his hospital bed to Lloyd about Britain's not going through with the venture and dispensing with Nasser. The Secretary of State later attributed his stand in the United Nations to his illness. Throughout Britain and the United States had the same objective: to dispose of Nasser. The only difference was in the timing.[35]

But that timing was crucial for Eisenhower. Few doubted that he would be re-elected, but Eisenhower felt that the least Eden owed him for arranging the summit conference in 1955 to help his general election was to hold off the Suez operation until after the presidential election. Shortly after the Anglo-French invasion Eisenhower confessed to Air Chief Marshal William Elliot that he had known that Britain intended to strike at Nasser, but had thought that it would be after the American elections.[36] London adhered to Dulles's wishes that no official information be passed about the military operation: both Eisenhower and Dulles were worried that Adlai Stevenson could use that against them in the election campaign if he found out. But Washington knew through unofficial contacts. By 2 November Eisenhower was aware of the Sèvres discussions; Dulles knew of the impending Israeli attack by 28 October;[37] Eisenhower was furious. With Dulles out of the way, he concerted action with the anti-British Humphrey and Hoover. Intelligence information was not passed to Britain, with the exception of the American assessment that the Russian nuclear threat was a bluff.[38] Eisenhower and Humphrey co-ordinated economic sanctions against Britain: the American Federal Reserve sold quantities of sterling; they held up emergency oil supplies to Europe; and in Macmillan's view almost illegally blocked Britain's drawing rights on the International Monetary Fund.[39] That act forced Britain to stop a successful military operation before it had secured both ends of the canal. The parity of sterling was considered important.[40] There was spectacular domestic opposition to the operation in Britain, but probably over 75 per cent of the population supported the venture.[41] Members of the Commonwealth disapproved.[42] But it was Eisenhower and Humphrey's action that forced the British withdrawal. The President's anger was not ameliorated as the news of unsatisfactory Republican returns in Congress were announced. Members of successive American administrations have publicly regretted Eisenhower's 'humiliation' of Britain and France: Henry Kissinger has argued that it forced the United States to take over Britain and France's burdens.[43]

Myths have proliferated about the Suez crisis. Often these were fuelled by Labour politicians for domestic political ends. Nutting resigned. Unlike Sir Graham Bower who, after the Jameson Raid in 1895–96, recorded his information about the complicity of Joseph Chamberlain and had his papers closed for fifty years,[44] Nutting published his account of Suez in 1967. This backfired on the sitting Labour government: it led to a spate of memoirs which, perhaps, undermined the sanctity of Cabinet confidentiality on which the British political system had been based for over 200 years. The 'Nutting attitude' was only partly balanced by another legend current in British political thinking in the 1950s: that of the iniquity of 'appeasement'. Both Eden and Macmillan emphasized reputations made on opposing Neville Chamberlain's policy of appeasement of Europe. This view was assisted by the perhaps rather hasty publication of the British documents

161

for 1938–39. It was only effectively undermined when Harold Wilson opened the actual records in the late 1960s. But, as the 'anti-appeasers' faded from British political life, another school of politicians emerged who had either supported Neville Chamberlain, like Sir Alec Douglas-Home, or who had not been involved. By the 1970s it was the Americans who persisted in perpetrating the myth of 'appeasement' –probably to draw attention away from Roosevelt's supposed 'sell out' at Yalta in 1945.[45] These myths have possibly obscured the realities of the British and French diplomacy that enabled Israel to launch the Suez–Sinai War.

Suez was not 'the lion's last roar'. Britain was already retreating from empire. Suez did not force Britain to turn to Europe: Macmillan only decided on that after South Africa's exclusion from the Commonwealth in 1961.[46] Suez was not an unfortunate break in the Anglo-American 'special relationship'. Britain had been demoted to the status of just one among a number of allies in December 1953. Rather Suez led to the revival of the special relationship on old terms. Macmillan was chosen Prime Minister by Queen Elizabeth II, acting on advice. Perhaps he was seen as the man best able to heal the breach with the United States. But it was Eisenhower who was particularly anxious to make amends. At the Bermuda Conference in March 1957 there was a return to an Anglo-American management of world affairs.[47] For a while this did not apply to the Middle East. After the Suez crisis Churchill wrote to Eisenhower about the dangerous vacuum in the Middle East into which Russia could move. The former Prime Minister urged, in effect, Anglo-American action to stop this.[48] Eisenhower agreed about the dangers of Russian penetration.[49] Dulles modified Chuchill's suggestions into unilateral American action with the Eisenhower doctrine for the Middle East. That was implemented in Jordan in April 1957 to restore a pro-Western government and to substitute American for British influence. But during the Syrian crisis of August 1957 there was close Anglo-American consultation, and that was maintained in 1958 during the crisis in the Lebanon and Jordan.[50] A government sympathetic to Britain was overthrown in Iraq in July 1958, but other than that there was no immediate significant lessening of British influence in the Middle East. British paramountcy in the area was over before Suez; perhaps Suez was an attempt to reassert it. Suez was not the last imperial war. It did not relegate Britain to minor power status, and was not the last wag of the lion's tail after which the British people were prepared to turn inwards and leave the upholding of the international system to others. Admittedly that view gained wider acceptance in Britain than abroad. But it was confounded in 1982 when troops returned from the Falkland Islands, 8,000 miles (12,900 km) away in the South Atlantic, having triumphantly fought both an imperial war, and one to maintain an international system as tenuous as that of the 1930s. On 11 July, as the *Canberra* berthed in

Southampton docks, the Royal Marine brass band played 'Rule Britannia'. It was loudly sung by over 2,500 marines lining the decks and waiting crowds waving Union flags as red, white and blue balloons were released into the air. This was followed by 'Land of Hope and Glory'. Over 250 British servicemen gave their lives and many more were terribly wounded to unseat another dictator.[51] It was possible partly because this time the United States backed Britain, in the words of President Ronald Reagan, 'its closest ally'. Macmillan later observed that if the Suez–Sinai War did nothing else it ended for at least ten years Nasser's claims to be a great Pan-Arabic leader. It arrested for a while the development of the Philosophy of Revolution.[52]

The immediate origins of the Suez–Sinai War lie more in the diplomacy of Britain, France and the United States than in the wish of Ben-Gurion and his colleagues for a pre-emptive strike against Egypt to enable Israel to force a peace on the surrounding Arab states. That Israeli policy had been decided in 1955; what was needed was the opportunity to implement it. As Dayan has observed, Israel was only able to launch the Sinai campaign because of the decision by Britain and France to use force to retake the canal. The origins of the Suez–Sinai War lie partly in a mythology, current in the West in the 1950s, of Chamberlain's policy for the appeasement of Europe, and in the perhaps dangerous and inaccurate idea that history can repeat itself – that historical analogy can be used to determine political policy. Britain and France, and Israel conducted their own separate wars. The outcomes of both were largely determined by the United States. It was that country which forced Britain and France to stop, and effectively secured Israel's rights to the Straits of Tiran. And American policy was influenced, if not decided, by domestic electoral politics and pressure groups.

REFERENCES

1. Leonard Mosley, *Dulles: A Biography of Eleanor, Allen and John Foster Dulles and Their Family Network* (London 1978), pp. 403–4; Anthony Nutting, *Nasser* (London 1972), pp. 141–6; Robert Stephens, *Nasser. A Political Biography* (London 1971), pp. 193–7.

2. Anthony Eden, *Full Circle* (London 1960), pp. 423–4; Roy Fullick and Geoffrey Powell, *Suez: The Double War* (London 1979), pp. 12–13; Selwyn Lloyd, *Suez 1956* (London 1978), pp. 74–5; Foster to Dulles, 27 July 1956, quoted by Kennett Love, *Suez. The Twice-Fought War* (London 1970), pp. 355–6; Earl of Kilmuir, *Political Adventure. The Memoirs of the Earl of Kilmuir* (London 1964), pp. 263–82; Jacques Georges-Picot, *The Real Suez Crisis. The End of a Great Nineteenth Century Work* (New York 1975), pp. 74–6.

3. Dwight D. Eisenhower, *Waging Peace* (London 1966), pp. 3–19; *FO*

371, 76386, PUSC 51 (Final) Second Revise, Anglo-American Relations. Present and Future, 1949.

4. Lloyd, op. cit., pp. 82–5; Eden, op. cit., pp. 424–8; Eisenhower, op. cit., pp. 36–7.

5. Eisenhower, op. cit., pp. 38–42; Eisenhower to Eden, 31 July 1956, pp. 664–5; Lloyd, op. cit., pp. 86–96; Harold Macmillan, *Riding the Storm* (London 1971), pp. 104–6; Eden, op. cit., pp. 432–4a; Robert Murphy, *Diplomat among Warriors* (London 1964), pp. 463–5.

6. Mosley, op. cit., pp. 411–13; Eden, op. cit., pp. 437–8; Lloyd, op. cit., pp. 97–100; Macmillan, *Riding the Storm*, p. 106.

7. *United Kingdom Parliamentary Debates House of Commons*, 557, cols. 1610–12, 2 Aug. 1956; Philip M. Williams, *Hugh Gaitskell: A Political Biography* (London 1979), pp. 421–2; Harold Wilson, *The Chariot of Israel, Britain, America and the State of Israel* (London 1981), p. 248.

8. Eden to Eisenhower, 5 August 1956, quoted by Love, op. cit., p. 394.

9. André Beaufre, *The Suez Expedition 1956* (London 1969), pp. 26–48; Robert Jackson, *Suez 1956: Operation Musketeer* (London 1980), pp. 14–23.

10. Macmillan, *Riding the Storm*, p. 108, Diary 24 Aug. 1956.

11. Eisenhower to Eden, 2 Sept. 1956, quoted in Eisenhower, op. cit., pp. 666–8.

12. Lloyd, op. cit., pp. 124–30.

13. Eisenhower to Eden, 8 Sept. 1956, quoted in Eisenhower, op. cit., pp. 669–71; see also pp. 11–19.

14. Macmillan, *Riding the Storm*, pp. 133–9, Diary, 24 Sept. 1956.

15. Lloyd, op. cit., p. 151, Eden to Butler, Sept. 1956; Macmillan, *Riding the Storm*, p. 128, Diary, 20 Sept. 1956; Eden, *Full Circle*, pp. 474–506.

16. Lloyd, op. cit., pp. 151–65; Eden, op. cit., pp. 507–9; Macmillan, *Riding the Storm*, pp. 139–45; Eisenhower, op. cit., pp. 52–45; Townsend Hoopes, *The Devil and John Foster Dulles* (Boston 1973), pp. 363–8.

17. Beaufre, op. cit., p. 63.

18. Shabtai Teveth, *Moshe Dayan* (London 1972), p. 252.

19. Sylvia Crosbie, *A Tacit Alliance. France and Israel from Suez to the Six Day War* (Princeton, NJ), pp. 68–71; Shimon Peres, *David's Sling. The Arming of Israel* (London 1970), p. 185.

20. Moshe Dayan, *The Story of My Life* (London 1976), pp. 151–73; Teveth, op. cit., pp. 251–8; Abba Eban, *An Autobiography* (London 1977), pp. 208–9, Beaufre, op. cit., pp. 64–9.

21. Beaufre, op. cit., pp. 69–73.

22. Lester Pearson, *The International Years 1948–1957* (London 1974), pp. 231–2; Lloyd, op. cit., pp. 123–4.

23. Anthony Nutting, *No End of a Lesson. The Story of Suez* (London 1967), pp. 90–9.

24. Lloyd, op. cit., p. 166; Nutting, *No End of a Lesson*, pp. 96–9; Geoffrey Warner, ' "Collusion" and the Suez crisis of 1956', *International Affairs*, **55** (1979), 226–39 at 233.

25. Lloyd, op. cit., pp. 173–5; Nutting, *No End of a Lesson*, p. 98.

26. Lloyd, op. cit., pp. 176–7; R. A. Butler, *The Art of the Possible* (London 1971), p. 192; Eden, op. cit., p. 514.

27. Nutting, *No End of a Lesson*, pp. 100–1, Lloyd, op. cit., p. 175; Dayan,

The Suez–Sinai War of 1956

op. cit., pp. 173–6; Wilson, op. cit., pp. 268–9.
28. Lloyd, op. cit., pp. 180–1.
29. Lloyd, op. cit., pp. 179–89; Dayan, op. cit., pp. 177–82; Fullick and Powell, op. cit., pp. 75–84; Christian Pineau, *1956 Suez* (Paris 1976), pp. 149–51; Nutting, *No End of a Lesson*, pp. 101–4.
30. Dayan, op. cit., pp. 185–6.
31. Dayan, op. cit., pp. 187–93; Lloyd, op. cit., pp. 187–8; Lloyd, *op. cit.*, pp. 187–8; Pineau, op. cit., pp. 149–53; Warner, op. cit., pp. 237–8; Fullick and Powell, op. cit., pp. 84–6.
32. Lloyd, op. cit., pp. 188–94; Warner, op. cit., p. 238; Michael Bar-Zohar, *Ben-Gurion* (London 1978), p. 243.
33. Mosley, op. cit., pp. 413–17; Pineau, op. cit., p. 124.
34. Eban, op. cit., pp. 222–58; Dayan, op. cit., pp. 195–217; Teveth, op. cit., pp. 259–80; Trevor N. Dupuy, *Elusive Victory: The Arab–Israeli War 1947–1974* (London 1978), pp. 145–208; Yigal Allon, *The Making of Israel's Army* (London 1970), p. 60; David Ben-Gurion, *Israel: A Personal History* (London 1971), pp. 507–36; Robert Henriques, *One Hundred Hours to Suez* (London 1957).
35. Hoopes, op. cit., pp. 369–93; Lloyd, op. cit., pp. 219, 257–8.
36. Lloyd, op. cit., p. 220.
37. Elizabeth Monroe, *Britain's Moment in the Middle East,* 2nd edn (London 1981), p. 207; Mosley, op. cit., pp. 416–17.
38. Chester Cooper, *The Lion's Last Roar* (New York 1978), pp. 192–200.
39. Macmillan, *Riding the Storm*, p. 164; Cooper, op. cit., pp. 192–200.
40. Fullick and Powell, op. cit., pp. 192–3.
41. D. A. Farnie, *East and West of Suez. The Suez Canal in History 1954–1956* (Oxford 1969), pp. 730–3; L. Epstein, *British Politics in the Suez Crisis* (London 1964); Russell Braddon, *Suez: Splitting of a Nation* (London 1973).
42. James Eayrs, *The Commonwealth and Suez. A Documentary Survey* (London 1964).
43. Henry Kissinger, 'Suez weakened Euope', *The Listener*, 20 May 1982, pp. 9–11.
44. *Bower Papers* (South African Public Library, Cape Town), 61, Bower to Montague Ommanney, 8 April 1905 (copy).
45. Althan G. Theoharis, *The Yalta Myths: An Issue in US Politics* (Columbia 1970).
46. Harold Macmillan, *Pointing the Way 1959–61* (London 1972), pp. 285–305.
47. Macmillan, *Riding the Storm*, pp. 180–205, 249–62; Eisenhower, op. cit., pp. 121–5; Richard Neustadt, *Alliance Politics* (New York 1970), pp. 30–1.
48. Macmillan, *Riding the Storm*, pp. 175–6.
49. Eisenhower, op. cit., pp. 680–1.
50. Macmillan, *Riding the Storm*, pp. 269–87, 313–41, 502–37; Michael Ionides, *Divide and Lose. The Arab Revolt of 1955–1958* (London, 1960), pp. 216–52; *United States Policy in the Middle East September 1956–June 1957 Documents* (New York 1968), *passim*; M. S. Agwani (Ed.), *The Lebanese Crisis, 1958. A Documentary Study* (Bombay 1965).

165

51.   *The Times*, 12 July 1982.
52.   Harold Macmillan, 'The Cuban missile crisis of 1962', *The Listener*, 30 Jan. 1969, pp. 142–3.

Chapter 10

TOWARDS THE SIX DAY WAR

The settlement that ended the Suez–Sinai War of 1956 provided the pretext for the Six Day War of 1967. Israel agreed to withdraw its forces from the conquered territories largely because of an under-standing with Washington that the United Nations Emergency Force would ensure freedom of passage through the Straits of Tiran. Egyptian forces did not re-enter the Gaza strip, and Israel was free from fedayeen attacks from that area between March 1957 and May 1967. Israel, furthermore, secured the understanding of the Eisen-hower administration. The sea route to Eilat was also a matter on which Israel could find sympathy from traditional maritime countries, including Britain. Trading nations had vested interests in issues like freedom of the seas, and these could override other considerations. Having achieved comparative security, Israel was able to concentrate on furthering its international status and internal development, as well as its military preparations.[1]

Nasser's gamble on the Suez War also paid off. Nikita Khrushchev warned Nasser, before the Anglo-French invasion, that Russia would not get involved in a Third World War for the Suez Canal. But Nasser decided to stay his ground: world opinion would evict the 'aggressors'. For a while Nasser's prestige was enhanced in Arab countries and throughout the Third World. Nasser seized this opportunity to try to implement the Arab circle of his Philosophy of Revolution. He did this when he was still courting Washington, and hoping for American finance for the Aswan dam, while striving to give the impression that he was not Khrushchev's puppet. But Washington was not sympa-thetic: it had agreed with the overall British objective behind the Suez operations – the unseating of Nasser – and, if anything, seemed aggrieved that Britain had not persisted in securing it. Jordan was first on Nasser's agenda: he tried to secure Egyptian influence through the Prime Minister, Suleiman Nabulsi, but in April 1957, Hussein, with American help, thwarted this. The King did not want to be dominated by Cairo, and he rid himself of both Nabulsi and his pro-Egyptian chief of staff. Cairo radio vented Nasser's spleen against Hussein. The domestic turmoil in Syria gave Nasser his next opportunity. By the end of 1957 Russia was aiding that country. The Left there liked ideas of Pan-Arabism. The Right wanted union with Iraq and the West. The Centre, supported by Saudi Arabia, hoped for Syrian neutrality. The Ba'ath were hesitant about pressing for union with Egypt as a solution, but early in 1958 a group of young officers asked Nasser for just this. Nasser consented. The union, largely on Egypt's terms, called the United Arab Republic, was proclaimed on 1 February 1958. In the terms of the Philosophy of Revolution Nasser was becoming the Arab 'hero'. Hussein and Feisal responded by joining together the Hashemite countries. In the Lebanon Chamoun became convinced that Nasser wanted to destroy the Christian ascendancy in that country. As Cairo and Damascus radios incited the Muslim community to revolt, Chamoun invited in the American marines. On 14 July an Iraqi brigade under Abdel Karim Kassim murdered Feisal and Nuri. Hussein asked for British assistance which was despatched immediately, the United States securing the overflying rights from Israel. Nasser, though he had no advance knowledge of the coup in Iraq, saw his Arab revolution threatened, and went in secret to Moscow. Khrushchev obliged with threatening noises. Britain withdrew its planes from Iraq; Nasser helped to choose the new President of the Lebanon; Cairo's dominance over the Arab world appeared, on the surface, to have increased.[2]

Nasser alienated the Ba'ath in Syria, plotted an abortive coup in Mosul against Kassem in Iraq early in 1959, and on 28 September 1961 army units marched into Damascus and proclaimed Syrian independence. Worried that increasing Russian influence in the Arab states would undermine his own revolution, Nasser tried to improve relations with the West. President John F. Kennedy seemed less hostile to the Third World and neutralism; he appointed an Arabist ambassador in Cairo. Britain re-established full diplomatic relations in March 1961 and sent Harold Beeley. Nasser, fearing that Russia wanted a 'Red' Fertile Crescent made up of Iraq, Syria, Jordan, the Lebanon and Kuwait, arrested Egyptian communists. But he still managed to secure Russian finance for the Aswan dam and Egypt's arsenal was stocked with Russian weapons. When Kassem of Iraq claimed Kuwait in June 1961, Nasser told Beeley he had no objection to British forces going to Kuwait's assistance. But Nasser did ensure that forces from the Arab League replaced those from Britain almost immediately in the new independent state. By this time the Arab circle of Nasser's Philosophy of Revolution was not progressing well. It was after all imperial British troops rather than Egyptian forces that had contained Kassem. Even in North Africa Nasser had alienated Bourguiba by harbouring the Tunisian President's enemy, Salah Ibn Yusuf. Indeed, the only Arab state with which Egypt had friendly relations was the Sudan. From November 1958 Nasser had successfully negotiated the apportionment of the Nile with the military dictatorship led by General Ibrahim Abboud.[3]

Thwarted in the Arab world Nasser tried to further the African circle of his Philosophy of Revolution. In July 1960 he supported Patrice Lumumba in the Congo. Cairo radio broadcast propaganda to Black Africa; even Emperor Haile Selassie of Abyssinia objected over this incitement to rebellion aimed at his Muslim subjects. Nasser tried to win the sympathy of Black Africa by breaking off relations with Pretoria on the apartheid issue. He courted the leaders of the former French colonies of Guinea and Mali. It seems that Nasser wanted a united African state of Egypt, the Sudan and the Congo with Cairo as its capital. His ambitions were partly countered by Israeli aid to Kenya, Tanganyika and Ghana, and by tribal rebellions against Arab rule in the southern Sudan, probably stirred up by Israeli agents. And Kwame Nkrumah was suspicious of Nasser's African adventures as they endangered the Ghanaian leader's ambitions to be the Black saviour of Africa.[4]

In March 1962 Nasser initiated a coup in Syria, and during the succeeding months an unsuccessful reunion with Egypt was attempted. But all this really led to was public exposure of Egyptian interference in Syrian affairs. Relations between Egypt and Saudi Arabia were already hostile and suspicious when, on 27 September 1962, army officers led by General Abdullah Sallal deposed the Imam al-Badr who had just succeeded to the throne of the Yemen. Cairo recognized Sallal; Riyadh supported the deposed Imam. Cairo and Sanaa had already broken off diplomatic relations when the Yemen supported Iraq over the Kuwait crisis in 1961. The Yemen bordered on Aden and the Aden protectorate. Nasser had openly proclaimed his intention to drive British forces from all Arab territory. The Yemen affair also seemed an opportunity to stop the spread of Saudi hegemony over the Arabian Peninsula. Hussein supported the Imam. In 1964 40,000 Egyptian troops were tied down in the Yemen; by 1970 they numbered 70,000 or nearly half the army. At the start of the Yemeni venture coups in Syria and Iraq returned regimes more friendly to Cairo; these were, however, achieved by the local Ba'ath parties and not Egyptian intelligence. This time Nasser resisted moves for a tripartite union. The Yemen, however, proved to be Nasser's Vietnam. To the British and American publics it seemed that once again Nasser was trying to pursue his revolution abroad. London did not like this threat to its position in Aden and the Aden protectorate. Washington was worried about Saudi Arabia's involvement and a possible threat to American oil interests there. When, in October 1963, Ben Bella asked Nasser for help in his dispute with Morocco, Nasser could only spare tanks and not men. Even so, Rabat was alienated from Cairo.[5]

Israeli military prowess during the Suez–Sinai War had convinced Nasser of the need to maintain peace on his borders with Israel. But, during his engagement in the Yemen, this policy was endangered by the new Israeli Prime Minister, Levi Eshkol. In August 1963 Israel started to divert 75 per cent of the waters of the Jordan for its own industrial and agricultural development. Syria sent troops; Israel threatened retaliation. Nasser tried to restrain Damascus, but it was the United Nations that achieved the cease-fire. Nasser, however, was worried about future Syrian action, and by the pro-Israeli stance of the new American President, Lyndon B. Johnson. Confronted by this new situation, the Egyptian President called an Arab summit conference in an effort to achieve unity.[6]

On 13 January 1964 the heads of thirteen Arab states met in Cairo. Nasser proposed that ways of stopping Israel's diversion of the Jordan River be studied, and that a unified Arab command be set up under General Ali Ali Amer of Egypt to protect Arab frontiers from Israeli attacks. Nasser secured the appointment of Ahmed Shukhairy as the Palestinian representative. Shukhairy proposed the establishment of a Palestinian national 'entity'. But Nasser's position in the Arab world continued to be undermined by the situation in the Yemen. Nasser did not want to appear too closely allied to Russia: Sallal, however, travelled frequently to Moscow and antagonized Washington. London was also annoyed by Nasser's financing of the Federation for the Liberation of South Yemen (FLOSY) which had its headquarters in Cairo and was dedicated to the expulsion of Britain from the Aden protectorate. In July 1964, however, Britain announced that Aden and the other territories making up the South Arabian Federation would become independent no later than 1968: Britain would retain a military base in Aden. But Nasser's dependence on Moscow increased. Khrushchev opened the Aswan dam and the Russians promoted industrialization in Egypt, but it became evident to Nasser that Russia hoped to replace Western influence in Egypt with Russian influence. It was against this background that Nasser was confronted with the Palestinian issue again.[7]

For eight years it seemed that Nasser had done nothing concrete to help the Palestinians regain their lost lands. Nasser had concentrated on his Philosophy of Revolution, on making Cairo the capital of the Arab world and, failing that, the centre of Black Africa. This was his personal mission. Initially, it might have seemed to him that Arab unity under Cairo was essential before anything could be done about Israel. Nasser did his best to ensure that the Palestinian refugees in Gaza were comfortable, but he deliberately avoided conflict with Israel and tried to see that other Arab countries did the same. This disappointed Yasser Arafat and his militant Fatah resistance group. At the Cairo summit in January 1964 Nasser had said that the liberation of Palestine was not an immediate issue. But, in May 1964, Shukhairy called a Palestine conference in Jerusalem, attended by all the Arab foreign ministers, and formed the Palestine Liberation Organization, the PLO. Its aim was to unite all expatriate Palestinians, including those on the West Bank. There would be a government in exile with headquarters in Gaza; an army would be recruited from the Palestinian refugees. Nasser offered the PLO Egyptian instructors and equipment. In September 1964, at another summit in Alexandria, Nasser secured endorsement of the PLO as the first step towards the liberation of Arab Palestine. In 1965 Nasser led the Arab world in breaking off diplomatic relations with West Germany; the latter country had been supplying Israel with American weapons from 1960 and had recognized Israel. But Nasser warned the third Arab summit in Casablanca in September 1965 that war against Israel would not be possible: the Arab countries lacked the necessary weapons and training.[8]

After the meeting in Casablanca there was a brief honeymoon with Britain. A cease-fire was achieved in the Yemen, and the new Labour government under Harold Wilson hoped for an end to Nasser's agitation in the Aden protectorate and improved relations with Egypt. But nationalist activities in Aden led to a suspension of the Constitution there, renewed suspicion of British imperialism from Nasser and eventually a break in diplomatic relations on the Rhodesian issue. In any case Nasser suspected the known Zionist leanings of the Labour Party and its leader. When Britain agreed to supply Riyadh with a sophisticated air defence system, and the Saudi King Feisal and the Shah of Iran announced they were calling an Islamic summit, Nasser saw his position in the Arab world challenged by a combination of Britain and reactionary forces. Cairo radio denounced British imperialism. Nasser sent renewed support to the guerrillas in the Aden protectorate and decided that Egyptian forces should stay in the Yemen to help FLOSY. At the same time Nasser developed a paranoia over Washington's hesitation to renew grain shipments to Egypt. Nasser began to suspect a conspiracy between a pro-Zionist American President and a pro-Zionist British Prime Minister that did not exist. When in February 1966 Britain announced that it would not need a base in Aden, Nasser was not pacified and stated that his troops would remain in the Yemen until the last British soldier had left Aden.[9]

At this time the new Boumedienne regime in Algeria allied itself with Nasser's enemies, Tunisia and Morocco. But changes in the leadership in Syria led Nasser, following the prompting of A. Kosygin, the Russian leader, to renew contacts with Damascus. Probably to prevent what he thought was a Western conspiracy to unseat him, Nasser resorted to using the one platform that he thought might achieve an Arab unity: attacking Israel. The Egyptian President started by attacking the pro-Western Arab governments: instead of concentrating their activities on the Israeli invader they had tried to undermine Egypt. Hussein was the first: he was an American protégé who refused to allow Shukhairy to recruit PLO forces on Jordanian soil. The Jordanian King feared Israeli reprisals for such activities.

Then there were clashes on the Israeli–Syrian border over Israeli fortifications in the 1949 demilitarized zone. With Russian prompting, on 4 November 1966, Damascus and Cairo signed a defence agreement: aggression against either state would be regarded as an attack on the other. On 13 November, in retaliation for an incident in which an exploding mine killed three Israeli soldiers near the Jordanian frontier, an Israeli armoured force attacked the village of Samu, just inside Jordan, destroyed 125 houses and killed 18 Jordanian troops. Palestinians in Jordan rioted against Hussein; Amman criticized Cairo for not sending assistance to repel the Israeli assault. The Jordanian forces and radio taunted Nasser: the United Nations Emergency Force secured Egypt's borders with Israel; Nasser was just allowing Israel to get military supplies through the Straits of Tiran to be used against Arabs. The unified command with Syria was just an excuse for Egypt not to protect its brothers in Jordan and elsewhere against Israel. The Arab world at the beginning of 1967 was torn by factionalism. This was largely the result of Nasser's efforts to promote his Philosophy of Revolution, and to make Cairo the centre of the three circles. Israel could only benefit from this division.[10]

Nasser secured his control over Egypt, but he failed in his attempt to lead a Cairo-dominated Arab world, to make Cairo the centre of an Islamic renaissance and the pivot of Black Africa. But, perhaps, Nasser's most serious shortcoming was his alienation of Western sympathies. His propaganda war was often directed against British imperialism; he sponsored guerrillas to fight British forces in the Aden protectorate. Nasser's activities throughout the Arab world and Black Africa probably seemed to an informed British and American public merely to confirm the diagnosis by Eden and Dulles of the Egyptian President's aims. By the beginning of 1967 the number of Palestinian refugees was well over 1 million, possibly as high as 2 million. The public of western Europe and the United States hardly knew of their existence, let alone their plight. Ethel Mannin, the novelist and travel writer, planned a script for a film, *The Road to Beersheba*, about the Arab flight from Palestine, and hoped that it would be made with Jordanian assistance. But it never appeared. Instead Western audiences saw the Hollywood blockbuster, directed by Otto Preminger, *Exodus*. Based on Leon Uris's best-selling novel, it starred the archetypal image of White Anglo-Saxon Protestant America, Paul Newman, as the Zionist commander. This was, admittedly, a fictitious account of the *President Warfield* incident. But the film and the novel created a myth that was so widely believed that it became the reality. A multi Academy Award winner, this emotional epic, with its rousing musical score, ranks as one of the most anti-British films ever made, rivalling even some of the efforts of John Ford. Whether intentional or not, it was also a successful instance of Zionist propaganda in the period between the Suez–Sinai War and the Six Day War. It is remarkable that its release in Britain, barely ten years after the Irgun's hanging of the two British sergeants, did not result in more of a public outcry. Possibly, at a time when a weekly visit to the cinema was still popular, it encouraged in a generation disillusioned with Nasser and Pan-Arabism a sympathy for Israel.[11]

Lenin considered the cinema a revolutionary force. In the 1950s and 1960s public attitudes in the West might have been influenced by this medium. The Hollywood industry had for decades been run by Gentile Jews and Jews. But until around the time of the creation of the state of Israel the Jew in the American cinema was largely a figure of fun. Shortly after the Second World War a series of films was made which bravely tackled the question of anti-Semitism in the United States: the exclusion of Jews from universities, country clubs and certain residential areas. After 1948 the Zionists in the American cinema industry acquired a new confidence and made a film attacking British policy in the Palestine mandate. This anti-British tradition was sustained in the 1950s, extending even to films about Zionists in North Africa during the Second World War with the British forces learning their trade for the real war against the British in Palestine. At the same time the popular Hollywood cinema projected the Arab as devious, sadistic and treacherous. American films, perhaps unconsciously, also reinforced the image of Jews as being virtually the only victims in Hitler's concentration camps. Both the State Department and the Foreign Office had been disturbed by this sort of publicity in the United States during 1944 and 1945. In the 1950s and 1960s the Western media seemed only conscious of Hitler's plans for the extermination of the Jews: gypsies, homosexuals and other racial minorities were not a suitable subject for the industry. Many of these American films were moving and of artistic merit. Leading directors tackled the subject with sensitivity: these included George Stevens with *The Diary of Anne Frank* (1959) and Sidney Lumet's *The Pawnbroker* starring Rod Steiger (1964). They were reinforced by offerings from Eastern Europe like *The Shop on the High Street* which, unusually for a foreign film in the 1960s, was widely seen in the United States and received major awards. Often this sort of cinema presented the Zionist case: Israel had to exist as a refuge for the survivors of the holocaust. It was only in the late 1970s that a play, *Bent*, opened at the Royal Court Theatre in London and presented audiences with the case that under Hitler's regime the homosexual's pink star placed him in an inferior position even to the Jews with the yellow star. The play did transfer to the West End, and late in 1979 opened on off-Broadway. The programme pointed out that Hitler had exterminated between a quarter- and a half-million homosexuals. In the early 1980s a much-publicized American television film, starring Vanessa Redgrave, about the Jews in the concentration camps did suggest an alternative to the Zionist solution, that urged by Bevin: the Jews should be able to continue to live in Europe. The selection of Miss

Redgrave for the part was condemned because she had, in 1977, made a film directed by Roy Battersby, *The Palestinian*, which carefully distinguished between Zionism and Judaism and presented a Palestinian case. Zionist elements in the Hollywood industry had tried to prevent Miss Redgrave being given an Academy Award because of this. But, on the whole, during the 1950s and 1960s the Hollywood cinema presented a selective view of the victims of Hitler's extermination policy, ignored the question of the Palestinian refugees and generally projected an unfavourable image of the Arab. Probably the major film of the period, however, was by a British director, David Lean: *Lawrence of Arabia*. One of the greater masterpieces of the cinema it won almost as many Academy Awards as *Gone With the Wind*. The script by Robert Bolt presented Arabs in a rather different way from the usual Hollywood offering. But audiences probably saw little connection with the modern Arab–Israeli question and went to see a visual depiction of one of the few legendary figures of the twentieth century.[12]

It is difficult to explain the shift in British public opinion over the two decades between 1947 and 1967. In 1947 the terrorist activities of Begin's Irgun, particularly the hanging of the two sergeants, had, in Bevin's view and that of the majority of the House of Commons, made any continuation of a British presence in Palestine impossible. Only twenty years later the blowing up of the King David Hotel, the flogging of British officers and the booby-trapping of the sergeants' bodies seemed to be forgotten. Begin's admission to the Israeli cabinet did not shake the overwhelming enthusiasm for Israel at the outbreak of the Six Day War. The opinion polls suggested over 50 per cent support for the Israeli cause, and only around 2 per cent for the Arabs. Sympathy for the underdog could account for some of this: Israel appeared beleaguered by massive Arab forces. One of the central issues also appeared to be that of freedom of the seas and maritime rights, a matter of concern to a trading nation. But Nasser's promotion of his Philosophy of Revolution was probably a primary factor. The Six Day War vindicated Eden's action over Suez. Certainly Nasser's activities had not promoted any sympathy for the Arab cause in Britain. And Israel appeared as Nasser's new victim. Another factor was the widespread respect in Britain for Jews in public life. Prominent Jews, and Zionists, held distinguished posts in universities, were television script writers, film directors, actors, conductors, pianists, cellists, authors, periodical editors, publishers, and managers of Britain's leading business houses, grocery chains and department stores. Their pre-eminence helped to create a climate sympathetic to Israel, as well as providing a ready market for Israeli manufactured goods and produce. British soldiers who had been shot at by Zionist terrorists in the 1940s presumably bought Jaffa oranges and ate McVities Jaffa Cakes in the 1960s.

On the whole British cinema and television depicted problems of anti-Semitism and the Jewish community in Britain in a sympathetic light, though the most outstanding examples came in subsequent decades with John Schlesinger's *Sunday, Bloody Sunday*, and the biggest box office British film ever in the United States, *Chariots of Fire*. The British Jew, however, was shown as the product of the Diaspora, owing allegiance to the sovereign and not Israel, perhaps having to fight for acceptance as a loyal British subject and achieving it – as in *Chariots of Fire* when *Jerusalem* was played at the Olympic victor's memorial service in the church in the Strand. Practically the only reminder of Zionist terrorism was a BBC play of the flogging episode, and, later, the television series on nannies. British attitudes were partly determined by the coverage of events on the wireless and television. In the 1960s many people seemed to have relied on the wireless for foreign news, and thus the BBC's coverage was particularly important. The BBC's man in Tel Aviv was Michael Elkins, an American Jew who had lived in Israel since 1963. His appointment was unusual in that the BBC tended to rely on foreign correspondents who did not have particular connections with the country from which they were reporting. During the Six Day War, however, the BBC did interview Arab sympathizers like Christopher Mayhew, a Labour Member of Parliament, and Anthony Nutting. It is impossible to estimate whether the British press, on the whole sympathetic to Israel, merely reflected public sentiment or helped to form it. There does not appear to be any substantial evidence of Zionist control of the British press at the time.[13]

As in Britain, the Arabs lost the propaganda war in the United States. American Jews and Zionists held pre-eminent positions. The Zionist lobby, even if not active, was a dominant factor in officials' calculations: its anticipated reaction could influence foreign policy. The media gave wide coverage to Israel, little to the Arab states and the Palestinian refugee question was almost totally ignored. The existence of Israel, and American sponsorship of that state, gave the Jewish community a new sense of security, if not of belonging. Most American Zionists contented themselves with sending tax-free contributions to Israel; few went to live there. By the 1960s the Jews had been increasingly absorbed into the American hyphenate culture. This was widely reflected in the American cinema of the time by films like Mike Nichols's *The Graduate*, and *Goodbye Columbus*. Public support for Israel during the Six Day War was almost universal and Johnson's fears of congressional hesitation proved to be unfounded. Indeed, sympathy for Israel was evident throughout the West during the Six Day War. There was even some outcry in France over General Charles de Gaulle's shift towards the Arabs. Arab propaganda, particularly that of Nasser, was unsubtle, often directed against Western imperialism and undermined the Arab cause. To many the Egyptian

175

President seemed to be implementing his Philosophy of Revolution and courting Russia. Israel appeared as an ally of the West.[14]

The image Israel projected after the Suez–Sinai War helped win Western sympathies at a time when Nasser's activities were alienating them. First under Ben-Gurion, then Levi Eshkol who was widely regarded as moderate and non-expansionist, the Israeli economy grew. Israel became an industrial nation. Agricultural advances in the barren desert seemed almost miraculous. Jewish culture thrived, and achieved international recognition. By the mid-1960s it was evident that the economy had been overheated and that the boom was over, but most Western countries were also facing similar difficulties and growing unemployment. On the political front factionalism developed and the Mapai split. Divisions were also evident between the founder population and the new immigrants from the Middle East. By 1960 it was clear that Israel offered little attraction to American and European Jews as a place to live; it was, however, largely with their financial support that the new state was able to absorb the Middle Eastern immigrants. The factionalism gave a disproportionate power to the minority of orthodox Jews and enabled them to press for the traditional Rabbinical Law. This was opposed by a younger generation who found it irrelevant in a modern society. But, to Western eyes, all this probably seemed to be part of an emerging democratic process. Little attention was paid to Israel's refusal to accept back Arab refugees, except on what the Arabs regarded as impossible terms, and the increasingly exclusive, if not theocratic, nature of the state.[15]

Between 1956 and 1966 Israel increased its military strength substantially and, even more important, developed a sophisticated military doctrine and organization. The doctrine was based on the assumption that a war with the Arabs should be avoided if possible, and that only an army which could win such a war could act as a deterrent. Israel had to be prepared to face attacks on all its borders simultaneously and be ready to battle on its own. Israel, with a population of 2½ million Jews, would have to be prepared to fight 100 million Arabs from a geographically unfavourable position. Because of the overwhelming numerical strength of the opponents, and the necessarily small size of Israel's standing army, it was necessary to develop a scheme whereby reservists were kept in a state of readiness by regular military training so that practically the whole population could bear arms in war. Israel also had to develop a territorial defence system relying on armed civilian settlements, and the strategic initiative of being able to do the fighting in the opponent's territory. This could only be achieved by giving priority to military expenditure, and preventing possible international isolation by winning friends in the smaller countries of the developing world who had voting rights in the United Nations. It was evident that Israel would be exposed if it relied on a defensive strategy; Israel had to be ready to take the initiative and make a pre-emptive counter-attack to destroy the opponent's forces. Any future war would have to be short, and fought on the opponent's territory. Israeli armies would have to advance so as to be able to defeat enemy forces, establish a defensive strategic position and hold enemy territory until permanent strategic boundaries were established. In the years following the Suez–Sinai War special emphasis was therefore placed on developing the offensive and striking power of the Israeli army. Air superiority was considered essential: the Israeli air force was considerably expanded to fulfil a multipurpose role. Helicopters were also acquired to drop troops behind enemy lines. The tank corps was developed to enable it to cover vast distances without interruption. The infantry became highly mechanized, and the paratroop corps was expanded for commando operations. A fast naval commando unit was also created. At the same time as expanding its conventional forces, Israel developed its nuclear technology with French help. In 1960, in his book, *Curtain of Sand*, Allon argued that the closing of the Straits of Tiran would be regarded by Israel as an 'act of open warfare'. Any such move constituted a declaration of war which would allow Israel to choose the place, size and time of its action. Israel secured most of the weapons on which this new strategy was based from the West, particularly the United States, but also Britain and France. HAWK missiles arrived from the United States in April 1965. Patton tanks, discarded by West Germany, were supplied through the United States. France provided Mirage jets.[16] At the outbreak of the Six Day War Israel had almost as many first-line troops as the combined Arab forces.[17]

At the beginning of 1967 Israel was in a strong military position, and also regarded sympathetically throughout the Western world. Both the American President and the British Prime Minister had pronounced pro-Israeli views. France, however, Israel's former patron, had been guided first under Maurice Couve de Murville, and then de Gaulle, away from the Franco-Israeli alliance. There were difficulties over nuclear collaboration, and Israel's diversification of its arms suppliers offended the French military establishment. De Gaulle refrained from commenting on the series of crises that preceded the Six Day War; indeed he warned Eban that Israel should not strike first.[18] The Arab countries had modern weapons from the United States, France and Britain. But, most important, they possessed some of the latest Russian T-54 and T-55 tanks and allied equipment together with sophisticated MiG-19 and MiG-21 aircraft. Much of this weaponry, however, was new, and the Arabs were not sufficiently well trained to handle it. The Arab states lacked an effective co-ordinated defence strategy, and had lost the propaganda war in the West. Russia was an uncertain sponsor, and though it might lend diplomatic aid, military intervention by Moscow was unlikely.[19]

During the early months of 1967 there was a series of clashes along the border between Israel and Syria. Eshkol had been attacked by Ben-Gurion and his supporters for endangering Israel's security: he had been forced to allow the chief of staff, General Itzhak Rabin, latitude in launching reprisals for Fatah attacks. On 7 April an exchange escalated into a tank battle and clashes between the Israeli and Syrian air force. Six Syrian planes were shot down and victorious Israeli jets swept over the suburbs of Damascus. Rabin stated that the Syrian government needed to be overthrown before Israeli security could be guaranteed. Damascus joined Amman in denouncing Nasser for doing nothing against Israel. Newspapers in some Arab countries suggested that Nasser was more interested in an Egyptian empire in the Yemen than in joining the Arab fight against Zionism. Through leakages to the Russians, and by absenting armoured formations from the Independence Day parade in Jerusalem on 15 May, Israel gave Nasser the impression that an attack on Syria was imminent. That day Nasser declared a state of alert in Egypt, and sent Egyptian troops into Sinai. On 16 May the UNEF commander was asked to withdraw a limited number of his forces so that Egypt could occupy certain positions on the border between Sinai and Israel. Nasser did not ask for the withdrawal of UNEF forces from the Gaza strip or Sharm el Sheikh. Late on 16 May U Thant, the Secretary-General of the United Nations, told the Egyptian ambassador that a partial withdrawal of UNEF forces was not possible. Nasser, unable to face further taunts from his fellow Arabs, asked for the total withdrawal of UNEF forces on 18 May. Nasser sent advance units to the Sinai border to replace UNEF, but not to Sharm el Sheikh. This hesitation met with scorn from Amman radio and some Eygpian officers. Nasser gave in, and on 21 May Egyptian troops occupied Sharm el Sheikh. On 22 May Cairo closed the Gulf of Aqaba to Israeli ships and others sailing to Eilat with strategic cargoes. The next day Eshkol told the Knesset that interference with shipping in the Gulf of Aqaba and the Straits of Tiran constituted a violation of international law, and an act of aggression against Israel. Nasser was suddenly hailed by the Arabs as their saviour.[20]

U Thant was in a difficult position. Canada demanded that its UNEF contingent leave in twenty-four hours. On 18 May, in reply to an Israeli protest about Egypt, the Secretary-General proposed that UNEF be moved to the Israeli side where it could do its work equally well, but Israel rejected this as an infringement of its sovereignty. In Cairo, Nasser accepted U Thant's suggestion that a United Nations representative go to Israel, Egypt and Jordan to arrange a settlement. Israel rejected this. Nasser accepted the proposal that the blockade of the Gulf of Aqaba be not tested for the time being, but Israel rejected this as well. Before the closure of the straits Eban had warned de Murville and George Brown, the British Foreign Secretary, that it did not intend to acquiesce.[21]

In the United States Johnson immediately declared Nasser's closure of the straits to be an illegal act. The American President approached London and Paris about invoking the Tripartite Declaration of 1950. Paris was cautious. The British Cabinet met on 24 May, and was concerned that reactivation could harm Britain's relations with the Arab states. Instead, it favoured a declaration that Britain, the United States and other maritime nations intended to establish a naval force to keep the Gulf of Aqaba opened to shipping, and assert maritime rights. This would avoid giving the impression of assisting Israel, and so not seriously affect Britain's relations with Arab states. Johnson pursued this idea with congressmen and other governments. On 30 May Eshkol indicated to the American President that the envisaged naval force should move through the straits within a week or two.

Eban returned to Tel Aviv on 23 May and attended a meeting at the Ministry of Defence: it was reported that the Egyptians were not yet ready for a full offensive; Syria was retreating; there was no movement in Jordan. Rabin had told him that time was needed to reinforce the south: the diplomatic establishment could help with that. Eban advised the gathering that Israel must think like a nation whose soil had already been invaded; but Israel's predicament was international not regional and it had to look to the United States to neutralize the Russian menace. Johnson had asked to be consulted, and for forty-eight hours' respite. Most of those present agreed on the need for a political phase before a military reaction. Dayan, however, favoured military action against Egypt after forty-eight hours on a battleground close to the Israeli border. It was agreed to mobilize the reservists. In Paris, on 25 May, de Gaulle warned Eban that Israel should not fire the first shot; the French President wanted four-power consultation. Wilson showed 'unembarrassed sympathy'; he had just been given the opposition's support by Edward Heath and Sir Alec Douglas-Home; the Cabinet had agreed that morning that the blockade could not stand. Surprisingly, it was Crossman who had struck a dissenting note. In Washington Eban conferred with State Department and defence officials, and finally saw Johnson on 26 May: the President wanted a little time and argued that Israel should not initiate hostilities. London tried to hold the situation. On 31 May Wilson flew to Washington. Johnson was disturbed by the resistance in the Senate to positive action.[22]

Threats against Israel from Arab radio stations reached frenetic proportions. Nasser moved further forces into Sinai, but these had instructions not to provoke Israel. The Egyptian President added to the propaganda war with a speech on 26 May to the Arab Trades Union Congress in which he said that the Arab states were determined to destroy Israel. Moscow tried to restrain Nasser, but the Egyptian emissary deliberately distorted the information. Hussein initiated a mutual defence pact with Egypt on 30 May, and on 3 June three

179

battalions of Egyptian commandos were flown to Amman. Charles Yost, a State Department official, negotiated in Cairo for modifications in the Egyptian blockade. It was arranged that Zacharia Mohieddin, the Vice-President of Egypt, would go to Washington to make arrangements. On 2 June Dean Rusk informed the Israelis of these developments.[23]

On 27 May Eban returned to a divided Israeli cabinet: some wanted immediate action; others favoured more waiting. The next day Johnson conveyed to Eshkol warnings from Russia; Israel must not take pre-emptive military action. The Cabinet almost unanimously rejected an immediate strike. By 31 May the pressure to include Dayan in the ministry was considerable: he was offered the deputy premiership but would only accept the Ministry of Defence. Begin was also invited to join. On 2 June Dayan argued for an attack without delay. The next day Meir Amit, just back from Washington, reported that he felt after seeing Robert McNamara, the Secretary of State for Defence, and others that the United States would not take the necessary action to open the straits, but if Israel went to war it would not act adversely and might even help in the United Nations. Dayan then advocated a pre-emptive strike to the ministerial defence committee on 4 June. While Eshkol was speaking a message arrived from Johnson that action to ensure the freedom of shipping through the Straits of Tiran could not be taken by the United States alone. The Prime Minister thought this disappointing: in effect he gave the army latitude to launch an attack when it considered the moment right. Dayan formally proposed this. Two ministers hesitated, but the cabinet agreed. On the morning of 5 June Israeli planes destroyed the Egyptian air force.[24]

A similar fate met the other three Arab air forces within twenty-four hours. By 8 June Israel controlled the area from Gaza to the Suez Canal and down to Sharm el Sheikh. By 7 June Jordan had ceded Arab Jerusalem, Nablus, Jericho and the rest of the West Bank. Israel pressed into Syria and secured the Golan heights on 10 June. Israel lost around 1,000 men; the Arabs around 18,000. Ten years of careful defence preparations, a carefully thought out military and political doctrine turned the Israeli 'pre-emptive counter-attack' into a spectacular military victory in the Six Day War.[25]

The origins of the Six Day War can be found in the settlement that ended the Suez–Sinai War. Nasser's pursuit of his Philosophy of Revolution provided Israel with the opportunity to prepare itself for a war based on a sophisticated military doctrine. This time Israel was prepared to fight on its own. Israel had won the propaganda war, and its shrewd foreign policy obviated the need for reliance on the active support of any foreign power. It wanted, however, at least the assurance that the United States would not intervene. Israel fought the Six Day War in a favourable international climate. The Arab states were afflicted by internal strife and Nasser's attempts to enforce his leadership. Nasser was pushed by his own ambition and vanity – he could not endure taunts from his fellow Arabs – towards a war he had tried to avoid as, conscious of Israel's power, he felt such an engagement could only be undertaken by an Arab world united under himself. Probably Nasser was hoping for a negotiated settlement, and the means of restraining his fellow Arabs. He was taken by surprise when Israel destroyed his air force. The diplomatic negotiations of May and June suggest that, for a while, both sides were playing for time. But Israel decided to fight before the Arabs could prepare themselves fully. It considered the closure of the Straits of Tiran as an act of war anyway. That gave it the right to choose the place, and time to retaliate.

REFERENCES

1. Abba Eban, *An Autobiography* (London 1977), pp. 242–58; Yair Evron, *The Middle East* (London 1973), pp. 47–51, 67–70; Shlomo Aronson, *Conflict and Bargaining in the Middle East. An Israeli Perspective* (Baltimore 1978), pp. 11–20.
2. Anthony Nutting, *Nasser* (London 1972), pp. 168–244; Malcolm H. Kerr, *The Arab Cold War. Gamal 'Abd Al-Nasir and his Rivals 1958–1970*, 3rd edn (London 1971), pp. 1–25; Mohamed Heikal, *Sphinx and Commissar. The Rise and Fall of Soviet Influence in the Arab World* (London 1978), pp. 76–117; Robert Stephens, *Nasser. A Political Biography* (London 1971), pp. 277–302.
3. Nutting, op. cit., pp. 245–85; Theodore C. Sorensen, *Kennedy* (London 1966), pp. 594–7; Arthur M. Schlesinger, Jr, *A Thousand Days. John F. Kennedy in the White House* (Boston 1965), pp. 566–7; Oles M. Smolansky, *The Soviet Union and the Arab East under Khrushchev* (Lewisburg 1974), pp. 157–221; Aryeh Yodfat, *Arab Politics in the Soviet Mirror* (Jerusalem 1973), pp. 206–13.
4. Nutting, op. cit., pp. 285–93; Stephens, op. cit., pp. 303–20; W. Scott Thompson, *Ghana's Foreign Policy 1957–1966* (Princeton, NJ 1969), pp. 50–1.
5. Nutting, op. cit., pp. 312–44; Kerr, op. cit., pp. 44–76, 107–14; Yodfat, op. cit., pp. 256–9; Evron, op. cit., pp. 61–2; Stephens, op. cit., pp. 378–410.
6. Nutting, op. cit., pp. 344–6; Walter Laqueur, *The Road to War 1967* (London 1967), pp. 49–50; Odd Bull, *War and Peace in the Middle East. The Experiences and Views of a U.N. Observer* (London 1976), pp. 72–8.
7. Nutting, op. cit., pp. 347–61; Kerr, op. cit., pp. 96–105; Stephens, op. cit., pp. 411–14.
8. Nutting, op. cit., pp. 361–8; Stephens, op. cit., pp. 414–15; Kerr, op. cit., pp. 114–17.
9. Nutting, op. cit., pp. 369–84; Harold Wilson, *The Labour Government 1964–1970* (London 1974), p. 186; Elizabeth Monroe, *Britain's Moment in the Middle East,* 2nd edn (London 1981), pp. 213–15.
10. Nutting, op. cit., pp. 385–93; Kerr, op. cit., pp. 117–25; Laqueur, op.

cit., pp. 58–9, 81–2; Aronson, op. cit., pp. 61–2; Stephens, op. cit., pp. 461–5.

11. *Exodus*, United States, 1960, directed by Otto Preminger, starring Paul Newman, Eve-Marie Saint, Ralph Richardson, music by Ernest Gold; V. F. Perkins, *Film as Film. Understanding and Judging Movies* (London 1972), pp. 96–7; Michael Kerbel, *Paul Newman* (London 1975), pp. 58–60; Jane Mercer, *Great Lovers of the Movies* (London 1975), pp. 153–9; Ethel Mannin, *The Lovely Land. The Hashemite Kingdom of Jordan* (London 1965), pp. 83–5; *The Road to Beersheba* (London 1968).

12. *The Diary of Anne Frank*, United States, 1959, directed by George Stevens; *The Pawnbroker* United States, 1964, directed by Sidney Lumet, starring Rod Steiger; *The Shop on the High Street*, Czechoslovakia, 1965, directed by Jan Kaddr and Elmar Klos; Alistair Whyte, *New Cinema in Eastern Europe* (London 1971), pp. 92–3; *The Palestinian*, Great Britain, 1977, directed by Rod Battersby, starring Vanessa Redgrave; *Lawrence of Arabia*, Great Britain, 1972, directed by David Lean, starring Peter O'Toole, Alec Guinness, Anthony Quinn, Jack Hawkins, Omar Sharif, José Ferrer, Anthony Quayle, Claude Rains, script by Robert Bolt, winner of seven American Oscars; Edward Said, 'The Arab portrayed' in Ibrahim Abu-Lughod (Ed.), *The Arab–Israeli Confrontation of June 1967: An Arab Perspective* (Evanston 1970), pp. 1–9. Films attacking anti-Semitism in the United States include *Gentleman's Agreement*, United States, 1947, directed by Elia Kazan; *Crossfire*, United States, 1947, directed by Edward Dmytryk; *From Here to Eternity*, United States, 1953, directed by Fred Zinnemann; *The Dark at the Top of the Stairs*, United States, 1960, directed by Delbert Mann, play by William Inge; Roger Manvell, *New Cinema in the USA* (London 1968), pp. 10–21. One British film not widely distributed was made with Israeli money about the last days of the Palestine mandate, *Hill 24 Doesn't Answer*, Great Britain, 1954, directed by Thorold Dickinson; *Sight and Sound*, XXV (1955–56), 148. This was more a speciality by the American cinema: *Sword in the Desert*, United States, 1949; *Judith*, United States/Israel, 1966, directed by Daniel Mann, starring Sophia Loren, Peter Finch; *Cast a Giant Shadow*, United States, 1966, directed by Melville Shavelson, starring Kirk Douglas, Angie Dickinson, Hyam Topol. Martin Sherman, *Bent*, opened Royal Court Theatre 1979, starring Ian McKellen.

13. Randolph S. and Winston S. Churchill, *The Six Day War* (London 1967), pp. 219–41; Michael Adams and Christopher Mayhew, *Publish it Not . . . the Middle East Cover-Up* (London 1975), pp. 3–105, 121–6; Laqueur, op. cit., pp. 191–5; *Sunday, Bloody Sunday*, Great Britain, 1971, directed by John Schlesinger starring Peter Finch, Glenda Jackson, Murray Head; *Chariots of Fire*, Great Britain, 1981, directed by Hugh Hudson, script by Colin Welland, starring Ben Cross, Ian Charleson, Nigel Havers.

14. Michael W. Suleiman, 'American mass media and the June conflict', in Abu-Lughod, op. cit., pp. 138–54; Laqueur, op. cit., pp. 184–227; M. Abdel-Kader Hatem, *Information and the Arab Cause* (London 1974), pp. 204–30; *The Graduate*, United States, 1967, directed by Mike

Nichols, starring Dustin Hoffman; *Goodbye Columbus*, United States, 1969, directed by Larry Peerce, starring Richard Benjamin and Ali MacGraw.
15. Laqueur, op. cit., pp. 26–30; Aronson, op. cit., pp. 39–56; Evron, op. cit., pp. 67–77; Terence Prittie, *Eshkol of Israel. The Man and the Nation* (London 1969), pp. 206–98.
16. Yigal Allon, *The Making of Israel's Army*, pp. 60–75; Edgar O'Ballance, *The Third Arab–Israeli War* (London 1972), pp. 37–55.
17. Trevor N. Dupuy, *Elusive Victory: The Arab–Israeli War 1947–1974* (London 1978), pp. 231, 337.
18. Sylvia K. Crosbie, *A Tacit Alliance. France and Israel from Suez to the Six Day War* (Princeton, NJ 1974), pp. 122–91.
19. Dupuy, pp. 234–8, 337.
20. Dupuy, pp. 225–9, Nutting, op. cit., pp. 394–401; Stephens, op. cit., pp. 466–76; Allon, op. cit., pp. 76–8; O'Ballance, op. cit., pp. 23–6; Laqueur, op. cit., pp. 71–96; David Ben-Gurion, *Israel: A Personal History* (London 1971), pp. 753–61; Eban, op. cit., pp. 316–26; Moshe Dayan, *Story of My Life* (London 1972), pp. 143–8.
21. Samir N. Anabtawi, 'The United Nations and the Middle East conflict of 1967', in Abu-Lughod, op. cit., pp. 122–37; Nutting, op. cit., pp. 402–4; Bull, op. cit., pp. 106–12.
22. Lyndon Baines Johnson, *The Vantage Point. Perspectives of the Presidency 1963–1969* (London 1972), pp. 287–96; Dayan, op. cit., pp. 253–5; Eban, op. cit., pp. 326–64; Harold Wilson, *The Chariot of Israel, Britain, America and the State of Israel* (London 1981), pp. 329–46; George Brown, *In My Way* (London 1972), pp. 126–32; Harold Wilson, *The Labour Government 1964–70* (London 1974), pp. 505–12; William B. Quandt, *Decade of Decisions. American Policy towards the Arab–Israeli Conflict, 1967–1976* (Berkeley 1977), pp. 37–71; Marcia Williams, *Inside Number 10* (New York 1972), pp. 192–3; Richard Crossman, *The Diaries of a Cabinet Minister*, Vol. II, *1966–68* (London 1976), pp. 352–9, 364–93, 513, 537.
23. Dupuy, pp. 229–30; Nutting, op. cit., 405–17; Stephens, op. cit., pp. 479–92; Laqueur, op. cit., pp. 288–311; King Hussein of Jordan, *My 'War' with Israel* (New York 1969), pp. 60–4.
24. Dayan, op. cit., pp. 270–80; Eban, op. cit., pp. 365–408.
25. Dupuy, op. cit., pp. 231–340; Churchill and Churchill, op. cit., pp. 78–191; O'Ballance, op. cit., pp. 62–267.

Chapter 11

ATTRITION, AND THE YOM KIPPUR/RAMADAN WAR

The Six Day War was fought by the countries in the Middle East for the possession of land. It was a Middle Eastern war and the Great Powers stood aside. As soon as it was over the Middle East once again became an area of Great-Power rivalry. Within eighteen months Russia had made good the military losses of the Arab states. To the United States this seemed to challenge Western interests. In the end Washington was always prepared to back Israel, but, under the influence of the State Department it also tried to woo the Arabs. Moscow saw the chance to establish a permanent Russian fleet in the Mediterranean, and probably hoped that its support of the Arab cause would give Russia access to a warm-water port. Britain, though involved in the international diplomacy, was only engaged in the sidelines: British paramountcy in the area had passed two decades earlier. France, with the Algerian War behind, tried to cultivate the friendship of the Arabs. Henry Kissinger, President Richard Nixon's White House adviser, attributed the British and French position to the 'deplorable' American attitude during the Suez crisis of 1956: the American humiliation of its allies had shattered their confidence, and awareness of a global role had left a vacuum in the Middle East which the United States had had to fill.[1] Israel fought the Six Day War in a favourable climate of world opinion. Its extension of Israeli sovereignty to Arab Jerusalem, and the picture of poor Arab refugees crossing from the West Bank into Jordan – even though Israel offered to have those new refugees back – soon dispelled this.[2]

Suddenly the Palestinian refugee question, ignored for twenty years, became an issue that concerned world statesmen. Arab propaganda shifted away from Nasser's promotion of his Philosophy of Revolution and acquired some subtlety: *The Times* carried a full-page advertisement asking for a Balfour to found a home for 2 million Arabs. Yasser Arafat, despite his terrorist activities, probably achieved more for the Arab cause than Nasser had ever done. Nasser might have been idolized in Egypt – the people refused his resignation after the Six Day War and there was national mourning after his death

– but his Philosophy of Revolution destroyed any form of Arab unity and alienated the West. It was Arafat who helped to bring the plight of the Palestinian refugees to the attention of the West. Nixon told a National Security Council meeting on 10 June 1970 that the failure to deal with this question was one of the major lapses of the post-Second World War era.[3] After their humiliation in June 1967, however, the Arab states were not prepared to condone even the existence of Israel. Leaders of Arab states met at Khartoum at the end of August 1967, and decided that there should be no negotiations with Israel; no peace with Israel; no recognition of Israel; and that Palestinian territory could not be subject to bargaining. In October 1968 Al-Fatah rejected all compromises that could halt the armed strife: it demanded a 'free, open, non-sectarian, non-racist society in Palestine'.[4] Israel had achieved more under Eshkol than during any previous premiership. On his death, Eshkol was succeeded by Golda Meir, a woman who had grown up amidst the pogroms in Russia and had helped to pioneer the Yishuv in Palestine. Through her direct approach, and feigning a disbelief in State Department strictures, she managed to convince Nixon that Russia had to know that the United States would not let Israel be destroyed. Meir managed to link Israel's survival with that of American interests in the Middle East.

At a time of waning enthusiasm for Israel's occupation of Arab lands, the United Nations Security Council, on 22 November 1967, passed resolution 242. This was a triumph for British diplomacy. In the early stages of discussion Britain refrained from supporting an American draft which the Arabs considered too favourable to Israel. George Brown, however, did assure Eban that Britain would only advocate Israeli withdrawal if agreed boundaries were secured to establish a permanent peace. On 18 November Eban rejected a British draft as he felt that it would give the United Nations representative the power to dictate a solution. Hussein and Mahmoud Riad, the Egyptian negotiator, however, secured from Arthur Goldberg, the American ambassador, the assurance that Johnson would guarantee the implementation of the final resolution, subject to boundary rectifications and a new status for Jerusalem. As it seemed that only the Americans could persuade Israel to withdraw from Sinai and the West Bank, Nasser and Hussein agreed to resolution 242, despite objections from Syria, Iraq and Algeria. The Americans told the British delegation that they could only accept a resolution that had Israeli endorsement. Under this pressure Lord Caradon changed his draft to stipulate that the United Nations representative would merely have to 'promote agreement between the states of the region'. This gave Israel the necessary assurance, and, in any case, the ambiguities of the wording provided the necessary loopholes for both sides. Resolution 242 provided for a 'just and lasting peace' within 'secure and recognized boundaries'; Israel was to withdraw 'from territories occupied in the

185

recent conflict' and there was to be acknowledgement of all states' 'sovereignty, territorial integrity and political independence'. The Arab states and Russia failed to have withdrawal from 'all' the territories occupied included. Johnson insisted the text be left as it was. Russia and India supported the resolution on the understanding that the withdrawal envisaged was from all the territories.[5]

Gunnar Jarring, the Swedish ambassador to Moscow, was appointed by U Thant, as the United Nations special representative. For over three years Jarring energetically flew from Arab capitals to Cyprus, where he was based, and to Israel. But little came of his diplomacy. Both sides had other interests.[6]

Nasser saw to the reconstruction of Egypt's armed forces, securing not only the latest Russian weaponry, particularly aircraft and missiles, but Russian technical assistance and help in retraining the Egyptian officer corps. This was the period of Nasser's maturity: he virtually abandoned promoting his Philosophy of Revolution and tried instead to further Egyptian neutralism. Nasser resisted Russian attempts to obtain a warm-water port and naval base in Egypt. He sought a *rapprochement* with Britain. The British withdrawal from Aden encouraged this, together with the announcement that British forces would leave the Persian Gulf. Indeed, when King Idris was overthrown by Muammar el-Ghadaffi in a *coup d'état* in September 1969, and American and British forces withdrew from Libya, Britain no longer seemed to have any imperial presence in the area. Beeley was welcomed back as British ambassador. The Egyptian economy was partly sustained by contributions from the oil revenues of some Arab states, together with Russian contributions. Nasser, to some extent working with Hussein, tried to heal breaches in the Arab world. Indeed, the Egyptian President took up the cause of the Palestinian refugees. In 1968 Yasser Arafat accompanied him to Moscow. Nasser finally acknowledged that a failure in the Arab struggle had been the absence of a Palestinian element. The Egyptian authorities, to the annoyance of the Jordanians, started training and equipping the members of Al-Fatah. After the Syrian experience, however, Nasser resisted premature efforts to join Arab states together. This disenchanted Ghadaffi, who hoped to unite Egypt and Libya. Cairo even thwarted Ghadaffi's attempt to sink the British liner, *Queen Elizabeth 2*, in the Mediterranean. In January 1970 Nasser secured the promise of the latest Russian missiles, SAM-3's, technicians to man them, MiG-25 reconnaissance aircraft and eighty other Russian planes, and the appropriate number of Russian technicians to handle them.[7]

During this period Nasser led a war of attrition against Israel. By the end of 1968 there had been almost 1,000 incidents along the Jordanian frontier and approaching 200 on the Egyptian border, as well as clashes involving Syria and the Lebanon, and also in Gaza. Perhaps the Canal Zone was the worst affected. After Israeli shelling Nasser evacuated the towns of Suez and Port Tewfik. In November 1968 and April 1969 Israeli commando units attacked bridges over the Nile and electricity plants in Upper Egypt. An Israeli force captured the island of Shadwan (Green Island) off the Red Sea coast in January 1970 and destroyed radar equipment. In February there were further deep-penetration Israeli strikes against SAM missile sites. Nasser had formally announced the war of attrition on 8 March 1969. He aimed to destroy the Bar Lev line fortifications that the Israelis had constructed on the east side of the canal. By the middle of 1970 it was evident that Egypt was having to sustain considerable losses.

Israel meanwhile, pursued the American connection. Johnson, in January 1968, assured Eshkol that the United States would supply Israel with Phantom jet fighters. The President anticipated that his successor would honour that agreement. Nixon conducted most of his foreign policy through the White House Office, but possibly because of the Jewish background of his special assistant, Henry Kissinger, the President left Middle Eastern affairs in the hands of William Rodgers and the State Department. On 16 January 1969 France proposed four-power consultation on the Middle East. Washington agreed, but also decided on simultaneous two-power talks with Moscow. The Zionist lobby objected to any substitute for direct talks between Israel and the Arabs. Celler and five other congressmen saw Kissinger and Nixon on 13 February. Eban protested in March. Washington found Nasser's attitude intractable, and attributed it to his Pan-Arab ambitions. Hussein, dependent on American aid, seemed more amenable when he met Nixon on 8 April. Against a background of a deteriorating situation in the Middle East, and a promise by Golda Meir to repay seventeenfold any Arab attacks on Israel, the State Department attempted several unsuccessful initiatives. In September Nixon assured Golda Meir that he favoured a strong Israel, and on 9 December Rodgers outlined a plan: both sides had to make concessions; the United States did not support expansionism, and boundary modifications should be confined to 'insubstantial alternatives required for mutual security'. The Israeli cabinet rejected these proposals. Nasser initially accused Washington of supplying planes to Israel to bomb Egyptian schools. Then on 23 July 1970 Nasser accepted Rodgers's proposal for a cease-fire: the President explained to Arafat that he needed time to finish his rocket defences, and to secure bridging equipment. Russia supported an American-sponsored cease-fire between Israel and Egypt on 8 August.[8]

A few weeks later Jordan exploded. The fedayeen resented Hussein's apparent attempts to achieve a political settlement with Israel. The King survived an assassination attempt in June, and took personal command of his army. Hussein retained the fierce loyalty of his bedouin followers. On 1 September Palestinians again attempted to assassinate Hussein, and there was fighting between the loyal army and the fedayeen. The King asked for American support and Iraq threatened to stop Hussein's attacks on the fedayeen, but the Jordanians had the situation under control. Then, on 6 September, members of the Marxist Popular Front for the Liberation of Palestine (PFLP) started hijacking aircraft to Dawson Field, a strip about 30 miles (50 km) from Amman. They demanded the release of fedayeen in British, German and Swiss gaols, and said they would keep Israeli and American–Israeli passengers until guerrillas were released from Israeli goals. Until this episode Arab terrorism had followed the sort of tactics used by Begin and the Irgun, with the connivance of Haganah, against the British in the Palestine mandate. On the whole terrorism had been directed against Israeli citizens and sympathizers. This new departure, involving Western nationals, was probably supported by a thinking which suggested Western responsibility for the Palestinian refugees: the Arabs had never been able to understand why they had been forced to give up their land to atone for Western feelings of guilt about Hitler's pogroms. To them the West seemed morally responsible for the Palestinian refugees, ar ⁴ was reluctant to apply the principles of the charter of the United Nations to achieve a solution. John Frankenheimer finally made this point to American audiences in his film, *Black Sunday*, in 1977.

The Western reaction to Dawson Field did not win the Palestinian cause many sympathizers, but it did instil into Western consciousness an awareness of the refugee problem. On the whole Western sympathy was rather selective: the murder of Israeli Olympic team members by Palestinian terrorists in 1972, partly as a result of bungling by the West German authorities, created far more of an outcry than the hanging of the two British sergeants in 1947, or the blowing up of the King David Hotel in 1946. On 9 September 1970 Washington investigated the consequences of a protracted military engagement in Jordan, and how Russian intervention could be deterred. The West European countries were persuaded that they should not hand over their fedayeen prisoners until all the passengers were released. The Palestinians blew up the aircraft, but secured no concessions. In the middle of September Hussein decided to establish order in his country: he asked Washington to restrain Israel, and warned that he might have to ask for assistance if other Arab states intervened. On 15 September Sir Denis Greenhill, the permanent head of the British Foreign Office, warned Washington that a battle between the fedayeen and Hussein's soldiers was likely; he asked about American intentions. Kissinger indicated that American military involvement could not be excluded. He also told the Washington Special Actions Group, the President's advisory body, that it was essential that Hussein should stay: it should be shown that friendship with the West and a moderate foreign policy would be rewarded with American support. This was also a chance to arrest extremism in the Middle East which had been encouraged by the arrival of Russian missiles and military officials in Egypt. Nasser's attempt to blackmail the United States with Russian threats also had to be exposed as futile. Nixon, however, involved in an election campaign, preferred unilateral American action to Israeli military moves. On 17 September Hussein ordered his army into Amman, and attacked Palestinian concentrations in the north of Jordan.

Washington kept in close touch with London, and assured Hussein that it sympathized with his efforts. American forces were rapidly deployed in the Mediterranean, and Nixon leaked to the press that he would make the Russians pay for their missiles along the Suez Canal. Golda Meir visited the President on 18 September, and said that Israel would inform the United States before it did anything. Moscow hoped for American prudence. On 20 September Syrian tanks invaded Jordan. Kissinger decided that Moscow and the Arab radicals should not have the initiative. Washington asked Moscow to impress upon Syria the need to withdraw its forces from Jordan, and to desist from further intervention there. An American brigade in Germany was prepared for an air drop. That evening Nixon became resolute. Greenhill passed on Hussein's request for immediate air strikes. Washington did not have the intelligence or target information: an Israeli move seemed essential. Israel was asked to make reconnaissance flights. Israel mobilized, and on 21 September two brigades moved towards the Golan heights. After this there were hints of Russian pressure on Syria. Hussein, encouraged by American backing, attacked the Syrian tanks; they started to withdraw from Jordan.

The Middle East had once again become an area of Great-Power confrontation. The hijack hostages were freed, some by Hussein's soldiers. Arab heads of state met in Cairo on 22 September, and on 25 September it was announced that an agreement had been reached between Hussein and the captured Palestinian leaders. Arafat, however, denounced this. Syrian reverses led to an effective change of government there: on 19 October the Defence Minister, Hafez al Assad, seized power. He refused to allow Palestinian activities in Syria as these could involve the Syrian army in clashes with Israel. In January 1971 Assad visited Moscow and obtained financial assistance and military aid including substantial numbers of aircraft, and technical advisers to rebuild the Syrian army. Early that same year Dr George Habash, the leader of the PFLP, founded the Free Jordan Movement with the aim of overthrowing Hussein. Arafat denounced Habash, but Hussein decided that no agreement was possible with the Palestinian guerrillas. In July 1971 he attacked their camps, and the guerrillas were moved to the Lebanon.[9]

On 28 September 1970 Nasser died. He was succeeded by Anwar el-Sadat, another of the free army officers who had overthrown Farouk in 1952. On 1 March 1971 Sadat went to Moscow. He wanted to ensure Egyptian equality with Israel on arms. On 8 March Sadat asked

189

Arafat what resistance Al-Fatah could provide in the event of a new war. The President advised against any provocation of Hussein. The next month the unity of Egypt, Syria and Libya was agreed. Sadat surmounted a threatened coup by pro-Russian elements and then, on 27 May 1971, signed a friendship treaty with Moscow, possibly to pacify Russian suspicions over the anti-Soviet purge. Sadat secured further aircraft and arms from Russia, while at the same time opening channels to Washington. Local tensions developed over the Russian presence in Egypt and, on 12 April 1972, Sadat told Leonid Brezhnev that the Russians had not supported their friends as actively as the United States had Israel. The Egyptian President complained about the flow of Russian Jews to Israel: many were intellectuals and scientists helping to build up the Zionist state. Sadat became disillusioned with Moscow: it delayed arms supplies; and five years after the Six Day War the Russian connection had not provided any solution to the Israeli problem. He informed Brezhnev that Egypt could not become a trusteeship territory of Russia. On 18 July Sadat announced that the 15,000 Russian military advisers and experts were to leave Egypt within a week; the equipment and installations established in Egypt after 1967 were to become Egyptian property. Possibly Sadat was worried that Nixon and Brezhnev had just agreed at their summit conference that there should be no war in the Middle East.[10]

While the United States was furthering relations with Egypt, Israel was building up its forces with American weapons. In January 1970 Nixon had threatened to delay the supply of Phantom jets to Israel in retaliation for Zionist demonstrations against President Georges Pompidou in Chicago. France had agreed to supply Libya with aircraft which the Zionists felt could be used against Israel. Nixon also hoped, by this gesture, to further diplomatic relations with Egypt and Syria. By the end of September, however, the Phantoms had started arriving in Israel. Nixon believed in a strong Israel. After Sadat broke the friendship treaty with Russia, Israel concentrated on anti-terrorist activities as Palestinian hijackings and murders spread across the world. But, at the beginning of 1973, Israel felt that American support and military aid, the decline in international pressure following the Munich Olympic massacre and Egypt's weakening links with Russia all made an Arab attack unlikely. The Arabs in the occupied territories seemed acquiescent. Dayan mentioned abandoning the remote prospects of peace, and, instead, drawing up a new map of Israel: he wanted to resettle Judaea and Samaria. On 14 May 1973, on BBC television, Dayan spoke of Israel remaining till the end of time on the West Bank: if the Palestinian Arabs did not like that they could go to another Arab country. He told *Time* magazine on 30 July that Palestine was finished. In April he had referred to his vision of a new state of Israel stretching from the Jordan River to the Suez Canal. Dayan's statements were not necessarily official Israeli poliy, but they projected an image. Sadat was particularly exercised by Dayan's designs for a new port of Yamit at Rafah which would isolate Egypt from the Gaza strip. There was also a degree of military euphoria in Israel: Allon said, on 4 June 1973, that Egypt had no military option at all. Israel's dramatic anti-terrorist activities helped: in April 1973 Israel even searched for terrorist leaders in the streets of Beirut. On 10 August Israeli jets forced a Lebanese airliner back to Beirut on the pretext that a Palestinian terrorist leader could be on board. Even American public opinion resented this sort of high-handed action, but it projected an image of Israeli power.[11]

Sadat was moving, and being moved, towards war. It was evident that Egypt had not achieved, and was not likely to reach, tactical military parity with Israel in the near future. Israel had adopted a status quo stance: for over five years there had been no concessions over the territories occupied during the Six Day War. It was evident that only pressure from Russia or the United States would secure serious Israeli negotiations on the basis of resolution 242. Given the reality that Egypt's military preparedness was not likely to improve, the evidence of Israeli designs for permanent control over the occupied territories and in particular Dayan's scheme for the port of Yamit, it probably seemed to Sadat that the only way of achieving a Middle East settlement was another war that might force the Great Powers and the United Nations to take more interest in the Arab predicament. Of course Sadat was principally worried about Egypt. The Egyptian economy was straining: there was the cost of the Aswan dam; the war in the Yemen; industrial development; and most of all the $8–9m it had cost to re-equip the defence forces between 1968 and 1973. Egyptians could not be expected to suffer austerity indefinitely. The army was showing the strains of almost five years of total mobilization and some of the conscripts had been in full-time service for the whole period. Egypt, particularly after Nasser's death, had enjoyed more international support for its cause, and some sympathizers felt that it was doing little to utilize this. Even the British Foreign Secretary, Sir Alec Douglas-Home, put on Arab clothes and rode a camel while on a goodwill visit to Egypt. But Egypt's sympathizers increasingly felt that Cairo was not taking advantage of this new mood. The emerging detente between Russia and the United States could also mean that Egypt would not have another chance. The superpowers could accept the status quo or impose a humiliating settlement in their own interests. A war, even if only partly successful, could lead to the opening of the Suez Canal and a source of revenue for Egypt. It could also restore Egypt's flagging position in the Arab world. Sadat had noted 30 November 1972 as the day he decided to go to war.[12]

In November 1972 General Ahmed Ismail Ali became commander-in-chief of the Egyptian armed forces, and Minister of War. With both British and Russian training, Ismail understood the relationship between war and politics, and developed a strategy band on the principle that the superpowers would prevent a complete military victory by either side. Egypt had to contend with both Israeli air, technological and tactical superiority. This had to be matched by exploiting Israeli weakness in manpower, and fighting a two-front war with Syrian assistance. Ismail also worked on the principle that Israel suffered more from the loss of its fighting men than territory or material. Surprise was to be the essential element. On 31 January 1973 the armed forces of Syria and Egypt were put under a unified command. Ghadaffi was excluded from the planning because of his ideas as to how the attack should be launched. Libya, however, made a substantial contribution to the cost of the weapons. Sadat warned Arafat to be ready to fight, but the Palestinian leader did not take much notice. The Egyptian President also tried to achieve a semblance of Arab unity. He worked closely with King Feisal of Saudi Arabia and President Boumedienne of Algeria. By doing this Sadat hoped for the support of both the conservative and radical elements in the Arab world. In May 1973, in Cairo, Sadat told Feisal that he was confident that the Egyptian army could cross the Suez Canal and advance into Sinai; at the same time Syria could cope with the Israeli forces on the Golan heights. Feisal agreed to provide money and restrict oil production and to see that the Gulf states co-operated in this. President Assad of Syria secured a promise of Russian support in the United Nations in the event of a possible war with Israel. Feisal made arrangements with Boumedienne to control the radical oil producers. Diplomatically, the Arabs scored another victory in May: most members of the Organization of African Unity meeting in Addis Ababa agreed to sever diplomatic relations with Israel. Egyptian and Saudi Arabian diplomats also travelled the world arguing the Arab case and suggesting that the prevailing situation could not continue. This helped to secure support in the United Nations. That same month, on the day that Israel celebrated its twenty-fifth anniversary, Arab oil producers stopped production for one hour to mark the anniversary of 'the usurpation of Palestine'. Feisal hoped, in vain, that this demonstration would stir Washington. Instead the King became increasingly disturbed over Washington's support for the Shah of Iran whose growing armed forces were challenging Saudi Arabian paramountcy in the Gulf. Riyadh moved towards Cairo. Syria also sacrificed several aircraft and pilots on 3 September to prevent Israeli reconnaissance planes from discovering the new SAM batteries around the port of Tartous. Syrian military intelligence also planned the raid by Palestinian commandos on the train taking Jews from Russia to Vienna which led to the closure of the transit camp at Schoenau Castle in Austria, to divert attention from the Arab military preparations. The Syrian plan worked: Golda Meir personally went to see the Austrian Chancellor, himself a Jew, in an effort to persuade him to reopen the transit camp. Israel and the

United States attributed Syrian military moves to defensive preparations in case Israel retaliated for the closure of the camp. A conference between Sadat, Assad and Hussein in Cairo led to the resumption of diplomatic relations between Egypt and Jordan. Egypt was preparing a united Arab front for the war.[13]

Between 22 and 28 August 1973 eight Egyptians and six Syrian officers meeting in Alexandria finalized the plan for a simultaneous attack on Israeli forces in Sinai and the Golan heights. The general operation had been agreed in April. They left with the day and the hour of the attack still to be decided. Signals came out of Cairo that war was not imminent: a contract for a pipeline was awarded to an American firm; it was announced that officers would be given special leave to go to Mecca. There were disagreements with the Syrians over the precise timing of the attack, but, by the middle of September Assad consented to 2 p.m. on 6 October: weather conditions, moonrise and tides would be favourable then for the crossing of the canal. It was Yom Kippur, the Jewish Day of Atonement, but this was not a primary consideration, if one at all. In the event the attack on that day only facilitated the call-up of Israeli reservists: they were either at home or in the synagogue and the roads were not congested. It was also Ramadan, the month of the Muslim fast – this did not help soldiers' fitness. On 1 October Sadat warned the Russian ambassador, Vladimir Vinogradov, that a breach of the cease-fire was likely. No precise dates were mentioned to him, or to his counterpart in Damascus. Hussein was only informed on the eve of battle, and then Sadat advised him not to commit his forces at that time. It was decided that the pretext for the battle would be an announcement that the Israelis had attacked Zafarana on the Red Sea.[14]

On 6 October 1973 Israel was almost taken by surprise. Dayan was told at 4 a.m. that Syria and Egypt were going to attack later that day. Reserves were mobilized immediately, and a pre-emptive strike by the air force was considered. On 3 October Dayan had advised Golda Meir, just back from her mission to Vienna, of Syrian and possibly Egyptian weapon reinforcements. Intelligence, however, thought that the Egyptians were just on annual manoeuvres. On 5 October the general staff ordered 'C' alert, the highest alert, for the army, and also a full alert for the air force. That was all that could be done short of mobilizing the reserves. Golda Meir gave her authority for the reserves to be mobilized on Yom Kippur if this was thought necessary. Preparations were also made to convene the full cabinet.[15]

Washington was taken by surprise when Meir warned of the imminent attack; Nixon was stunned by the failure of Israeli intelligence. The President's immediate concern was the Russian position. The initial Arab successes excited even their own leaders. The operation had been well planned, and was executed by the Arab soldiers with tenacity, courage and skill. Sadat and Assad turned down Russian offers to arrange a cease-fire. The United States convened a meeting of the Security Council, but there was little interest in arranging a cease-fire. Britain and France, perhaps conscious of the significance of Arab oil, stood aside. But Douglas-Home told the Conservative Party at Blackpool on 12 October that the combatants would need the help of others to reach a settlement. He had 'been certain that it would not be psychologically possible for the Arabs to go on gazing indefinitely at their own lands without the eruption of war'. The British Prime Minister, Edward Heath, embargoed spares for the Centurion tanks Britain had supplied to Israel. The Labour opposition did not think this even-handed. Nixon's dilemma was greater: faced with the domestic turmoil of Watergate, he knew he had to sustain Israel while at the same time not permanently alienating Egypt, Syria and other Arab countries. There was also the danger of an Arab oil embargo. But four days of Israeli reverses convinced him that Washington would have to make good their losses, and he instructed Kissinger to work out the necessary logistics. He also knew that Congress did not want American involvement in a Middle Eastern war: it could be another Vietnam. On 10 October Golda Meir thanked Nixon for his offer of material: Israel, however, was confident that it would win. Nixon overrode Pentagon obstacles and insisted that Washington send everything it could fly to get the equipment to Israel. He sent an extra ten Phantom jets and mounted an operation larger than the Berlin airlift of 1948–49.

By 18 October Israeli forces were driving back the Arab armies and Moscow proposed a joint Russian–American cease-fire resolution. Nixon, however, did not like the terms: it implied pre-1967 boundaries. On 17 October the Organization of Arab Petroleum Exporting Countries decided to reduce oil production. Two days later Nixon asked Congress for $2.2bn. for emergency aid for Israel. Abu Dhabi, Libya, Saudi Arabia, Algeria and Kuwait embargoed oil for the United States. Kissinger flew to Moscow on 20 October, and together with Brezhnev drafted a cease-fire agreement: a cease-fire in place; a general call for the implementation of resolution 242 after the cease-fire; negotiation to establish a just and durable peace in the Middle East. This was accepted by both sides and set for 22 October, but there were violations, and the Egyptian Third Army of 20,000 men was encircled by Israelis on the east bank of the Suez Canal. A second cease-fire was effected on 24 October. American intelligence, however, reported that seven Russian airborne divisions, 50,000 men, were on alert, and 85 Russian ships were in the Mediterranean. Sadat asked for a joint Russian–American peacekeeping force. Nixon did not like the idea: it would mean a return of Russia to the Middle East. Brezhnev continued to insist that Israel was fighting, and that the United States and Russia should immediately send military forces to the Middle East. Washington took this as a threat of unilateral Russian intervention: shock tactics were decided on and American bases throughout the world were put on nuclear alert. Brezhnev gave way. There were further threats at the end of the month over supplies to the trapped Egyptian Third Army, but nothing very substantial. Golda Meir travelled to Washington at the beginning of November to say thank you. Kissinger started his shuttle diplomacy between the Arab countries and Israel on 5 November. Egypt and the United States resumed diplomatic relations after a break of six years on 7 November 1973.[16]

Sadat emerged from the October War a world statesman, something Nasser had aspired to but never achieved. Relations were established between Washington and Cairo: Sadat perceived that only the United States could effectively persuade Israel to make concessions in the occupied territories. The calculation that the superpowers would prevent a victory by either side proved correct, as did the hope that another war would force the powers and the United Nations to take an interest in the Arab predicament. The October War secured serious Israeli security negotiations on the basis of resolution 242. The Security Council resolution 338 of 22 October called for the implementation, after the cease-fire, of resolution 242 'in all of its parts', and decided on 'negotiations between the parties concerned under appropriate auspices, aimed at establishing a just and durable peace in the Middle East'.[17]

REFERENCES

1. Henry Kissinger, *The White House Years* (London 1979), p. 347.
2. Moshe Dayan, *The Story of My Life* (London 1972), pp. 311–34; Abba Eban, *An Autobiography* (London 1977), pp. 438–9.
3. Kissinger, op. cit., p. 577.
4. Eban, op. cit., p. 445; Kissinger, op. cit., p. 345.
5. Eban, op. cit., pp. 426–53; Anthony Nutting, *Nasser* (London 1972), pp. 436–9; Kissinger, op. cit., p. 345; George Brown, *In My Way* (London 1972), pp. 225–7; William B. Quandt, *Decade of Decisions. American Policy towards the Arab–Israeli Conflict, 1967–1976* (Berkeley 1977), pp. 65–6.
6. Eban, op. cit., pp. 452–6, 470–80; Mohammed Heikal, *The Road to Ramadan* (London 1975), pp. 56–9; Nutting, op. cit., pp. 438–9.
7. Heikal, op. cit., pp. 46–90; Malcolm H. Kerr, *The Arab Cold War. Gamal' Abd Al-Nasir and his Rivals 1958–1970*, 3rd edn (London 1971), pp. 129–56; Robert Stephens, *Nasser. A Political Biography* (London 1971), pp. 510–44; Nutting, op. cit., pp. 440–2.
8. Dupuy, *Elusive Victory: The Arab–Israeli War 1947–1974* (London 1978), pp. 343–69; Kissinger, op. cit., pp. 346–79; Eban, op. cit., pp. 460–70; Quandt, op. cit., pp. 72–104; Heikal, op. cit., pp. 90–7; Mahmoud Riad, *The Struggle for Peace in the Middle East* (London 1981), pp. 103–81.

9.   Kissinger, op. cit., pp. 594–631; Dupuy, op. cit., pp. 378–83; Quandt, op. cit., pp. 105–27; Heikal, op. cit., pp. 95–103; John Bullock, *The Making of a War, The Middle East from 1967–1973* (London 1974), pp. 49–86; Richard Nixon, *The Memoirs of Richard Nixon* (London 1978), pp. 483–5; *Black Sunday*, United States, 1977, directed by John Frankenheimer.

10.   Heikal, op. cit., pp. 114–84; Kissinger, op. cit., pp. 1276–1300; Quandt, op. cit., pp. 128–64; Riad, op. cit., pp. 183–242.

11.   Nixon, op. cit., pp. 479–83; Eban, op. cit., pp. 468–94; Heikal, op. cit., p. 205; Dayan, op. cit., pp. 380–1.

12.   Anwar el-Sadat, *In Search of Identity* (New York 1978), p. 237; Heikal, op. cit., pp. 204–6; Dupuy, op. cit., pp. 387–8.

13.   Bullock, op. cit., pp. 202–9; Dupuy, op. cit., 388–405; Eban, op. cit., p. 497; Heikal, op. cit., pp. 12, 20; Robert Owen Freedman, *Soviet Policy towards the Middle East since 1970* (New York 1975), pp. 125–35.

14.   Eban, op. cit., p. 504; Heikal, op. cit., pp. 11–45; Bullock, op. cit., pp. 210–11.

15.   Dayan, op. cit., pp. 375–87; Dupuy, op. cit., pp. 406–10; Eban, op. cit., pp. 500–2.

16.   Nixon, op. cit., pp. 920–43; Harold Wilson, *The Chariot of Israel, Britain, America, and the State of Israel* (London 1981), pp. 362–72; Eban, op. cit., pp. 505–30; Heikal, op. cit., pp. 207–61; Dupuy, op. cit., pp. 411–622; Shlomo Aronson, *Conflict and Bargaining in the Middle East. An Israeli Perspective* (Baltimore 1978), pp. 168–211; Quandt, op. cit., pp. 165–206; Dayan, op. cit., pp. 388–444; David Downing and Gary Herman, *War Without End. Peace Without Hope. Thirty Years of the Arab–Israeli Conflict* (London 1978), pp. 221–45; Golda Meir, *My Life* (London 1975), pp. 358–61.

17.   Walter Laqueur, *Israel–Arab Reader*, 3rd edn (New York 1976), p. 481.

Chapter 12

CONCLUSIONS

This is a story of men and women, of their ideas and beliefs, their power and vision as well as personal ambition and treachery. Sometimes it is an account of how they perceived their countries' interests could best be served, imperial, strategic and economic, at other points it relates how these became submerged in individual gain and even a desire for re-election. The important decisions were taken by a small number of people: they were open to persuasion, lobbying and blackmail. Chance and accident played a part, but so far as it is possible to discern the course of events[1] there is no evidence of blind impersonal forces, or of an inevitable progression.[2] The Arab–Israeli Wars can be attributed largely to the actions of people and the decisions they took at particular points in time.

The background to the wars forms an episode in imperial history: it is an account of how Britain tried to exercise paramountcy over both Arabs and Zionists. In the era of proconsuls surprisingly few statesmen were able to divide a vast area of the world, without consulting the inhabitants as to their wishes, with a view to relations with France and a possible future war with Germany. British paramountcy over the Middle East lasted until the end of the Second World War: it was undermined by an American President obsessed with his re-election prospects, Zionist terrorism that wore down domestic morale, and an exploding sense of nationalism among a new generation of Arabs who were just as disillusioned with their hierarchical leaders as with the colonial powers. The attempt to reassert British suzerainty was thwarted in 1956 by another American President and his election. After this, the Middle East increasingly became an area of superpower confrontation as Russia and the United States competed with one another for control of what was considered to be the principal reservoir of the world's oil. It was a difficult game for the United States to play during decades when many of its citizens ceased to think of themselves as being principally American and discovered hyphenate identities. This meant that administrations were faced with powerful electoral groups who threatened punishment through the ballot box not so much

197

on American issues, but on those affecting their other, and often principal, loyalty.[3] But, in the end, the Arab states retained a surprising degree of independence, resisting both American and Russian dominance.

It was the existence of Israel that precipitated the Arab–Israeli Wars. The idea of the Zionist state was promulgated by Herzl late in the nineteenth century. Almost fifty years later Ben-Gurion proclaimed its birth under Herzl's portrait. Weizmann, whose very Jewishness seemed to make him attractive to the British Establishment, nurtured the growth of the Yishuv in Palestine by winning the sympathy of influential people in British public life. But his gradualist tactics seemed inadequate during the Second World War, and were replaced by Ben-Gurion's activism. The Zionists used Weizmann again, however, in 1947–48 to persuade Truman to support the creation of Israel, and, appropriately, it was he who handed the American President the scroll of the law. Israel came into being largely through Ben-Gurion's policy of using the Zionist pressure groups in the United States to persuade that government to instruct Britain to implement a policy favourable to Zionism in Palestine, together with his policy of wearing down British morale in the mandate. Ben-Gurion was helped by Begin's Irgun and its terrorist activities: it was the hanging of the two sergeants and the booby-trapping of their bodies that ultimately forced the British government to withdraw. Israel was initially nurtured by Ben-Gurion, but probably its most successful leader was Eshkol: under his guidance Israel achieved a state of military preparedness that enabled it to occupy territories necessary for secure boundaries during the Six Day War; with his premiership Israel also obtained international recognition and even sympathy. Allon and Dayan played important roles in the military planning and its execution. It was Golda Meir, though, who finally achieved the development of American sponsorship into an assurance that the United States would guarantee Israel's survival. It is perhaps significant that the Zionist founders of Israel, and its early leaders, were either east European or Russian Jews, victims of anti-Semitism and pogroms.

In the eyes of many Arabs it was Britain that was responsible for the creation of the state of Israel. It was the British government that issued the Balfour Declaration in 1917, held the mandate and admitted the Jewish immigrants who took over the Arab land. There was widespread sympathy within the British establishment for Zionism both in Conservative and Labour circles. In the case of some this was to compensate for guilt feelings over latent anti-Semitism, for others like Harold Wilson, and possibly Lloyd George, it was a consequence of the teaching of Old Testament religious history in schools and churches. Until the 1960s there was a tendency for even the Anglican Church to use the Judaic Ten Commandments, rather than Christ's injunctions, in the eucharist service. Officials taking key decisions were often converted to Zionism by shrewd lobbying, though many later became disillusioned. But, by then, they had served their purpose. It is often said that the British Foreign Office was pro-Arab. A surprising number of its officials were Zionists, or Zionist sympathizers. And, on the whole, the Colonial Office was always sensitive to Zionist demands. There is at least one instance of a British politician, Richard Crossman, who placed his loyalty to Zionism before his loyalty to king and country. British official policy, however, was not to support a Zionist state: British declarations always emphasized that the Balfour Declaration safeguarded the existing rights of the indigenous inhabitants. Churchill's White Paper stressed this, it was implicit in the terms of the mandate, and only wavered for a short period after Ramsay MacDonald's letter to Weizmann, and then the Arabs themselves secured a rapid reversal of policy. The British government, possibly because of its strategic concerns and relations with the Arab world, severely restricted Jewish immigration into Palestine. After 1945 it fought at considerable cost to sustain this policy, under the threat of Truman's displeasure and Zionist terrorism. Bevin felt that the Jews should be able to stay in Europe: if they had to leave that would defeat one of the objects of fighting the Second World War. He feared that the creation of a Zionist state would destroy British paramountcy in the Middle East. After the First Arab–Israeli War, when unjustly accused of anti-Semitism, the Foreign Secretary lamented the plight of the Arab refugees, far exceeding the number of Jewish refugees in Europe in 1945, but largely ignored in the West.

Rather than Britain, it was the United States that fathered Israel. The State Department, opposed to the creation of a Zionist state as officials thought it would undermine the United States' strategic position and destroy relations with the Arab world, referred to Truman's determination to be its foster-father. Truman's private correspondence has overtones of anti-Semitism, and suggests little sympathy for the Jews themselves, but an alliance between Roman Catholics under Wagner (who did not want Jewish immigrants to use up quota certificates available to Roman Catholics in Europe), Gentile anti-Semites, and the Zionist lobby headed by Silver, Wise and Rosenman, used by Clifford and Niles, convinced Truman that the Jewish vote was a determining factor in American elections. As Marshall observed, domestic political considerations overrode both American national security considerations and those of the West. The United Nations vote for partition which secured international backing for a separate Zionist state was achieved by blackmail on the part of American citizens. Election politics also appear to have determined Eisenhower's stand over Suez in 1956. As Kissinger has noted, the American humiliation of Britain and France led, in the end, to the United States having to assume those countries' responsibilities in the

Middle East. It was largely tax-free contributions from American citizens that enabled Israel to absorb the immigrants from the Middle East during the 1950s, and industrialize and rearm during the 1960s. The American media which selectively emphasized the holocaust helped to create a favourable climate for this. Old Testament Christianity was also a factor. Johnson was openly sympathetic to Israel, but it was Nixon, a Republican who had not been supported by the Zionist vote in his presidential election, who finally identified Israel's existence with that of the United States.

Russia, too, at the time of the joining of the Cold War, contributed to the foundation of Israel. Partition was supported by Russia: possibly it hoped, through the Zionist state, to establish a bridgehead in the Middle East. But, as the Middle East became an area of superpower conflict, Russia sided with the Arabs.

Most of the modern Arab states were British or French creations. They were born in the era of imperialism, and emerged into the modern world under a form of tutelage. Many were a consequence of the personal relationships formed between British officials and the Arab leaders whom they later installed as rulers. T. E. Lawrence felt that, through doing this, he discharged his debts to the Arabs incurred during the Middle Eastern campaign of the First World War. During the last decades of the nineteenth century Arab secret societies and writers probably floated the idea of an Arab identity. But it was Lawrence, and the legend that grew up around him, who brought a consciousness of the Arabs before people in the West. Zionists have often complained about a sympathy between British Foreign Office officials and the Arabs: one has attributed this to the public school education system and a common preference for homosexuality and horses.[4] Apart from Lawrence, who was in the Colonial Office anyway, there is little if any evidence of homosexual proclivities on the part of the officials concerned. And it seems an irrelevant consideration anyway. It is true that most were products of Arnold's educational system but some, like Sykes, came from a merely Bohemian background. The public school system of the time was designed not only to enable its recipients to exercise authority, but also to understand the suffering they might inflict. On the whole it produced dedicated officials whom the Arabs in Arabia respected, and even admired. The exception was Egypt, where the British developed a separate social society comparable to that in India. This alienated the young generation.[5] In particular, the resentment over the activities of Lampson was a formative influence in Nasser's experience, that of the free officers and other Egyptian nationalists. Back in London, however, it was the Eygptian hands, including Lampson, who were the most ardent advocates of the Arab cause in Palestine. The nationalism that emerged in the Arab world in the early 1950s, particularly under Nasser, was not directed so much at Israel as at getting Britain out, and the promotion of the Philosophy of Revolution. Nasser only discovered the Palestinian refugee question after the Six Day War. Divisions in the Arab world, fostered by the promotion of the Philosophy of Revolution, meant that the Arabs not only lost the propaganda war, but were unable even to agree among themselves as to how to deal with the existence of Israel.

Israel was build on Arab land. The Arabs could not understand why they had been selected by the West for this particular treatment. At the time of the Balfour Declaration Arab leaders were concerned about the nature of a possible Jewish homeland or commonwealth. They feared that it would not be just another Middle Eastern state, but would be one of a very special nature, possibly exclusive and even theocratic. As the number of Jewish refugees into Palestine increased with Hitler's persecutions, Arab resentment grew. The Arabs argued that Palestine could not absorb the refugees anyway, and that they would have to be settled on Arab land. After the Second World War Arab leaders complained to the Anglo-American commission of inquiry that they could not see why they, who had no anti-Semitic traditions, should be made to pay for the sins of Christian Europe. In a way Israel came into being as a refuge for the Jewish survivors of Hitler's persecutions. The Anglo-American commission in April 1946 estimated that there were 226,000 Jewish refugees in Europe, of which 100,000 were in camps. The creation of the state of Israel, and the First Arab–Israeli War, left almost 1 million Arab refugees. Over the following two decades their numbers doubled. But during Nasser's attempts to lead the Arab world, the promotion of the Philosophy of Revolution took precedence, and there was little awareness in the West of the plight of the refugees. It was only when the leaders of the Palestinians started using, with variations, the terrorist tactics Begin had employed against the British that concern was aroused in the West over their plight. To some extent this also coincided with the Arab use of the oil weapon. Arafat did more to promote the Palestinian cause than Nasser. But the Palestinians' tactics often alienated the leaders of Arab states in which they based themselves, and attacks on Western citizens estranged Western sympathy. Western citizens could not accept the concept of collective guilt for the Palestinian refugee question. The Arab states, after all, had largely ignored it for almost two decades.

The Arab-Israeli Wars resulted from great, and then superpower, policies. Domestic considerations, particularly in the United States, were often a determining factor. But the wars were also the consequence of Israel's determination to secure the right to exist, and to establish the defensible boundaries that would make this possible. That and Arab opposition to the presence of what they considered an alien Zionist state on Arab land.

REFERENCES

1. See R. G. Collingwood, *The Idea of History* (Oxford 1961), pp. 205–31; Carl Becker, 'Everyman his own historian', *American Historical Review*, 37 (1931–32), 221–36; Charles Beard, 'Written history as an act of faith', *American Historical Review*, 39 (1933–34), 219–31; E. H. Carr, *What is History* (London 1964), pp. 7–30.

2. See Isaiah Berlin, *Four Essays on Liberty* (London 1969), pp. 51–81; Ernest Nagel, 'Determinism in history', *Philosophy and Phenomenological Research*, xx (1960), 219–317; Carey B. Joynt and Nicholas Rescher, 'The problem of uniqueness in history', *History and Theory*, I (1960–61), 150–62; Edmund Wilson, *To the Finland Station. A Study in the Writing and Acting of History* (London 1974).

3. Inis L. Claude, *National Minorities, an International Problem* (Cambridge, Mass. 1955); Lawrence H. Fuchs, *The Political Behaviour of American Jews* (Glencoe, Ill. 1956); Louis L. Gerson, *The Hyphenate in Recent American Politics and Diplomacy* (New York 1964); Ben Halpern, *The Classic American Minorities* (New York 1971); Samuel Halpern, *The Political World of American Zionism* (Detroit 1961).

4. Ian Mikardo, Sept. 1970, quoted by Michael Adams and Christopher Mayhew, *Publish it Not . . . the Middle East Cover-Up* (London 1975), p. 26.

5. See Trefor E. Evans, *Mission to Egypt (1934–1946): Lord Killearn, High Commissioner and Ambassador* (Cardiff 1971), pp. 3–25.

BIBLIOGRAPHY

A: MANUSCRIPT SOURCES

BRITAIN

CAMBRIDGE

Churchill College, Cambridge
Alexander of Hillborough Papers
Attlee Papers
Halifax Papers

LONDON

British Library
Oliver Harvey Diaries

British Library of Political and Economic Science
Dalton Papers
McKay Papers
James Meade Diaries

Public Record Office
(a) *Cabinet Papers*
   Cab 16; Cab 21; Cab 23; Cab 24; Cab 27; Cab 37; Cab 42; Cab
   65; Cab 66; Cab 128; Cab 129
(b) *Colonial Office*
   CO 537 Palestine Files; CO 733 Palestine Correspondence
(c) *Foreign Office*
   FO 2; FO 78; FO 195; FO 226; FO 371; FO 594; FO 608; FO
   686; FO 800; FO 882
(d) *Military*
   AIR 8
(e) *Prime Minister's Office*
   Prem 1; Prem 4; Prem 8
(f) *Accessions*
   PRO 30

203

OXFORD

Western Manuscripts Department, Bodleian
Attlee Papers

UNITED STATES

BURLINGTON, VERMONT

Guy W. Bailey Library, The University of Vermont
Senator Aiken Papers
Governor Ernest Gibson Jr Papers
Warren R. Austin Papers

CHARLOTTESVILLE, VIRGINIA

Aldeman Library, University of Virginia
J. Rives Childes Papers
Louis Johnson Papers
Edward R. Stettinius Jr Papers

CLEMSON, SOUTH CAROLINA

Robert Muldrow Cooper Library, Clemson University
James F. Byrnes Papers

HYDE PARK, NEW YORK

Franklyn D. Roosevelt Library
Harry L. Hopkins Papers
Henry M. Morgenthau Jr Papers
Samuel I. Rosenman Papers
Anna Eleanor Roosevelt Papers
Franklin D. Roosevelt Papers
War Refugee Board: Records 1944–45

INDEPENDENCE, MISSOURI

Harry S. Truman Library
Dean Acheson Papers
Clark M. Clifford Papers
Jonathan Daniels Papers
Elsey Papers
Edward Jacobson Papers
Herschel V. Johnson Papers
Howard McGrath Papers
Harry S. Truman Papers: Foreign Affairs Files; *Official Files*: United
    Nations Special Committee on Palestine; *President Secretary's Files*:
    Palestine–Jewish Immigration; *General Files*: American Christian
    Palestine Committee; American Zionist Emergency Council; Jews May

1944; Jews; Eddie Jacobson; United Nations Relief and Work Agency for Palestine Refugees in Near East; Zionist Organizations; Zionist Organization of America
MHCD 184: Correspondence between Merriam and Henderson
MHDC 250: Material on Palestine donated by E. M. Wright, Department of State official
MHDC 259: Epstein Correspondence
PPF 1296: Alex F. Sachs Files
PPF 1395: Rabbi Samuel Thurman Files
PPF 2513: Herbet H. Lechman Files
Rosenman Files
Henry L. Stimson Diaries
Copies of Papers in the Weizmann Archives, Rehovoth, Israel, relating to Relations between the United States and Palestine and Israel 1945–52.
Oral Histories: Mathew J. Connelly; George M. Elsey; Mark Ethridge; Loy W. Henderson; John D. Hickerson; Max Lowenthal; Evan M. Wilson

LEXINGTON, VIRGINIA

George C. Marshall Library, Virginia Military Institute
Marshall S. Carter Papers
George C. Marshall Papers
Kenneth W. Condit, *The History of the Joint Chiefs of Staff. The Joint Chiefs of Staff and National Policy.* Vol. II *1947–1949* Historical Division. Joint Secretariat. Joint Chiefs of Staff 22 April 1976.
Op-35-ohn Ser 000687P35(SC)EF52 Papers relating to the Chiefs of Staff Xerox
WDCSA 381 Papers relating to Security Xerox
Secretary's Weekly Summaries 19 May 1947–3 January 1949 Xerox 2055
Record Group 59, General Records of the Department of State, Records of Charles E. Bohlen 1942–52 Xerox 2061
Record Group 59, General Records of the Department of State, Records relating to Palestine Reference 'File' of Robert McClintock Xerox
Record Group 59, Department of State, Policy Planning Staff
United States National Security Council: Papers of the National Security Council Xerox
United States Joint Chiefs of Staff White House Records of Fleet Admiral William D. Leahy 1942–49

PRINCETON, NEW JERSEY

Princeton University Libraries
Bernard M. Baruch Papers
John Foster Dulles Collection
Louis Fischer Papers
James V. Forrestal Diaries
George Kennan Papers
Arthur Krock Papers
Adlai E. Stevenson Papers

Harry Dexter White Papers
The John Foster Dulles Oral History Collection: Robert R. Bowie; Herbert
Brownell; James F. Byrnes; Andrew W. Cordier; Hugh S. Cumming
Jr; Thomas E. Dewey; Clarence Dillon; C. Douglas Dillon; Allen
Dulles; Eleanor Lansing Dulles; Ernest A. Gross; Raymond A. Hare;
W. Averell Harriman; Loy W. Henderson; John D. Hickerson;
Douglas G. Mode; Harold Stasson; Thomas E. Stephens; James P.
Richards

WASHINGTON, DISTRICT OF COLUMBIA

Georgetown University Library
Robert F. Wagner Papers

Library of Congress Manuscript Division
Emmanuel Celler Papers
Tom Connally Papers
W. S. Culbertson Papers
Felix Frankfurter (Zionism) Papers
Theodore F. Green Papers
Jessup Papers
James M. Landis Papers
Francis Bowes Sayre Papers
Laurence A. Steinhart Papers

National Archives
Record Group 59, General Records of the Department of State, Decimal Files
1945–49, 501.BB Palestine; 711, 741, 867N; OSS Bureau of Intelligence Research; Records of Charles E. Bohlen 1942–52; Office of
Near Eastern Affairs Palestine; Records of Policy Planning Staff 1947–
53; Records Relating to Palestine. Palestine Reference 'Book' of Dean
Rusk, 15 February–19 April 1948

Washington National Records Centre (Suitland, Maryland)
Record Group 000319 Entry 00082 Army Staff Intelligence (G2) Library 'C
File' 1946–51
Record Group 84 Entry 57A-446 (Cairo Embassy)
Record Group 84 Entry 59A543 part 5, 800 Palestine (London Embassy Files)
Record Group 165 G2 Regional File 1933–44 Palestine 2800–900

B: A SHORT LIST OF FURTHER READING

Abu-Lughod, Ibrahim (Ed.), *The Arab–Israeli Confrontation of June 1967.
An Arab Perspective*. Evanston 1970.
Adams, Michael and Christopher Mayhew, *Publish it Not . . . the Middle East
Cover-Up*. London 1975.
Adelson, Roger, *Mark Sykes. Portrait of an Amateur*. London 1975.
Allon, Yigal, *The Making of Israel's Army*. London 1970.

Antonius, George, *The Arab Awakening. The Story of the Arab National Movement.* London 1938.

Arendt, Hannah, *The Origins of Totalitarianism* (2nd edn). New York 1958.

Bawden, Liz-Anne (Ed.), *The Oxford Companion to Film.* London 1976.

Beaufre, André, *The Suez Expedition 1956.* London 1969.

Ben-Gurion, David, *Israel: A Personal History.* London 1971.

Bethell, Nicholas, *The Palestine Triangle. The Struggle between the British, the Jews and the Arabs 1935–48.* London 1979.

Bullock, John, *The Making of a War. The Middle East from 1967 to 1973.* London 1974.

Cohen, Michael J., *Palestine: Retreat from the Mandate. The Making of British Policy, 1936–45.* London 1978.

Crosbie, Sylvia K., *A Tacit Alliance. France and Israel from Suez to the Six Day War.* Princeton, NJ 1974.

Darwin, John, *Britain, Egypt and the Middle East. Imperial Policy in the Aftermath of War 1918–1922.* London 1981.

Dayan, Moshe, *The Story of My Life.* London 1976.

Dupuy, Trevor N., *Elusive Victory: The Arab–Israeli War, 1947–1974.* London 1978.

Eban, Abba, *An Autobiography.* London 1977.

Farnie, D. A., *East and West of Suez. The Suez Canal in History 1954–1956.* Oxford 1969.

Friedman, Isaiah, *The Question of Palestine, 1914–1918.* London 1973.

Gilbert, Martin, *Exile and Return. The Emergence of Jewish Statehood.* London 1978.

Glubb, John, *Britain and the Arabs. A Study of Fifty Years 1908 to 1958.* London 1959.

Glubb, John, *A Soldier with the Arabs.* London 1957.

Heikal, Mohammed, *The Road to Ramadan.* London 1975.

Hirst, David, *The Gun and the Olive Branch.* London 1977.

Hoopes, Townsend, *The Devil and John Foster Dulles.* Boston 1973.

Ingrams, Doreen, *Palestine Papers 1917–1922.* London 1972.

Ionides, Michael, *Divide and Lose. The Arab Revolt of 1955–1958.* London 1960.

Johnson, Lyndon Baines, *The Vantage Point. Perspectives of the Presidency 1963–1969.* London 1972.

Kayyali, A. W., *Palestine. A Modern History.* London 1978.

Kedourie, Elie, *In the Anglo-Arab Labyrinth.* Cambridge 1976.

Kent, Marian, *Oil and Empire. British Policy and Mesopotamian Oil 1900–1920.* London 1976.

Kerr, Malcolm H. *The Arab Cold War. Gamal 'Adb Al-Nasir and his Rivals 1958–1970* (3rd edn). London 1971.

Kissinger, Henry, *The White House Years.* London 1979.

Laqueur, Walter (Ed.), *The Israel–Arab Reader* (3rd edn) New York 1976.

Lilienthal, Alfred W., *The Zionist Connection.* New York 1978.

Lloyd, Selwyn, *Suez 1956.* London 1978.

Love, Kenet, *Suez. The Twice-Fought War.* London 1970.

Mansfield, Peter, *The Arabs.* London 1978.

Meir, Golda, *My Life.* London 1975.

Monroe, Elizabeth, *Britain's Moment in the Middle East* (2nd edn). London 1981.

207

Mosley, Leonard, *Dulles: A Biography of Eleanor, Allen, and John Foster and their Family Network*. London 1978.
Nevakivi, Jukka, *Britain, France and the Arab Middle East 1914–1920*. London 1969.
Nixon, Richard, *The Memoirs of Richard Nixon*. London 1978.
Nutting, Anthony, *Nasser*. London 1972.
Ovendale, Ritchie, *'Appeasement' and the English Speaking World. Britain, the United States, the Dominions and the Policy of 'Appeasement', 1937–1939*. Cardiff 1975.
Quandt, William B., *Decade of Decisions. American Policy towards the Arab–Israeli Conflict, 1967–1976*. Berkeley 1977.
Sachar, Howard M., *Europe Leaves the Middle East*. London 1972.
el-Sadat, Anwar, *In Search of Identity*. New York 1978.
Schechtmann, Joseph B., *The United States and the Jewish State Movement*. New York 1966.
Snetsinger, John, *Truman, the Jewish Vote and the Creation of Israel*. Stanford 1974.
Stephens, Robert, *Nasser. A Political Biography*. London 1971.
Stewart, Desmond, *T. E. Lawrence*. London 1977.
Stocking, George, *Middle East Oil*. London 1970.
Sykes, Chistopher, *Crossroads to Israel*. London 1965.
Tibawi, A. L., *Anglo-Arab Relations and the Question of Palestine*. London 1977.
Vital, David, *The Origins of Zionism*. Oxford 1975.
Vital, David, *Zionism: the Formative Years*. Oxford 1982.
Wasserstein, Bernard, *The British in Palestine. The Mandatory Government and the Arab–Jewish Conflict, 1917–1929*. London 1978.
Wilson, Harold, *The Chariot of Israel, Britain, America, and the State of Israel*. London 1981.

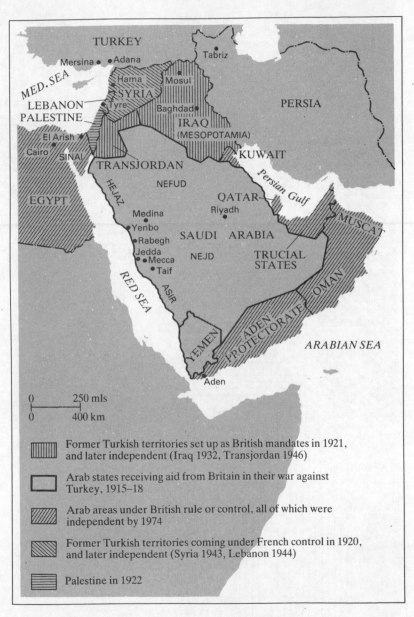

Map 1 Britain and the Arabs 1917-74 (after M. Gilbert)

Former Turkish territories set up as British mandates in 1921, and later independent (Iraq 1932, Transjordan 1946)

Arab states receiving aid from Britain in their war against Turkey, 1915–18

Arab areas under British rule or control, all of which were independent by 1974

Former Turkish territories coming under French control in 1920, and later independent (Syria 1943, Lebanon 1944)

Palestine in 1922

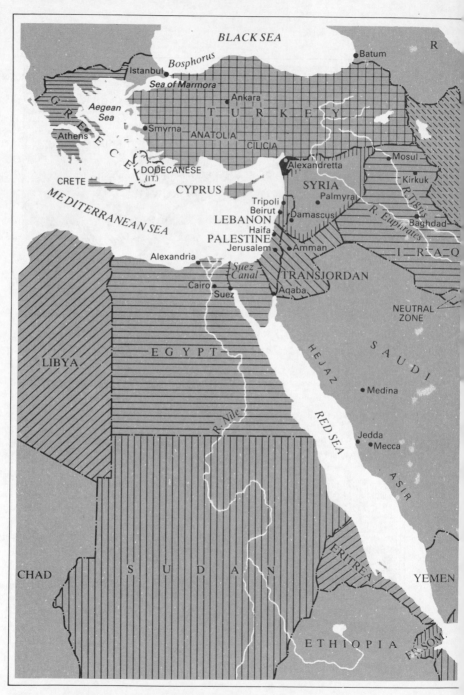

Map 2 The Middle East in 1936

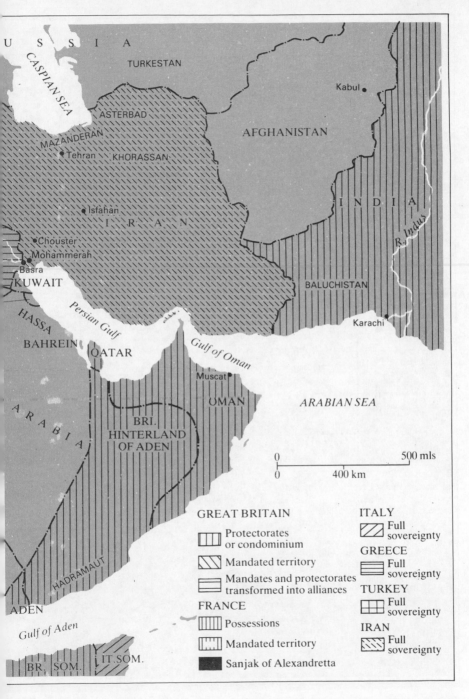

U S S I A

CASPIAN SEA

TURKESTAN

Kabul

ASTERBAD

AFGHANISTAN

MAZANDERAN

Tehran   KHORASSAN

I   N   D   I   A

Isfahan

I   R   A   N

R. Indus

Chouster

Mohammerah

Basra

KUWAIT

BALUCHISTAN

HASSA

Persian Gulf

BAHREIN   QATAR

Gulf of Oman

Karachi

A   R   A   B   I   A

Muscat

OMAN

ARABIAN SEA

BRI.
HINTERLAND
OF ADEN

| 0 | | 500 mls |
| 0 | 400 km | |

HADRAMAUT

ADEN

Gulf of Aden

BR. SOM.   IT. SOM.

GREAT BRITAIN

Protectorates
or condominium

Mandated territory

Mandates and protectorates
transformed into alliances

FRANCE

Possessions

Mandated territory

Sanjak of Alexandretta

ITALY
Full
sovereignty

GREECE
Full
sovereignty

TURKEY
Full
sovereignty

IRAN
Full
sovereignty

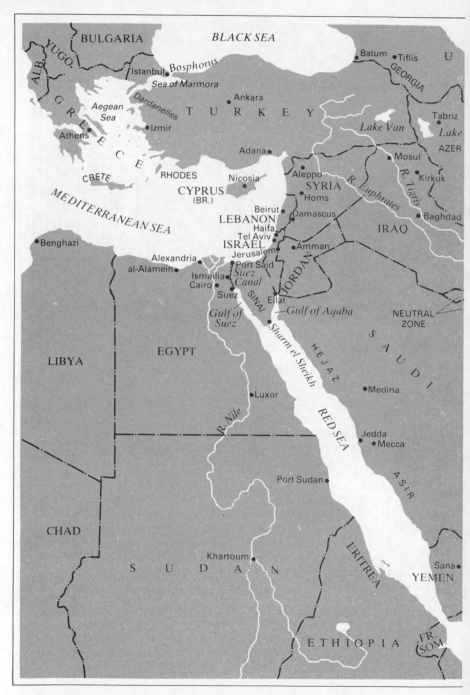

Map 3 The Middle East in 1954

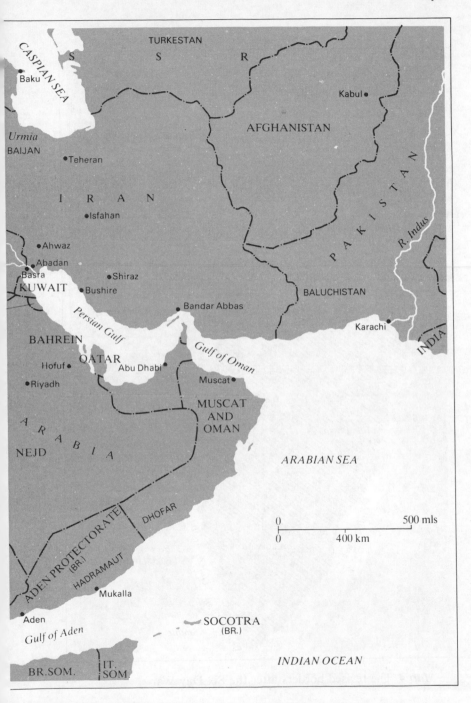

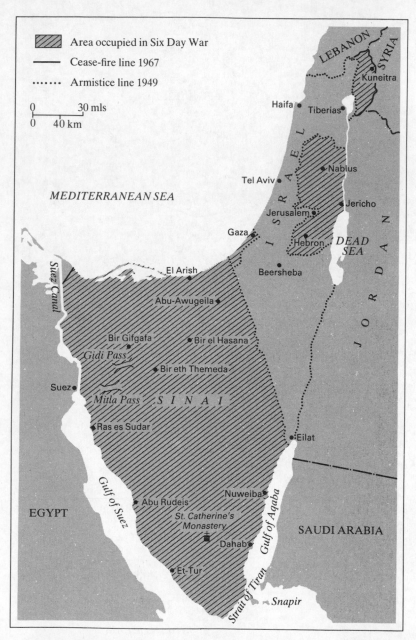

Map 4 The revised borders after the Six Day War

INDEX

administration, 82-3
and illegal immigrants, 100
Haifa, 16, 17, 20, 23, 114, 119, 120, 129
Haining, Lieutenant-General Robert, 68
Haj Amin (Mufti of Jerusalem), 50
Haiti, 105
Halifax, Lord, 69, 75, 81-2, 85, 86
Hall, George Glenvilla, 94, 95, 96
Hall, Sir Reginald, 40
Hama, 21, 23
Hamburg, 102
Hammarskjöld, Dag, 145
Hankey, Sir Maurice, 19, 40
Hannegan, Robert E., 97
Haram esh-Sherif, 63
Hardinge, Lord, 17, 31
Harriman, Averell, 136
Harris, Sir Douglas G., 84, 95, 97
Harrison, Earl G., 84-5
Harrow, 59
Hartford, 95
Harvard Law School, 29
Hashemites, 121, 122, 123, 168
'Hatiqva', 5, 64, 119
HAWK missiles, 177
Head, Anthony, 159
Headlam-Morley, Sir James, 44
Heath, Edward, 179, 194
Hebrew, 41, 45
Hebrews, 3, 19
Hebron, 64
Hecht, Ben, 101
Heimstätte, 5
Hejaz, 16, 18, 21, 50
Hellenism, 3
Henderson, Arthur, 28, 64
Henderson, Loy W., 96, 100, 136
'Hep! Hep!' riots, 2
Herod's temple, 63
Herzl, Theodor, 1, 52, 119, 198
   regarded as father of political
      Zionism, 3
   and *Der Judenstaat*, 4-5
   and negotiations with British
      statesmen, 6-7
Hess, Moses, 4
Hilldring, General John, 104, 104-5, 115-16
Hirsch, Baron Maurice de, 1, 8
Hirtzel, Arthur, 23, 44
Hitler, Adolf, 59, 63, 64, 69, 70, 77, 79, 98, 99, 115, 124, 132, 145, 151, 152, 173, 174, 188, 201
Hogarth, D.G., 24, 41
Hollywood, 173, 174
Home, Lord (Sir Alec Douglas-Home),

150, 156, 162, 179, 191, 194
Homs, 21, 22, 23
Hoover, Herbert, Jr, 141, 143, 151, 161
Horowitz, David, 92
The Hour of the Wolf, 27
Hourani, Akram, 131
House, Colonel Edward M., 31
House of Commons, 2, 51, 65, 66, 78, 85, 86, 94, 96, 98, 100, 105, 115, 124, 138, 140, 151, 152, 153, 158, 174
House of Lords, 51
House of Representatives (United States), 76, 79, 86, 95, 105
Hull, Cordell, 76, 77
Humphrey, George, 141, 161
Hungary, 2, 160
Hurst, Cecil, 6
Hussein, King, 131, 142, 167, 168, 169, 171, 179, 185, 187, 190, 193
Hussein, Ahmed, 143, 149
Hussein, Ibn 'Ali, the Sherif of Mecca, 15, 20, 21, 22, 23, 26, 27, 28, 43, 49, 50, 54
   and Germany, 15
   and Sykes-Picot agreement, 24, 39
   meets Hogarth, 39
   Britain's pledge that Palestine be
      'Arab' and independent, 41
   supported by Foreign Office, 42
   correspondence with McMahon and
      Palestine, 43, 66, 69
Hutcheson, Judge Joseph C., 92

Ibn Rashid, 9
Ibn Saud, 9, 16, 49, 50, 62, 66, 67, 80, 94, 97, 136
   and Germany, 15
   supported by India Office, 42
   as King of Saudi Arabia, 50
   Roosevelt's promises to, 1943, 75, 80, 85
Idris, 16
Idris, King, 186
Illinois, 81
Iman al-Badr, 169
Imperial Conference (1921), 47
Imperial War Cabinet, 28; 29
India, 16, 32, 41, 52, 53, 93, 103, 130, 138, 186, 200
   government of, 18, 19
   Muslims in, 42-3, 70, 85, 86
   social snobberies in subcontinent, 59
   and Baghdad Pact, 139
India Office, 23, 34, 42
Indian army, 17
Indian Ocean, 9, 21, 53

wanted immigration restrictions in
Palestine relaxed, 48
and Samuel, 48
and Passfield White Paper, 64-5
speech in Tel Aviv, 23 April 1935, 66
at Biltmore Hotel, 1942, 75
and Bevin, 86
and Truman on Negeb, 104-5, 113
to Truman on recognition of Israel,
117
no place for signature on scroll pro-
claiming Israel, 119
Welles, Sumner, 75
West Bank, 171, 180, 184, 185, 190
West End, 173
West Germany, 171, 177, 188, 189
West Point, 122
White Anglo-Saxon Protestant, 79, 172
White House, 81, 93, 101, 104-5, 184
White House Office, 187
'White Man's Burden', 53
White Papers
June 1922, 51, 52, 54, 63, 199
Passfield White Paper, 64
1939, 69-70, 71, 72, 76, 78
Wilson, A.T., 48
Wilson, Harold, 38 n29, 162, 171, 179, 198
Wilson, President Woodrow, 31, 32, 39,
41, 53
Wingate, Captain Orde, 68
Wingate, Sir Reginald, 18, 20, 22, 26, 39,
52
Winterton, Lord, 48
Wise, Stephen S., 29, 76, 77, 78, 79, 82,
96, 199
Wolf, Lucien, 24
Woodhead, Sir John, 68
World Bank, 141
World Zionist Organization, 5
Wright, Michael, 81
Würzburg, 2

Yadin, Yigael, 122
Yale, William, 83-4, 95
Yalta Conference, 162
Yamit, 191
Yemen, 62, 169, 170, 171, 178, 191
Yenbo, 26
Yishuv, 63, 67, 82, 119, 185, 198
Yom Kippur
28 September 1928, 63
October 1946, 97
1973, 193
Yom Kippur/Ramadan War, 193-5
Yost, Charles, 180
Yosuf, Salab Ibn, 168

Young Turk movement, 9
Yugoslavia, 120, 149

Zafarana, 193
Zaghlul, Sa'd, 52-3, 60
Zangwill, Israel, 7
Zeid, 42
Zetland, Lord, 70
Zionism
origins of Zionist movement, 1, 3
and proposals for land in Egypt, 6
Manchester School of, 7
support for Germany during First
World War, 15-16
conversion of C.P. Scott, 18
Sykes impressed by, 24
Meinertzhagen and, 27
possible importance for Britain's
strategic requirements, 28
and British political thinking in 1917,
29
and Russian jews, 30
Cornwallis and Clayton on, 40
Balfour on, 45
Curzon on, 47
Samuel and, 48
Deeds and, 48
Churchill and, 50, 78
White Paper (1922) and, 52
lobby in United States, 53
Malcolm MacDonald and, 68
pressure groups in United States, 79,
105, 187
new Zionism, 84
and Creech Jones, 99
and 1948 presidential election in
United States, 112
forces in Palestine, 115
and military preparations for First
Arab-Israeli War, 119-20
propaganda, 172
in United States, 175-6
Zionist Commission in Palestine, 51
Zionist commission to Palestine, 1918, 39,
48
Zionist Congress, first, 5, 6
Zionist Congress, July 1905, 7
Zionist Congress, seventh, 7
Zionist Congress in Prague (1933), 65
Zionist International Committee, 29
Zionist Organization, 64
Zionist Organization of
America, 29, 77
Zionists, German, 15
Zionists, Russian, 7
Zola, Emile, 1